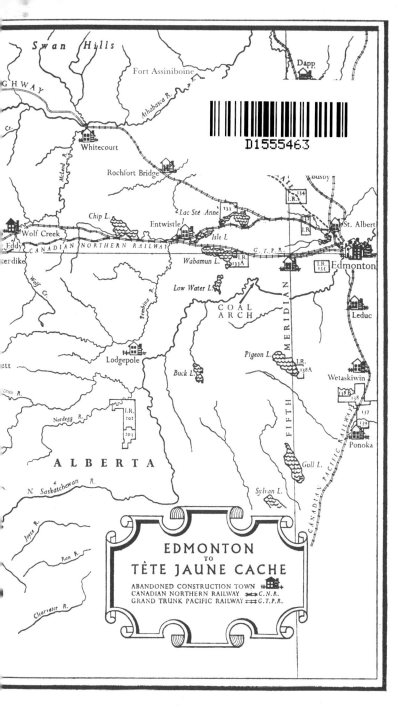

EDMONTON
TO
TÊTE JAUNE CACHE

ABANDONED CONSTRUCTION TOWN · · ·
CANADIAN NORTHERN RAILWAY · · · C.N.R.
GRAND TRUNK PACIFIC RAILWAY · · · G.T.P.R.

Brad. Anderson

PACK SADDLES TO TÊTE JAUNE CACHE

JAMES G. MACGREGOR

PACK SADDLES TO TÊTE JAUNE CACHE

HURTIG
Publishers
EDMONTON

DESIGN : FRANK NEWFELD

International Standard Book No. 0-88830-066-2
First Hurtig edition, 1973

PRINTED IN JAPAN

DEDICATED
TO THE MEMORY
OF
E. L. SMITH
WHO
ALSO LOVED
THE FOOTHILLS COUNTRY

INTRODUCTION
TO THE
NEW EDITION

Thereare two sides to this story. In this case that is no cliche.

One is the story of the exploration and development of a great stretch of the prairies and mountains of the Canadian West as told by the author, James G. MacGregor, a man with great knowledge of such things.

The other is of the fortitude and love of independence possessed by James Shand Harvey, whom Mr. MacGregor has made the eyes of the reader.

James Shand Harvey, whose departed soul and heart were those of an almost forgotten and certainly a legendary breed, had known the hospitality of Queen Victoria at Windsor Castle, yet he was happiest in his log cabin above the Athabasca River.

Years before, he had decided he was content to face whatever his chosen future held and embarking upon it, he deposited $200 in a bank at Jasper, Alberta. He stipulated it was to be used for his burial. He was no man content to become a public charge if things did not work out by reasons of circumstance or lack of planning, although it is doubtful Shand Harvey ever planned beyond the dawn of another day.

When he died in 1968 the man whose family was listed in *Burke's Peerage* left his modest cabin to the daughter of a grocer at Entrance, Alberta, who had delivered his groceries after Shand Harvey could no longer visit the store.

James Shand Harvey was in his eighties when he died. He left little in the way of material goods, but he did leave many friends among the neighbourhood's whites, Indians and Métis with whom he shared his cabin and the countryside. The cabin's shelves held books in the original Greek and such works as those of Thomas Gray, yet Shand Harvey himself occupied this humble domicile through the kindness of its original owner who requested that, upon his death, the cabin be left to Shand Harvey.

Shand Harvey also entertained many strangers after the first edition of *Pack Saddles to Tête Jaune Cache* appeared. They were tourists from faraway places, travellers whose greatest difficulty in making their way through the Yellowhead Pass was in refolding the road map.

Publication of the first edition of this volume made Shand Harvey a local celebrity. The people of Hinton held a dinner for him. He was reluctant to attend and when he did, he was wearing his only suit, purchased in the 1920s, and he was uncomfortable in shirt with collar buttoned and tie askew.

On that occasion he spoke in public probably for the first time in sixty years. He remembered his family home, Castle Semple, a place of antiquity in Aberdeenshire, Scotland. He recalled coming to Canada in 1905 to make his way by whatever means he could that appealed to him. It had to appeal to him. There was little at home apparently because, as he once told Mr. MacGregor, his father and his father's father had been fond of the gaming tables and the family home had been lost.

He was happy and content in his new home of spruce logs, a one room cabin, a bed at one end. He was a confirmed bachelor but in the manner of many he was also a good housekeeper. Through the cabin's single window he could see the world he loved, and his books were reminders of his boyhood in another when his closest chum at Eton was a grandson of Queen Victoria with whom the two boys visited.

The end of Shand Harvey's story was the beginning of another for James MacGregor. He visited Scotland to learn of the man's fortunes and misfortunes from parish families of long standing. It came to light that Mr. MacGregor's own grandfather had been a gamekeeper on the Shand Harvey estate. An aunt had lived in the dower house on the grounds of what was called a castle but which was in reality a three-storey fieldstone house with detached quarters for the servants.

The land had been divided into separate farm units and the National Trust (keeper of that country's heirlooms) had taken over the house. Fortunately, the valuable paintings it contained had been moved to Edinburgh before the property itself was destroyed by fire.

When the MacGregors took their leave of Shand Harvey's cabin in the mountainous country of the Canadian West it was to wonder why the host of whom they had grown so fond had chosen the life of "a typical old bushman, utterly honest and willing to share whatever he had."

Whatever the motive, it was fired by a spirit that led the explorers and traders into the mountains and guided those settlers who followed across the plains.

In *Pack Saddles to Tête Jaune Cache* Mr. MacGregor tells both sides of the story.

KEN LIDDELL

Calgary, Alberta
November, 1972

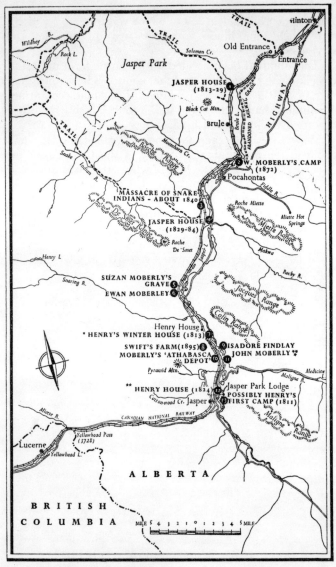

*—Also "Campement de Cardinal"

**—Also called "Miette's House" and "Rocky Mountain House"

*
**—Possibly Henry's first camp (1811)

IN a cosy trapper's cabin perched above the ghost town of Old Entrance, Alberta, lives Shand Harvey. Now over eighty, the slightly built woodsman looks back with clarity and zest to over fifty-five years spent as packer, ranger and trapper in the Iroquois country at the gateway to the famous Yellowhead Pass. When, in 1907, he turned his steps west along the barely discernible Indian trails, through the muskegs and thick forest, and reached the mountains, civilization lay two hundred miles behind in the embryo city of Edmonton. Since then, two railways and a magnificent paved highway have followed the paths he pioneered. Mills have cut the timber he cruised, mines have opened up the coal seams he explored, and a pulp mill, with its town of three thousand people, straddles one of his old camp grounds. Now the splendours of Jasper Park are available to the world's tourists where once Harvey and the legendary Lewis Swift camped with their Iroquois friends in the shelter of the Palisades.

In all of this development, Shand Harvey and his pack horses and a host of unsung men, Indian and white, have had a hand. And therein lies the purpose of this book – to recall at least in part the epic labours of the unknown men, sometimes even nameless men, who by their toil and grit opened up the foothills region. Of these multitudes a few, shaking off the shackles of conformity, had the rare luck to remain to live in it. They are a select breed and they enjoy a choice land. For this is a unique and a fine country, this country of the foothills, chinook winds, mountains and passes.

It has been my good fortune to see it through the eyes of Shand Harvey, as rare an individual as one is likely to meet. Through his eyes I have seen the unfolding drama of the opening up of the high country leading from the prairies to Tête Jaune Cache. Through his tales I have heard the tinkle of the lead mare's bell as the pack trains slithered over Roche Miette, the braying of the mules at noontide break and the roar of explosives among the rocks as rival railways blasted their way through the cliffs. Through his recollections I have lived again with some of the great surveyors, Bob Jones and Arthur St Cyr and many others; with packers and freighters, Montana Pete and Scissorbill Smith; and the Iroquois of the foothills, Vincent Wanyandi, Ewan Moberly and Adam Joachim.

In recent years my wife Frances and I have been installed on the roster of Shand's visitors. For years I had heard of James Shand-Harvey and planned to go and see him. Finally, after much urging by his neighbour Bill Hanington, I did so, and resolved to go back at the first opportunity and to take Frances and her shorthand book.

Now Frances, being a woman, is curious – sometimes very curious. When I listen to old-timers I'm content to beat around the bush and let their stories take shape gradually while I try to guide them, but her approach is more direct. She asked questions which I would have been weeks getting around to, and in half an hour she and Shand were firm friends. While I sat fascinated, he spoke of his years at Eton and of his chum there, Queen Victoria's grandson, whose father the Duke of Connaught was later to be Governor-General of Canada. Then, reaching back over sixty years, Shand recalled how the old Queen used to drive up to the school in her carriage to visit her grandson, and spoke of the times when the two boys together had called at Windsor Castle to have tea with her.

Then Shand, noticing that I had been left out of the conversation, looked at me and, reaching to a shelf above his head, brought down an Indian hide scraper. "But you," he said, "will be more interested in this *mich-ich-qun*, which belonged to my old friend the Stoney squaw, Anne Cardinal."

In one breath he spoke simply of these two he had known long ago, Queen Victoria and the Stoney squaw.

Our visits continued over many months, and our affection grew. Here was a man proud of his long experience in the bush, reticent, yet without any tinge of falseness in his modesty. "He doesn't talk much," said Billy Magee, his closest neighbour, "but you can believe every word he says. So many old-timers will tell you tall tales, but when Shand tells you anything you can depend on what he says. He either knows what he's talking about or he doesn't talk. You can't go wrong with Shand."

So, as one year merged into the next, we learned his story starting back fifty-five years ago. As is natural during the earlier years, one event crowded upon another, and as each year went by there was less to record. To Shand each year, although largely a repetition of the last, was nevertheless filled with a deepening contentment. For he was wedded to the wilderness, to the high hills and sparkling streams. And, like a happy husband, each year his enchantment grew until it merged into a mystic worship. Each spring with its aromatic freshness seemed fairer than all other springs. Each fall with its oreate flame glowed brighter than all other falls.

Shand Harvey typifies to me all the men who opened up Alberta. He homesteaded, surveyed on the Victoria Trail, ran base lines, packed for railways and for mountaineers, and became a forest ranger and a trapper. He arrived in Alberta when Edmonton was still in the Northwest Territories. His are not tales of murdering six-guns in smoke-filled saloons or of supermen stretching redskins in the dust. They are of men building railroads with hand shovels or men buried beside the grade, or of horses straining through sucking muskeg or plunging from pack trails clinging precariously to cliffs, of Indian women setting out alone for two-hundred-mile pack trips, or escaping, unarmed and unclothed, to endure in solitude the rigours of two Canadian winters. Little people, ordinary people, or, if you will, common people enjoying everyday challenges, enduring everyday hardships, and sometimes, at the end, dying in foaming rapid or howling blizzard.

Such men as Shand, cautious from long contact with the surprises of the wild, are slow to talk. "Shand," I say, "that time in 1909 when you took the pack train from Lac Ste Anne to Mount Robson and were on the trail from July to October – that trip must have been full of excitement?"

"No, not really," he replies. "It was uneventful, and we got back with all the horses safe and sound."

I have tried to ferret out Shand's story and by means of it to trace the gradual development of the area west to Yellowhead

Pass during these fifty-five years. And since the natives of the Smoky River country had a hand in this development and were such close friends of Shand's, I have tried to show them in their true light as friendly, sociable people, asking, as Shand says, "for nothing more than the right to live their own lives quietly and unobtrusively in the vast territories which their ancestors claimed as their hunting grounds."

I count myself fortunate to enjoy the confidence of such a man and to be able to take time on weekends to drive four hours in my car to hear his tales of taking thirty days with his horses to make the same trip. Surrounded as I am by cars, conferences and civilization, I can never equal his fortune in spending a lifetime free of these trammels. For few men have received more from life or now at four score years want less than he. A cut of cow moose now and then, a cup of tea and two fingers of his native Scotch – and his material needs are met. For more than five decades his spiritual needs have been met by an intimate harmony with the vast wilderness about him and by the friendship of kindred spirits who also called it their home.

In front of his cabin flows the angry Athabasca, hemmed in on either bank by a railway grade. One was abandoned long ago; the other is the great transcontinental Canadian National Railway, filling the narrow valley with a mighty roaring as the giant diesels thunder by. And in the west, just beyond the immediate valley, rises the vast misty blue wall of the Rocky Mountains. All of these things are part and parcel of the well-chinked cabin and its master. The cabin, the river, the railways, the mountains and the man are somehow one with the eternal verities. Surely he might say in the words of the Duke in *As You Like It* :

> *And this our life exempt from public haunt*
> *Finds tongues in trees, books in the running brooks,*
> *Sermons in stones, and good in everything.*

I N August 1905 James Shand-Harvey, armed
with a ·450 double-barrelled Express rifle and secure in the possession of a return ticket to Scotland, stepped off the CPR train at
Strathcona. It was raining heavily. Amongst the assortment of
vehicles drawn by horses and oxen which were tethered in the
black rutted mud, he sought vainly for a cab to take him to Edmonton. Finally he obtained a ride across the river in a long,
three-seated democrat. The trip through the mud holes down
Strathcona Hill was a cheerless introduction to Edmonton. After
a struggle the horses finally gained the top of McDougall Hill,
and he found himself safe at last at the old Windsor Hotel at the
corner of what is now Jasper Avenue and First Street.

The wet, the mud and the discomfort of the democrat were
mere incidentals. Even the chilly reception of the rain splashing
off the muddy boardwalks and spreading out into the mud holes
on Jasper Avenue, the main street of this frontier town of eight
thousand souls, could not dampen his joy at having achieved his
purpose. For he was, as he says now, "glad at last to be beyond
the end of a railroad with only trails ahead."

To reach the end of steel and to be at last at the edge of the
vast wilderness was the goal of hundreds of young men who came
to Edmonton. The trails ahead, the very few trails out north and
west into the great forests, called to many. No one felt the
appeal more than Jim Shand-Harvey. For him, who for fifty-five
years was to spend much of his life on these trails and who was
so often to enjoy the thrill of being the first white man to tread
them, the appeal was to turn into destiny. In 1905, however, what
form this destiny should take and in what direction it should
beckon mattered little. He was here at Edmonton. Outside it lay
the forest and the trails, and somewhere beyond lay the mountains. He was twenty-five and single. At that age the lure of new

places, of far-off valleys, of rivers not yet named and mountains shining in the sun, is irresistible.

James Shand-Harvey's choice of Edmonton had not been fortuitous. He had already seen something of the cultured countries of Europe. To him they were too civilized, too circumspect. One city was like another, and all of them hemmed him in. He decided he would come to Canada, and he studied the maps and literature to pick his destination. Wherever he went, it must be the end of steel.

Any part of the world or almost any occupation would have been available to him, for he had come of a prosperous Scottish family and had been born on his father's sugar plantation in Mauritius. In due course he had been sent to England and at eighteen had completed his schooling. Like all other Eton boys and like his father before him, he had received the customary richly bound volume of Gray's works, duly inscribed by Dr Edmund Warre, the Headmaster. Then for a while he had dallied with the thought of going to Virginia where he had relatives. Back in his grandfather's time one brother had gone to Mauritius, while another branch of the family had moved to America.

The West had won out over Virginia. But now that he was actually at Edmonton, he had yet to see whether or not he would like it. If he did not, the return portion of the ticket would take him home and then he could seek out some other corner of the world. Would the reality of the new freedom and of the trails beyond the end of steel match the rosiness of the dream?

Today, as he sits smoking on the porch of his log cabin perched high above the angry waters of the Athabasca at Entrance and watches the sun set over the mighty wall of the Rockies only twenty miles away, he says, "When the time limit of my ticket was close to expiring, I sold it to buy a horse and some clothing for my first Canadian winter. That was the best decision I ever made."

When Shand-Harvey woke up on his first morning in Edmonton, it was still raining. Seen through the narrow window of his room, the muddy prospect was not cheering. He wondered if he should have stayed in the Calgary area. He had broken his journey there for a few days and had gone out with Guy Warner, an old school friend, to his Bow River Horse Ranch. The weather had been clear and sunny, and from the ranch the Rockies stood out sharply. He was surprised to find that they were four times as far away as he thought. He had been urged to remain in the ranching country but had stuck to his original intention, and after a few days lay-over at Calgary he now found himself in muddy Edmonton. He wondered.

While the mud was unpleasant, the difficulties of some of the teamsters interested him and he observed the matter-of-fact way in which most of them accepted the situation. He paused on the wooden sidewalk on the south side of Jasper at 100A Street to watch a team which was stuck in the middle of the main street. He admired the quiet skill of the teamster. First he pulled the pin out of the doubletrees to allow his team to move forward to firmer ground. Next he produced a logging chain and hooked it into the front of the wagon tongue. After that, when his horses, by plunging and straining, succeeded in dragging the wagon to firmer ground, he calmly put away the chain, backed his horses up till he could replace the pin in the doubletrees, and in a few minutes was on his way.

This, of course, was on Jasper Avenue, where the city had made every attempt to keep the street in good shape. During the rainy spells it was bad, but the side streets were far worse. Any team straying off Jasper was almost certain to get stuck. One of the notorious mud holes was at the bottom of McDougall Hill at the terminus of the Edmonton, Yukon & Pacific Railway. Flanking the sidings were roadways so that wagons could draw up on either side of the boxcars to receive freight. During wet spells, wagons mired down and stuck in the mud beside the tracks. Doubling up teams and snaking the wagons out was almost routine procedure.

But in those days, if slipping around in the mud did not appeal, one could at least slip into a bar for a drink. The bars and waiting rooms of Edmonton's hotels were crammed with interesting characters. Edmonton was the gateway to the north, and these men had either just returned from a trip far back into the hinterland or were on their way to some far-off region. Their talk was of dog teams and pack horses, of steamboats and canoes on the northern rivers. Their tales were of remote places: Great Slave Lake, Chipewyan, Fort McMurray; of the prairies of the Peace

River country – Dunvegan, Spirit River and Pouce Coupe; of Roche Miette, Prairie Creek and Tête Jaune Cache. Some were from the wild west of Montana, some had been in the Klondike rush seven years ago, and others told of trap lines and Indians on the Smoky and the Wapiti Rivers. Very few at the hotel talked of land or farming. Because they could not afford the luxury of hotels, the bulk of the homesteaders were camped at various places around the outskirts of the city.

Shand-Harvey talked little and listened a lot. There was so much to hear of land, timber and coal out somewhere along the trails, and even of oil seepages recently seen at Egg Lake near Morinville and at Pelican Rapids on the Athabasca River. During August, Colin Fraser, who he found was the son and namesake of Sir George Simpson's old piper, had come in from Fort Chipewyan to sell the furs he had traded during the previous winter. The middle-aged trader, who had been born at Jasper House in 1850, had a fascinating collection of furs, including twenty-four silver fox skins. After a few days when his furs were put up for auction they brought nearly $19,000. For a week this was the talk of the town, and for the first time Shand-Harvey came into actual contact with the ages-old fur trade.

And everyone – fur trader, businessman, surveyor or prospector – was so friendly. Nearly all were young men ready for any new sight, new adventure or new friend.

"What's your moniker?" asked a young stranger beside him at the bar.

"I'm sorry," smiled Shand-Harvey, "but I don't understand."

"What's your name?"

"Oh, Shand-Harvey."

"Glad to meet you, Shand. Mine's Tom Carter."

"Well, my first name is Jim. Shand is part of my last name – Shand-Harvey."

"Oh, one of those double-barrelled names, eh? Well, I'll call you Shand, and everybody calls me Tom. Have a drink, Shand."

Thus was James Shand-Harvey given the name he was to bear through more than half a century in the West.

Edmonton was not only friendly, it was booming. Located as it was, with all the farming land anyone could want south and east for two hundred miles and all its timber and minerals north and west, it was destiny's child. And beyond all these, the riches of the far north poured into its lap.

Hitherto Edmonton had been neglected by fate. The Canadian Pacific Railway had planned to run through it, but at the last moment had been diverted through the south of the province. For a while Edmonton had languished, but in 1891 when the Calgary & Edmonton Railway reached Strathcona, it had taken on a new lease of life while it fought for supremacy with its rival on the south side of the river. The keen business sense of Edmonton's merchants had turned the tide in its favour when they capitalized on the influx of money in the hands of the Klondikers of 1897–1898. Then, since Edmonton seemed determined not to die on the vine, a railway had crawled slowly from the Strathcona station of the CPR down the Mill Creek Ravine and across the Low Level Bridge to its Edmonton terminus at the foot of McDougall Hill. At last Edmonton had a railway – one basking in the most grandiloquent name on the roll call of magniloquent titles, the Edmonton, Yukon & Pacific – but earthbound by the fact that in a straight line its termini lay one and a quarter miles apart.

Now in 1905 Edmonton's doldrums lay in the past along with the days of railways that promised but never performed. Even as Shand Harvey arrived at the Windsor Hotel two transcontinental railways were speeding west across the prairies as rapidly as men could build grades and lay steel. In fact, the Canadian Northern Railway was due to reach Edmonton before Christmas. Burns, its construction engineer, arrived in Edmonton that very week to look over a possible route to Stony Plain. McCrimmon's construction camp was on the point of moving out to Morinville for further work in that direction. Moreover, Shand had already spent an idle afternoon watching the river drivers assembling the timbers which were to be floated off downstream for the temporary railway bridge at Fort Saskatchewan. The Grand Trunk Pacific Railway, the other transcontinental, was not so near to Edmonton, but it was on its way, striding west two or three miles a day over the great plain.

Shand's first week in Edmonton was more or less typical of any other week during those early years, yet it was witness to more activity than occupied a full year in regions more staid. The new steamer *Alberta*, larger and more impressive than the older boats, completed its maiden voyage from its launching site at Prince Albert. New coal mines were opening up downstream, just at the edge of the city limits. That week the Reverend John McDougall, the famous old missionary who could look back to over forty years in Alberta, arrived in the city from Calgary. Fletcher Bredin of Lesser Slave Lake was in town on business, and G. A. McLeod, in charge of a government party, had returned after making a report on the Peace River block in the vicinity of Fort St John.

Jasper Avenue rejoiced because the crop outlook was good. Indeed, on August 14 the farmers out Belmont way were already cutting barley. A few days later at Stony Plain wheat was being harvested. As Shand wandered about watching and listening and pausing now and then to talk to anyone who came along, the feel of this Edmonton was beginning to seep in. This embryo city, its interests interwoven with those of the vast undeveloped hinterland, was a vibrant, pulsing frontier community. It was animated by its role of outfitting new settlers and stimulated daily by never-ending reports of vast new riches. At the market square, where produce was traded, horses, mules and oxen, as well as wagons and farm machinery, were available. Huge livery barns catered to this civilization made mobile by the sweat and patience of horses. Blacksmiths divided their time between shoeing horses and repairing wagons and farm machinery. Shand was fascinated by the smiths' role of breaking range horses. He could seldom pass the square without seeing a blacksmith leading an unbroken horse rigged up in casting ropes. The rugged discipline of these ropes was applied time and again until the bronco was brought to realize that he must submit to the man's will. When he would allow his feet to be lifted and held without too much struggle, he was considered to be broken and was then led into the shop to be shod.

In this small city everyone knew everyone else, or so it seemed from the easy familiarity that prevailed. While only at fleeting moments in the history of any region can there be complete freedom from class distinction, Shand had found Edmonton at this stage. He saw one instance of this one day while looking down from his hotel window. Two men with picks and shovels were digging a basement when one of the three men in the city police force stopped to talk to them. In a moment he was joined by no less a personage than the mayor, Charlie May, his shirt open at the neck. He too stopped, and it was obvious from the ensuing banter that all four men knew and liked each other. Someone in this assemblage of the mayor, the representative of law and order, and the two navvies made a suggestion which appeared to meet with general approval, for the two men climbed out of the excavation and, joined by the mayor, adjourned to the hotel bar, leaving the policeman standing alone. To Shand it seemed a pity that the rigorous conditions of his office should debar the policeman from the consummation of fellowship which was obviously going on inside. His pity was short-lived, however, and totally uncalled for, because after a careful look up and down the street, the policeman joined his companions in the bar.

This incident pointed up for Shand one of the outstanding characteristics of this new land, a fellowship that was not hindered in its expression by reason of social or official position. Even legal convention was not taken too seriously if it threatened to interfere with that free association which appeared to be much more important.

Somewhat later Shand went downstairs and looked at the notices on the bulletin board. One announcement stated that Madam Bayla had been induced by popular demand to remain at the Windsor Hotel for another week while she continued the practice of palmistry and fortune telling. Shand smiled. The recent demonstration by the mayor, the policeman and the navvies had settled his future. If any doubts had remained, this display of Western camaraderie had settled them. As a city maybe Edmonton left something to be desired, but its cordiality could not be surpassed. Every day the West was opening up new vistas.

In a day or so the rain let up, and Shand wandered around the embryo capital. Its busy streets were redolent with the smell of fresh lumber which was being literally thrown up into new homes and into pretentious false-fronted stores. For a few blocks south and west of the business section, a few brick houses peered out of the poplars. The Empire Building diagonally across from the hotel had just been erected and was the finest building in the city. But most of the houses were of wood, and there were a great many log shacks. Shand, who for most of the unknown years ahead was to live in log cabin or teepee, was struck by the lack of permanence in these wooden buildings.

Everything here was new and different, and Shand had come to partake of its newness, even rawness. This new freedom, this absence of convention, was what he had hoped to find. Now he enjoyed it, and grinned as he applied one of the new expressions he had already picked up in the West. He hoped soon to be "in cahoots with it."

So many little things were new. Rings let into the wooden sidewalks, to which horses were tethered, struck him as odd. So for that matter did the strap with the heavy weight attached to it which was snapped to the bit of a buggy horse to keep him from wandering. The crowds on Jasper Avenue were new to him – new in variety, cosmopolitan. There were Scandinavians and Slavs, Dutch and Germans, Irish and Italians, Armenians and Israelites, as well as the various branches of the Anglo-Saxon family. The proportion of Gaelic and Gallic was very high, and so were the clearly discernible shadings of these two into the duskiness of the aboriginal Albertans. Besides these mixtures of peoples on Jasper Avenue, Negroes from the far south strolled along, while Chinese, already established in cafés and laundries, jogged by with their bundles, making way now and then for a stately Blackfoot or a silent Cree. Many races and all colours were represented, except the turbaned East Indian with whom Shand had been familiar in Mauritius. Perhaps, he thought, the conforming product of the ages-old civilization of India had no place in this polyglot assembly of opportunists who were free for the reason that they were mainly nonconformists.

Being of Scottish ancestry, although with a burr softened by years at Eton, Shand felt at home in this Edmonton which teemed with clannish Scots. The city was full of them, either as craftsmen, shopkeepers or homesteaders. The railway companies' surveyors, engineers and contractors were mainly Scottish – McCrimmons and McLeods, Mackenzies and Manns. There was money to be made in railroad construction, planning and finance, and the Scots, aggressive and canny, planned to make it.

On September 1, while the steel of the Canadian Northern was approaching at the rate of two or three miles a day and a temporary bridge was being built near Fort Saskatchewan, the citizens of Edmonton were jubilant. At long last the transcontinental railways were on their way. At long last also the southern half of the old Northwest Territories, some 500,000 square miles, was about to be carved into two vast self-governing regions, which were to be erected into the provinces of Alberta and Saskatchewan. Edmontonians had correctly assumed that their city would become the capital of the western province.

Even Shand, who from his years with the Argyll and Sutherland Highlanders and his association with London and Windsor Castle was steeped in the fanfare and precision of military ceremonial, was caught up in the general jubilation of his fellow Albertans. He watched the procession as it formed up at the old Columbia Hotel – the official party, the old-timers, the Jean Baptiste Society, the Boer War Veterans and many others. To the music of the Edmonton, Strathcona and St Albert bands, together with that of the 15th Light Horse Band from Calgary, he marched off to the Exhibition Grounds then located on the flats below McDougall Hill. Commissioner Perry and Superintendent Primrose of the Mounted Police were there with their troops, which performed with remarkable precision. One of Canada's three greatest prime ministers, Sir Wilfred Laurier, was there that day to add his benediction. Courtly of figure, with finely chiselled face, he rose to speak. All was hushed. "I see everywhere hope. I see everywhere calm resolution, courage, enthusiasm to face all difficulties, to settle all problems." He spoke to this people of many nations, urging them to be British subjects, to take their share of the life of this country, whether it was municipal, provincial or national. "We do not anticipate, and we do not want, that any individuals should forget the land of their origin or their ancestors. Let them look to the past, but let them also look to the future; let them look to the land of their ancestors, but let them look also to the land of their children."

The ceremonies continued until, at high noon, in the presence of twelve thousand loyal Albertans, the oath of office was read to the Lieutenant-Governor elect, George Bulyea. He kissed the Bible, and Alberta became a province.

As the day wore on, Shand found his most absorbing interest

in the four polo teams, from Calgary, Cochrane, Alix and Edmonton. Their competition ended with a win for Calgary, much to the chagrin of Edmontonians in general and in particular to F. C. Jamieson of the Edmonton team.

Eventually the celebrations of the day drew to a close. While the people prepared for the dinner and the evening's festivities, Shand went for a walk towards Fort Edmonton. Beside the little ravine near 109th Street he passed one of the Indian camps. He was amazed by the multitude of dogs and surprised at the inferiority of most of the horses tethered to wagon boxes or trees, and at the untidiness and apparent dirtiness of the people. The scent of the smoke rising from the teepees and cooking fires, however, appealed to him. Some of the white man's whisky had spilled over to these people, and a few of the younger men were maudlin. But in general the group was a happy one. In God's name why? thought Shand. Propped against the tents, babies dozed in their backboards or peered with wide-eyed scrutiny at the activity around the fires. The young boys and girls, black-eyed and button-nosed, played happily about or watched him uncertainly. The adolescent girls were comely and trim, but beyond that age all the women, except the very old, seemed to be fat. The old crones sat smoking quietly or busied themselves with some light household chore. Their faces, wrinkled and thin, seemed to exude the patience and the wisdom of the ages. What passions and privations, Shand wondered, what joys and sorrows over the long years in the bush had added up to the patience and the humour in these faces and had etched these wrinkles?

Shand's thoughts as he left the camp were a mingling of pity and depression. In themselves these people were not pitiable, but fate in the form of the inrush of intolerant white men had engulfed them. Of the twelve thousand people in Edmonton for the day's ceremonies, none but a handful of priests and missionaries gave any thought to these dispossessed owners of all the West. Even the kindly and tolerant Sir Wilfred Laurier had said "I see hope everywhere." What hope was there for these Indians, whose roots went thousands of years back into Canada's past? Laurier's advice to Canadians to look more to the land of their children than to that of their ancestors overlooked these Indians for whom this was the land of their ancestors but would nevermore be the land of their children.

Shand walked on until at the edge of the high terrace west of the Fort he sat down to soak in the sublimity of a September evening on the Saskatchewan River. Far below in its magnificent valley, where dark spruces were interspersed with the yellows of the poplars and the reds of ripening shrubbery, the mighty river swept towards him from far out of the west. At his back lay the old Fort, and beyond it the city of Edmonton, filled this evening with rejoicing and bustle. Ahead lay this great river, bringing tidings from countless unknown lakes, unscaled hills and untrodden valleys. From hundreds of miles to the west it flowed, even from the very tips of the mountain crags that marked the Continental Divide. Some two hundred miles upstream lay the next fur trade post, Rocky Mountain House. Nearer at hand, for perhaps thirty miles, white settlers were scratching clearings out of the bush. And beyond that, for maybe sixty miles, only solitary sawmills desecrated the silence and the tidiness of the forest. Except for these petty pinpricks, the vast forest to the west lay untouched, serene and mysterious. Behind, far far away, lay the confining fetters of Europe. Behind and much nearer at hand lay the frantic, money-mad civilization of eastern North America. Behind and only half a mile away lay the friendly frontier settlement of Edmonton. But tonight, even there, what masked struggles were going on in the turmoil of social, political and financial strivings?

Ahead lay the West and this vast river, its valley a deepening purple as, for a few brief moments, the sun, sliding behind unknown hilltops far to the west, cast its glory on the red and gold clouds in the western sky. When the last thin streak of gold had faded to a cold blue cloud and had dissolved into gathering darkness, Shand stood up to return to his hotel. His mind was made up. All doubts were gone. This land of wilderness and mountains was to be his land.

J OBS were easy to get in September 1905, but
Shand did not want to work in Edmonton. Before long he met
Alfred Driscoll of the surveying firm of Driscoll & Knight. When
he asked for a job that would take him out of town – anywhere,
so long as it was out in the country – Driscoll assigned him to a
party under his assistant Bob Heathcote, who was to make an
official survey of the Old Victoria Trail.

Alfred Driscoll could understand the desire of a young man to
get out into the country. His own working years had been spent
in journeyings across the vastness of the Northwest Territories.
Even though as a surveyor he was doing all he could to fetter the
great outdoors by parcelling it into pieces hedged in by cut-lines,
survey mounds and stakes, Fred Driscoll knew and loved the
unexplored wilderness.

He typified a generation of great land surveyors. About 1869
it had become evident that the old Rupert's Land of the Hudson's
Bay Company would be transferred to Canada and that a rush
of settlers might be anticipated; the Dominion government then
set in motion the process of subdividing the prairie and parkland regions of the Territories into sections of 640 acres and
quarters of 160 acres. Throughout the vast area of some 300,000
square miles a system of survey, unsurpassed in its consistency
and exactitude, was adopted.

In the remarkably short space of thirty-five years the laying
out of most of the sections of land was accomplished by the
surveyors of Fred Driscoll's generation. First the prairies were
subdivided in an effort to keep ahead of the influx of hundreds
of thousands of settlers. In the years after 1900 these surveys were
pushed into the forested lands north of the North Saskatchewan
River and west towards the foothills. Even in this area some
settlers, in their hunger for farms, squatted on land not yet sur-

veyed. It was hard to predict what rumours of hay meadows or of enticing valleys might lure them into some hitherto inaccessible valley ahead of the surveyors. On the other hand, some forest lands had been surveyed years before settlers came to search out the iron corner posts of the sections.

Year after year the surveyors went about their task of subdividing in the heavy forest where they prophesied that no one would ever settle. The old-time Dominion land surveyors may have believed that their work would be wasted, but they did a meticulous job. In the middle of winter they could run a line ten miles or so through the forest, over hill and dale, crossing muskeg and lake, and at the end of it have an error that could only be measured in inches. The survey parties went out each winter, travelling what trails they could till they came to the end of the trail, and then struck out for the township where they were to work. When they had finished, the forest was everywhere intersected by cut-lines, four or five feet wide and running for miles. In the spring they returned to Edmonton to check their calculations and to draw their plans and maps.

The old-time land surveyors were a rare breed – quiet, thoughtful, accurate. Quiet, because for nearly a year at a time they worked perhaps hundreds of miles from the nearest settlement and with very few people to talk to. Thoughtful, for the star-studded skies, the great silences and the empty spaces induced profound thought, unhampered by the jabbering crowds of civilization. Accurate, as with almanac, chronometer and transit they marked the times and the seasons of the stars, making intricate calculations in their carefully kept field books. Far out in the forest, two hundred miles from the nearest settlement or survey monument, they extracted information from the inscrutable stars. With Castor and Pollux, Sirius and Polaris as guides they chopped a line through the forests or scratched it over rocky cliffs, and marked it with pits, cairns, mounds and pins, to testify to all men for all time that this meridian was exactly where they said it was. For all time, their fellows would judge them by the accuracy of this line.

Such men were Alfred Driscoll and Bob Heathcote, with whom Shand Harvey began his apprenticeship. With wagon transport and camping equipment and a cook, the party set off one fall morning along the Old Victoria Trail. Past the contented farms of Belmont and Horse Hills they rode, travelling now and then parallel to the almost completed grade of the Canadian Northern, making its way from Fort Saskatchewan to Edmonton. The Sturgeon River, the old Namao Seepee of the Crees, was crossed on a wooden bridge, and the party began its work in the area of rich soil beyond it.

In places the trail kept to the high land, looking down hundreds of feet to the silvery river. In other stretches it descended to the very banks of the river, while the valley walls far above, dark and mysterious on the south side of the river but open and welcoming on the north side, glowed in their autumn magnificence of yellows and reds. On these banks, midst grotesque jack pine and stately spruce, the glory of yellow aspens was trimmed by the red of cherry, saskatoon and dogwood. Along this trail Shand saw the Alberta countryside at its best in all the spiciness and the richness of early fall.

At intervals along the river a few planks had been laid over piles pounded into the river mud to form a landing for the stern-wheel river steamers. Although this late in the season the steamboats had been taken off, it was obvious that the Saskatchewan River was the chain of communication for all settlers venturing into the forests on either side. From their homesteads back in the deep forest the settlers came to these landings to ship any produce they had for sale and to pick up needed supplies. From these landings each spring and summer new settlers set out into the adjoining country to try their luck. In the fall and winter when the stern-wheelers did not run, the line of communication lay along the Victoria Trail. No new settlers were coming in this late in the year, but the survey party met many of the pioneers busily preparing their crude but snug homesteads to withstand the shock of an Alberta winter.

Life on a survey party was very much to Shand's liking. With his good education and knowledge of mathematics, he spent his evenings in camp helping the surveyor with his computations. Fred Driscoll suggested that he should study for two or three months and assured him that, if he did so, he could pass the Alberta Land Surveyor examinations without difficulty. Then he would be able to set himself up in a highly respected profession, one in which he need never lack lucrative employment and which would ensure enjoyable work out of doors. But Shand was not ready to be tied down and he postponed any such decisive step.

As the year 1905 drew to a close, survey work came to an end for another season, and Shand had some time on his hands. Of the many hotels in Edmonton at that time, the Alberta, the Queens and the Windsor were the better ones, and the Windsor was the newest and the most pretentious. The others supplied good rooms and wholesome board at a dollar a day, with a cheaper rate for those who paid by the week. Shand's earnings sufficed to keep him in comfort at the Windsor.

The hotel registers themselves were great books like ledgers, lying open in elaborately embossed metal frames, holding in one corner an inkwell and in the other a push bell. On these, open for all to see, were the signatures of the guests who, on one errand or another, had come and gone or were still in the house. Such a register as that of the Windsor displayed the names of men who had a hand in opening up the West – the adventurous, the great, the near great, and the merely wealthy. These men came seeking the best accommodation the city could afford. Some of them had not slept in a bed for months, and when, on returning to the city, they blew off steam, nothing was too good for them.

To the Windsor came the explorers, the railway engineers, surveyors and contractors: the rich men from older Canada, seeking new adventures or a new way of life. In these Western hotels contacts were made between men of funds and men of ideas, and many a life-long partnership or friendship had its birth in names displayed on the same page of a hotel register. Everyone signing it flipped over the pages to see who was in town, for it was a bulletin board of all the adventures afoot.

It was due to the Windsor register that Shand set out on his second adventure into the area east of Edmonton. Charlie Ward, an Irishman who had come in from his homestead at Sick Man Lake in the Lavoy-Vegreville country, spotted Shand's name. Possessed of a similar background and having known him in England, he hastened to look up his old friend. Ward, who was well fixed and single, had decided to try his hand at farming, and in addition to his homestead he had bought some Canadian Northern Railway land. He suggested that Shand come out to his place and help put up some buildings and corrals. Since this would show him more of the country, and would be added experience, he was glad to go.

In December these two set out by team and cutter. By lunch time they reached Fort Saskatchewan, the village that had grown up around the Northern Alberta Headquarters of the Mounted Police, which had been established there in 1875.

From Fort Saskatchewan, Shand and his friend followed the old fur trade trail in a direction slightly north of east for about twenty miles to the hamlet of Star, in one of the new farming communities which were springing up adjacent to the trail. Here, after a long drive, they rejoiced in the hospitality of Swan's Stopping Place.

Eventually they reached Vegreville, another oasis of settlement and apparent prosperity in the vast area of parkland. The hamlet of Vegreville and its immediate community had been started in 1895 by a group of French Canadians from Kansas. That fall these hardy pioneers, the Poulins, Dumonts, Tetréaults and Lamberts, had established a post office. Several years later, in 1900, the first English-speaking settlers, mostly from the midwestern states – the Coles, Trenhailes, Leaches, Tierneys, Dennises and Wilsons – arrived to start farming on a relatively large scale.

At the time of Shand's visit, quite a village remained here on the banks of the Vermilion River. There were general stores, a doctor, a dentist, and of course a blacksmith, as well as a one-man police detachment, but an air of doom hung over the hamlet. The Canadian Northern had passed it by and had set up a station which it called Vegreville, also on the river but some three or four miles north and east. Even as Shand and Charlie Ward dined with the hotelkeeper, Mr St Hilare, other hotels and stores were being rushed to completion in the new town, while most of the businesses in the old town had already moved or were on the move to the railway.

In fact, St Hilare's hotel had been built with this doom hanging over it, and many of its appointments were of a temporary nature. The bedrooms upstairs, besides having no doors, were very small, only about three feet wider than the beds. The only partitions between them consisted of building paper suspended from the ceiling without any supporting framework. When Shand was undressing for bed he had a misadventure. Why he did not sit down on the bed to take off his socks he doesn't know, but for some reason he tried to remove them while he was standing up. He lost his balance, burst through the flimsy wall and fell onto the bed next door, which fortunately was empty.

In the morning Shand and Charlie were amused by one of the true stories told at breakfast. Pete More, as the sole Mounted Policeman at Vegreville, maintained law and order over a vast territory. He was liked and respected by all, even by those who from time to time encountered him in his official capacity. Part of the Mounted Police establishment was a log jail some ten feet long and six feet wide. Inside there were two bunks, one over the other, and above them the roof of poles was covered with sods. When the jail had no occupants, the travelling public used it as a bunkhouse.

One night Pete had been relaxing in the hotel bar enjoying the normal pleasures of the place. One of the guests took on too big a load and, in spite of the efforts of his friends to keep him under control, he created such a disturbance that Pete had no choice but to arrest him and put him in the cooler for the night. A short time later Pete was called into the country on some official errand. While he was away, his prisoner began to miss the good fellowship of the bar. The more he thought of it, the more his thirst grew. Finally climbing to the upper bunk, he proceeded to break jail by pushing the roof poles aside and removing enough sods so that he could scramble through. Back to the bar he went, to rejoin his friends.

They were aghast at seeing him. Pete More was everyone's friend, and they all took it upon themselves to point out to the prisoner what a really low-down trick it was to escape from Pete's jail. He considered the matter while he absorbed another drink or two. By now his aggressive mood had softened into a more sentimental stage. Then, convinced that arguing with Pete or fighting with him was all in a day's work but that only a low-down skunk would escape his custody, he crawled back through the roof and filled in the hole as best he could. He slept peacefully through the night and appeared before the Justice of the Peace next morning. This incident, unlikely perhaps in any other country, is a clear illustration of the deep respect the early settlers had for law and order. Many may have brought this respect with them, but much of it came from the calibre of the Mounted Police who carried out the administration of the law.

After a good and an entertaining breakfast, Shand and Charlie resumed their trip. Going around by the new town, and then east over the hill some ten miles farther, they reached Charlie's place, near the shore of Sick Man Lake. This was in the vicinity of the newly created town of Lavoy, named after Joseph Lavoy, who some years previously had taken up a homestead, operated a stopping place, and kept the post office. Before the advent of the railway the post office had been called Dinwoodie.

This trip to Sick Man Lake, some seventy miles straight east of Edmonton, gave Shand a good look at that part of the country. All the available land for several miles on each side of the trail from Edmonton to Fort Saskatchewan and as far east as Star was already fully settled. Little produce was grown for export any farther than Edmonton, and, as a result, the farms were operated largely on a basis of self-sufficiency. There were a few nice farm houses, although the bulk of them were built of logs. From Star east, most of the land was occupied but it was obvious that the settlers were in their first year or so on the land. Little land was cultivated, and many of the log shacks were mere crude beginnings of homes thrown up hastily as a temporary shelter from the rigours of the climate. Many of these newcomers were Ukrainians, but that was a term not used in those days, as these peasant people were generally known as Galicians. To many Canadians who had been domiciled a generation or two in the Dominion and who did not like this influx of "foreigners," they were known as Bohunks. Nearly all of these people were practically penniless when they reached Edmonton. Anything they had acquired in the year or so since had been gained by the labours of their bare, unaided hands. Their farmsteads testified to their extreme poverty but also to their optimism and their willingness to make any sacrifice in the way of comfort so long as they might gain a foothold on this splendid soil and in this air of freedom. The extent of the freedoms of this new land was not yet clearly understood, but in spite of the smarting intolerance of the English-speaking element, it seemed almost too good to be true.

Many of the temporary homes of the settlers of Canadian, American, German or Scandinavian extraction were built of the light poles available in the parkland and were roofed with sods. Most of the homes of the Ukrainians were equally crude, but already here and there, when a Ukrainian farmer had been on the land long enough to harvest a cut of long rye straw, the thatched roofs, that for years kept these people warm and dry, were beginning to make their appearance. Trim and clean they were too, these two-roomed, thatch-roofed, mud-plastered and clay-floored houses, built to face south, with one window on the left as you entered the house and two on the right. Tidy and clean, too, were the neat clay, open-air bake ovens in the corner of the yard. But in the first year before some of these people had time to build much of a house, some of their homes were crude in the extreme. Shand wondered how anyone could live under such conditions, even for a short time, but he concluded that at times necessity brings us all to strange passes.

Charlie Ward gave Shand his first experience as an axe man as they worked together felling trees for building logs and erecting them into various stables and corrals. But as well as building, there was time for frequent sallies into the adjacent bush in search of bush partridges or for a stroll over Sick Man Hill, where, in the most open parkland, prairie chicken abounded. At first Shand enjoyed himself killing these birds with a shot gun – on the wing and in the approved manner. Soon, however, he was satiated with this sport and subsided to the status of a pot hunter with a ·22 rifle. While the two men lived mainly on chicken or partridges, the few they killed made scarcely any impression on the abundance of these birds.

Shand had heard dire prophecies of the rigours of the Canadian winter, but the mild winter of 1905–1906 he enjoyed. There were two or three light falls of snow, and once he had been initiated into the mysteries and excellence of Indian moccasins in dry snow, he found the weather delightful.

Each evening Shand looked forward to his stroll after partridge just before sunset. The adjacent woods and the willows around the shore of the lake were full of them. The light fall of snow had covered up the bare leaves so that a man could stroll about without making any noise. The crisscross tracks in the snow indicated the abundance of rabbits and partridges, while here and there weasel or coyote tracks made it plain that other hunters were abroad. The red cranberries and flaming rose hips glowed against the white snow, and occasionally Shand scared up a partridge which had been adding these berries to his bulging crop. For the most part, however, the partridges seemed to prefer willow buds. Many a time after shooting all the birds he needed off one willow tree, Shand stood to watch the unperturbed calm with which the remainder of the birds in this same tree kept on with their leisurely feeding. Instead of taking the few he needed, he might have killed several times as many, but already he was beginning to get the feel of the bush and a feeling of somehow being allied to these birds and of partaking of their enjoyment of nature's abundance. How little it takes, he reflected, to keep a man in food.

In a similar mood and with equal enjoyment he set forth over the open spaces of Sick Man Hill as dawn was breaking to exact his quota of prairie chicken. Here, too, as the December sun in a burst of magenta and gold set aflame the ribbons of cloud in the eastern sky, he marvelled at the flocks of chickens roosting in the poplars. All around for a distance of perhaps half a mile the trees were crowded with family groups of these beautiful birds, which, in their inexperience, paid little attention to the crack of the hunter's ·22. Often, after shooting three or four, Shand sat down to revel in the sight of the plenty of the parklands. In the Old Country, crowded with people, grouse-shooting was necessarily the prerogative of the few who could preserve them. And there it was pursued with a finesse unknown to pot hunters in this land of plenty. Here, over untold square miles of parkland, these uncounted flocks of prairie fowl fed unmolested, and here the shadowy recesses of the forest teemed with partridges.

While partridges and chickens were shot sparingly and almost with regret, the primeval hunting instinct of the two bachelors was allowed free rein when coyotes were the game. Since rabbits were plentiful, lynx and coyotes likewise abounded and gave Shand and Charlie many a merry chase. The bright winter's day was often spent in this sport. At the same time, coyote skins were worth money. A good one brought in a day's wages and could be sold for a dollar and a half. And in those good old days a quart of Seagrams 83 – used, mind you, to ward off possible rheumatism contracted in the pursuit of coyotes – cost one dollar.

Perhaps Shand's most lasting impressions of this area were his walks through the trees where the stark shadows cast on the crisp snow by the full moon contrasted with the ethereal mystery of the evening landscape. On such nights when the rabbits were hunched beside the path and the partridges and prairie chicken were black silhouettes against the bright sky, the silence and the solitude of the undisturbed forest struck deep into his soul.

During one of these walks he resolved that immediately after he reached Edmonton he would sell his return ticket to England. So after a New Year's celebration, made merrier by the refreshments provided by the sale of coyote pelts, he returned to Edmonton. This trip was done in one day in all the luxury of a train, for in December the Canadian Northern had commenced running regular trains into the city. From Lavoy west to Lamont the route of the railway lay some miles distant from the old trail, but from that point into Edmonton the two were seldom out of sight of each other. What a difference this railway was making. Every few miles embryo towns were springing into being – Vegreville, Mundare, Chipman and Lamont – and the inhabitants of the former hamlets were moving their businesses and skidding their buildings over to the new towns. Of these, Old Vegreville and the hamlet of Star, which moved in to Lamont, were the two main examples. From now on, everything was oriented towards this new railway, and of course new post offices were being set up in these growing centres.

The railway was a great economic boost to all the region. It would provide access to markets for grain and cattle, which before could not be marketed economically and, therefore, were raised on a very limited scale. The new villages meant stores where supplies and even luxuries could be had, and to them came doctors, lawyers, dentists. Even before its completion, the railroad had made a major contribution to the economy of the settlers. Most of them, by working with the construction crews, had been able to feed their families and to save a little money towards buying stock and machinery. The money the railways spent was the means of setting many a hard-pressed pioneer upon his feet.

But with the coming of the railway much of the old freedom of pioneer life passed, and with it went some of the spirit of the open door. As more people came in, the cares and even the dregs of civilization came with them. Before the railway, stealing was almost unknown. Shand recalls the indignation of one settler who had lost a set of eveners and doubletrees. He had left them at the edge of his field, and when he returned for them a few days later they were missing. If the owner of such items was not at home, a neighbour might borrow them but at the first opportunity brought them back, or else explained that he had taken them. But in this case these eveners had been stolen. The owner was aghast. It was not the value – three dollars would buy another set – but the thought that someone had stooped to stealing. What hurt everybody was the feeling that the whole character of the area had been damaged.

As soon as Shand reached Edmonton he sold his return ticket, thereby cutting a symbolic link with the Old Land and setting his feet for good upon the trails that lay beyond the end of the railways. As he folded up the money and stepped out onto Jasper Avenue, he strolled west. From here on, this land, rough and raw but vigorous and free, was to be his land. He tried to define his feeling of freedom. It was not the freedom from serfdom or despotism that many of the so-called "foreigners" on Jasper Avenue enjoyed. It was not freedom from the rule of law and order, for these, the essence of British tradition, he was glad to discover, were still with him. It was a freedom of the soul, a freedom from crowding, from conventionality and from artificiality. So long as a man earned his keep and obeyed a few laws, so long as in time of need he extended a helping hand, so long as he left his door unlocked, he could come and go as he pleased, do or refrain from doing as he chose; and no man would question whence he came or whither he was going. And whether along busy street or backwoods trail, every man, high or low, rich or poor, wise or witless, would raise his hand in glad and genuine greeting.

Shand looked west along the packed snow of Jasper Avenue. It is but a step, he thought, from the whistle of trains and the rattle of telegraph keys – a short step to the silence of the wilderness. For a few blocks the sidewalks extended. Beyond that for a few more blocks spruce and poplar trees crowded close upon the wide trail. At its end the line of sight continued as a broad cut-line eight feet wide, carrying the vision up and down over hill and valley, and on towards the West. Towards the mountains. After a few miles, somewhere lost to vision, this cut-line too would stop, and beyond that, far into the West, what unknown valleys and meadows, what unknown cascades or crags lay waiting to commune with any man whose heart would leap at the sight of them?

CHAPTER
THREE

———⊶❁⊷———

In 1906 Shand became a homesteader. "That," he says now, "was in the spring when a young man's fancy turns to many things, including daydreams of pastoral pleasures."

Before homesteading he stayed in Edmonton for the rest of that short, mild winter. There life was comfortable and exciting, and through the doors of the Windsor Hotel passed all the adventurers of the time. One of these was the daring and eccentric Jackie Hornby. He and Shand had similar cultural backgrounds. Both had left these behind, preferring the challenge beyond the end of steel. While Shand was to seek his in the forests in the shadow of Roche Miette, Jackie was to become a legend of eccentricity and endurance where the last stunted trees give way to the moss-girt rocks of the Barren Lands.

Many an escapade filled in the idle days as these young men waited for the coming of spring and the start of another season's activities. One day in the Alberta Hotel Jackie Hornby had been telling of some of his experiences and of how he planned to go into the far north. Jim Depasse, who appeared dubious, brought him up short. "Why, you'll never be able to stand a winter up there. A stiff winter here is as much or more than you can stand. Up there you'll have to travel by dog team and you'll have to run miles and miles to keep up with them."

"Well?" retorted Hornby.

"Yes, well!" said Depasse. "It's not really cold today, but I'll bet you couldn't run at a good clip from here to the Windsor Hotel even at this temperature."

"Like to race me?"

"Sure would. Just to show you up," laughed Depasse. "Huh! By the time you get there you'll be panting so hard you won't be able to talk."

Some of the other young bloods entered the discussion, and

soon it was agreed that the contestants should not only dash down the centre of Jasper Avenue, but that part of the contest would be the drinking of a quart of beer. The victor would be the one who got to the Windsor and drank the quart of beer before his opponent downed his. Shand Harvey went to the Windsor to have the flagons ready and to be the judge of the contest, and many others from the Alberta Hotel went with him.

After a proper interval the two runners started out abreast down the centre of Jasper Avenue. In a moment Depasse took the lead, dodging in and out amongst the grocery vans, farm sleighs, cutters and beer wagons. In an instant these two were the centre of interest. Horses shied, dogs barked and children yelled, and it looked as if Depasse was running for his life from some obviously crazed trapper. Then as Hornby overtook Depasse without harming him, it was realized that this was some prank. As the pair neared the Windsor, the crowd there cheered them on. The two ran up the steps almost in the same breath, although sadly short of that substance, as they soon realized when their lungs rebelled at any attempt to drink. Amid gasps, splutters and foam and hearty laughter, Hornby was adjudged the winner, and drinks were set up all around.

In such carefree company the winter days passed quickly. March arrived, and with it the influx of the twenty-four recently elected Members of the Legislative Assembly. From time to time Shand and his cronies went down to listen to their discussions and came away impressed with the obvious ability of most of the pioneers who composed it. Some of the niceties of debate may have been missing, but on the whole these men knew what they wanted and were clear in their thinking and forthright in their speaking.

In April, Shand went north to Edison to find a homestead for his new-found friends Arthur Lucas and his young wife. Lucas suggested that Shand might also like to file on a quarter-section. Shand was not too keen on the idea. The hope of most settlers was that, after putting in a few years of hard work on a homestead, they would be rewarded by becoming prosperous farmers strolling about their expansive acres, tallying their riches of fat kine. Shand felt that, while such an ambition was commendable, he was not ready to be incarcerated in one spot, especially if the sentence involved not only confinement but continuous hard labour. He had toyed with the idea of working on some railway survey party which would take him out to Yellowhead Pass. The Canadian Northern was already building into Stony Plain and carrying out surveys towards Lake Wabamun.

In the end he threw in his lot with the Lucas family and set out for what was then known as the Little Grand Prairie, a small area between the present towns of Clyde and Westlock, where at some time in the previous twenty years a fire had killed the forest. Since that time about a township of land had grown up to willow brush, young poplar and open grassy places. This, according to the rumour, lay some twenty-five miles north of Morinville. It was to this little prairie that Jack Edgson had gone in 1902 and it was here that George MacLachlan and his friends had decided to try their luck.

The road was good to St Albert and on to Morinville, but after that became more difficult as it swung through the heavy forest around the west side of Egg Lake, passed the sawmill at Casavant and crossed the Redwater River and Hay Creek to emerge into the Edison settlement. The trail from the sawmill was very crude. Shand learned afterwards that less than four years before, when Jack Edgson and his brothers, the first homesteaders, had come in they had opened this route into the Westlock country. It wound around trees and over stumps. The half-buried logs and the tree roots gave a jarring, rocking motion to the wagon as the wheels hit the roots first on one side and then on the other. The trees on each side got their bark rubbed off as the axles scraped against them in squeezing by. The floor of the forest was nearly always wet, but at first a lightly loaded wagon could get through easily enough. Most wagons passing over it, however, cut through the soft humus and began to wear holes and ruts. These filled with water, and each succeeding wagon found the road more difficult, until in the lower spots teams began to get stuck in the mud holes. Often the settlers had to cut a short bypass around the mud hole and used this until it too got into the same state. The next teamster who came along was faced with the dilemma of trying to choose the better of two mud holes that looked equally bad.

The Lucases stopped a day or two at the little log shack that was owned by Jack Edgson and was known as the Edison Stopping Place. Shand was puzzled by the discrepancy in names – Edison Stopping Place and Edison Post Office, kept by Jack Edgson, the first settler and after whom the district appeared to have been named. He asked Jack about it.

"Well," Jack replied, "I guess it's a bit hard to understand. My brothers and I came in here in 1902 and we opened up the trail from Casavant and picked out this land. The second group to work their way in here were Neil Forbes, George MacLachlan and his brother, who came out and settled three or four miles over east. After that, many others came in, especially in 1903 – the Maloneys, the Garrisons, the Wests and so on. Nearly all of them stopped at my place till they could get a shack up."

"This area used to be called the Little Grand Prairie?" interrupted Shand.

"Yes, but since everybody stopped at my place it wasn't very long before the area was in effect named after me, and became Edison. You know, several of the early settlers couldn't write. Spelling was not their long suit and anyway it's hard to pronounce Edgson right, and much easier to say Edison. All of America was agog over the inventions of that great man Thomas Edison, so most people called me Jack Edison and this place Edison."

"Well," said Shand, "the post office here now makes the name Edison official, doesn't it?"

"Yes. When we first came in, we got our mail at Egg Lake Post Office – you know, some thirty miles back along the trail. A year or so later, as this area settled up, mail came addressed to the Edison Settlement, Egg Lake Post Office. The official government mail carrier brought it to Egg Lake. Then, whenever anyone was coming out here, he called at the post office there, put all the mail for the settlement into a bag and brought it on. When he stopped at the first farm, he dumped the letters out on the table so that the settler could pick out all of his mail. The rest were carefully gathered up and taken on to the next place, and so on. Finally, what was left was taken over to Joe Maloney's store or to my stopping place, since both of them were convenient unofficial post offices."

"When did you get an official post office?"

"Oh, that was in 1904."

"And you didn't bother to get the name corrected to Edgson?"

"There's a bit of a story to that too. You know, at first in any community everybody is everybody else's friend. Later on, tiffs develop. By the time we were granted a post office, it was decided that my place was centrally located and that I should operate it. But there were some who from jealousy or dislike objected to naming it after me and my brothers and suggested other names. So you see, we compromised," continued Jack Edgson dryly, "and named it after the inventor."

When a log cabin had been built for the Lucases, Shand, refusing Arthur's proffered help, moved on to put up a shack of poplar poles on the quarter he had selected. Like Thoreau, he preferred doing this himself. So, moving north through the trees and the deadfall in what he hoped would be a straight line and for a distance which he hoped would turn out to be about a mile, Shand selected a slight rise in the land, overlooking a brook, and set to work. This, the first home he was to own in Canada for many years, was small, and, even if it was crudely constructed, was nevertheless built with joy. Spring was on the way, yet he did not notice the passage of time until the sod roof was in place and he had a chance to relax.

But the whole effort had been extremely relaxing. The first night that he camped on his homestead was the first time in his whole life that he had spent a night all alone and far from any other human being. He awoke next morning signally refreshed. After a quick rinse at the creek, he cut and fried a bit of bacon and hung his tea pail over the open fire. How little it takes, he reflected, to provide for a man's wants: a dry place to sleep, a bite to eat and a drink from a brook, and occasionally the solace of the company of one's fellows. That is it, he thought, occasionally – not always and continuously at every turn, but once in a while when one wanted it.

He thought of the fire he had built the night before – a little fire to make tea – and how he had sat beside it as the dark came on. A genial fire, smelling of spruce bark and pine needles and willows. As the darkness deepened, the breeze died down, the birds of the bushes and of the marsh fell silent, and finally the last croaking frog had said his say. Even the cheerful crackling of the fire subsided and was silent, except when a pocket of sap in a willow twig exploded and sighed as it was released . . .

And leaves the world to darkness and to me.

Shand lay back with his face turned from the glowing coals and marvelled at the host of stars, countless and fresh, as if tonight they had been newly made and he was the first of all men to see them. Surely this was the first night he really had seen them . . .

And all the air a solemn stillness holds.

After Shand finished his shack, he took his gun and wandered north to where the great forest had been left untouched by the fire since the day over five thousand years ago when the first spruce tree had sprouted at the very edge of the retreating glacier. For all these years there had been uninterrupted growth and decay. Giant trees had grown for two or three centuries and then, overthrown by old age or the wind, had rotted and enriched the earth. During scores of centuries the lesser plants – red willows, hazels, roses, raspberries, dewberries, the trailing honeysuckles and even the lowly grasses – had grown, ripened, and fallen in their turn. The leaf mould and humus was a foot deep. On it, ferns and toadstools and the tiny twinflowers had flourished in the forest's shady depths.

Shand's walk through the woods disclosed an infinite variety in the arrangements of the hundreds of plants that made up the quiet gloaming. Here were open glades and aisles, here low spots five feet deep with peat, its top covered with bright red cranberries snuggled against the moss. A hundred yards away he entered a grove of giant spruce two hundred years old, standing so close that he could almost reach from one to the other. Their great trunks rose straight to the unseen sky bare of limbs for sixty feet and disappeared in a canopy of branches far above the lesser trees. Up there, towering tops swayed and sighed in the breezes or swung and creaked in the gales; below all was calm and quiet as his feet sank into the piles of shelled cones and the mosses of hundreds of years.

Today in spring's hectic puberty the forest was alive as buds swelled and burst, sending their balmy aroma far afield, as flowers sprung full-bloomed from the retreating snowbanks, birds sang and mated, and squirrels challenged. Today the forest was vibrant.

As Shand stood watching some redwing blackbirds on a meadow fringed with willows, another wanderer stepped into view at the other side, a young, scrawny bull moose. In an instant Shand brought his gun up and blazed away. Several things happened. Thinking of it afterwards, he could never seem to work out their exact sequence. The recoil of the gun up-ended him over a log. Its roar deafened him and scared from all adjacent pot-holes a swarm of assorted ducks and blackbirds, which milled around protestingly. As he looked across the meadow, there was no sign of the moose. "Missed him," he thought, but he picked up the gun and hobbled across the meadow. There, hidden by a clump of willows, lay the moose, stone dead, not a muscle jerking. Shand was so busy rubbing his sore shoulder, caressing his swollen cheek and swatting at mosquitoes that he had little time to gloat over this, his first moose. And anyway, this scrawny, shedding, long-legged thing was far from his story-book conception of the majestic, antlered monarch of all the deer tribe. "And I used a howitzer to kill this thing!" he mused. "Must get a smaller gun. This elephant gun nearly killed the hunter as well as the hunted."

Maloney's store and the Edgsons' house were favourite meeting places. Shand went from one to the other to see if anyone had brought out mail for him and to enjoy the discussions that went on there. Jack Edgson often remarked about how easy things were becoming. The Lucases, for instance, had made the trip to Edison in three days. But Jack recalled one of his earlier trips from Edmonton, along the Egg Lake Trail. Trees had fallen over it and had to be chopped through and removed. The endless series of mud holes, where time and time again the wagon had got stuck and the load had to be taken off and carried across to dry land, was heart-breaking. And then it had taken them nearly a day to ford the Vermilion (Redwater) River. The flood waters had swept one of his horses off its feet and nearly drowned it before Jack could find a place to get it up the bank. The trip to his homestead, a straight line distance of forty-five miles, had taken twelve days.

Shand talked also with George MacLachlan, who had home-steaded in 1902. George had fought his way in along the same trail, and laughed as he told of the unnecessary hardships he had endured.

"Why," he said, "we came in by the Egg Lake Trail. We were too green and too independent to ask if there was an easier way. We only found out about the old Athabasca Trail by accident.

"Some months after we were all settled around here, Jack Edgson received a Land Office map. I was over at his place one Sunday when he hung it up on the wall. We all crowded round to look at it.

" 'George,' said Jack, 'what's that heavy line on the map that runs north out of Edmonton and passes up through the sand hills five or six miles east of your place?'

"I looked more closely and there as large as life on the map were the words 'Landing Trail.' 'Well, I'll be damned,' I said, 'that's the Athabasca Landing Trail.'

"So," said George, "right then Jack and I took a buggy and headed through the open spaces and along the edges of the meadows, and a few miles east came to a homesteader's shack. This man explained that he had settled there in the Halfway Lake area two or three years previously, and showed us the good road leading from his place a mile or so to connect up with the Athabasca Trail. For years freighting teams had used this trail, which was high and dry and had bridges and ferries on it.

"Here was this good road where a team could haul a ton, and all the while we had been swinging round west of Egg Lake where a team was lucky if it could pull about five hundred pounds. We weren't long in clearing out a way over to the Landing Trail."

Most of the settlers in the Edison district lived under primitive conditions, but on the whole enjoyed a deep-chested freedom that more than made up for the hardships. Friendliness, helpful-ness and the sharing of good or ill luck bound them into a united community. Of course there were some who, through ignorance of the frontier or bad luck, suffered deep distresses.

This was brought home to Shand when he met the Reverend Robert Telfer, who not only ministered to the less fortunate but bore his own burden of misfortune. He was then renting one of the Edgson boys' farms and was hobbling around with a stick to ease the burden of a leg recently broken.

A Scottish lay preacher of the Presbyterian faith and father of ten living children, he had gladly answered the call for volunteers to work in the homestead areas of Alberta. In February 1904 he had reached Edmonton, and a few days later had crossed the thick ice of Lac La Nonne on his way to settle on land as yet unsurveyed at McDonald's Crossing of the Pembina River. The following April his wife, herding her flock onto steamship and train, reached Strathcona. In London she had enjoyed the services of two maids, and the Bell tents pitched in the bush were a startling change. So was the trip to the homestead when the ox team took most of the month of May plunging through mud holes. In the first two winters the family lived almost wholly on rabbits – rabbits day after day – rabbits actually by the hundreds. Sometimes with a sigh Mrs Telfer thought of their comfort and security in the Old Land, but like her husband, having put her hand to the plough, she never really looked back.

Mr Telfer encountered in February 1906 an extreme case of suffering and fortitude. Three young people from Iowa had settled in Manola – a newly married couple and the husband's best friend. They planned to get rich by selling lumber, and so homesteaded in a stand of magnificent spruce near the Pembina River and far beyond land that would have been more easily cleared. They had arrived in the summer with supplies to last them six months.

Their log cabin was surrounded by the forest. Trees a mere arm's length away, and nothing but trees, hemmed in the young wife left alone during the day while the men went about their tasks. The men dug a well and broke a trail to a hay meadow on the river flat where they cut and stacked a winter's fodder.

Mr Telfer in his ministry followed every newly cut trail, and he came across this one which ended at the hay meadow. Retracing his steps, he saw the cabin. But the lack of new tracks in the melting snow made him think that these settlers, like so many others, must have left their homestead. Nevertheless he went on to the shack. To his horror he saw half-buried in the snow beside the door the body of a young man. Sensing tragedy, he knocked and was answered by a young woman. Upon entering, he found another young man in delirium, tied by sheets to the bed. Typhoid had laid both the strong young men low. Only the wife had escaped the disease. Her husband had died, and she had carried out his body and buried it in the snow. For some days afterwards she nursed the other, not knowing where to turn for help. Supplies had run low, and she was reduced to oatmeal from which she made gruel for herself and gruel water for the patient. Mr Telfer left some medicine and hastened away for supplies and help. In a few hours he returned with a neighbour couple. The woman tended the patient and cared for the exhausted girl, while the neighbour and the preacher buried the young man.

Of such mettle were pioneer women – ordinary folks like you and me, but tested in the crucible of crises and found whole.

It was three years later that Douglas Telfer – who after his father's death followed in his steps – inquired about the welfare of the young widow and heard the sequel. In the spring after her husband's death, she had filed on a widow's claim, taking the quarter which adjoined both the original homestead and that of her husband's friend. Some months later she married the other young man, and at the time of Douglas Telfer's visit they owned three quarters of land and a comfortable home, and ahead lay the prospect of a fine farm and a happy life. But the memory of those dreadful days must have been deep within them.

A few weeks after this episode Mr Telfer, who had so often reached out to ease the distress of others, found himself borne gently to a settler's shack where his own wounds were tended. After leaving the young widow he kept on his rounds, knocking on pioneers' doors all along the fringe of settlement north and east of Manola. Just east of the present town of Westlock his horse slipped on the ice and fell on him, breaking his leg in two places. The horse struggled to his feet beyond the rider's reach. Fortunately the rail fence of the Shutts' farm was close by, and Mr Telfer, calling for help, pulled himself through the drifts for half a mile along it. Mr Shutts finally heard him, took him in and put splints on the smashed leg. Next morning he bundled the minister up in blankets in his straw-filled sleigh-box and drove the thirty miles to Riviere Qui Barre. By chance his son Douglas had just arrived from Belvedere with the mail. Arrangements were made to take Mr Telfer to hospital in Edmonton, where he remained for several weeks.

Next morning Douglas started the return trip of thirty miles to Belvedere, reaching home at dusk with the mail and with the news of his father's accident. Before daylight the following morning, the Telfer house caught fire. And in an hour the large family was homeless.

Shand Harvey was impressed by Mr Telfer's earnestness and his devotion to this new country and its inexperienced settlers. The older man made light of his own accident, and Shand recalled the lines of Thomas Gray in his poem "On A Distant Prospect of Eton College":

> To each his suff'rings: all are men,
> Condemn'd alike to groan;
> The tender for another's pain,
> Th' unfeeling for his own.

By July Shand's doubts about farming had crystallized into some definite opinions. Being a hewer of wood and a drawer of water was not too bad, but being a tiller of the soil had obvious drawbacks. He was glad he was single and could move on. His brief experience as a homesteader had been worth while, and he had learned much about the fortitude of pioneers and the hardships they suffered. Barring bad luck, he had concluded that hardship was proportional to greenness. Green he admitted himself to be, and he was not averse to hardships, but he had no intention of undergoing them on a homestead. True, a homestead in the bush held all the pleasures of solitude and freedom to breathe, but the servitude of clearing 160 acres outweighed these advantages. There must be other vocations offering solitude and freedom where an axe was a companionable piece of equipment and not a nagging reminder that 160 acres of forest was to be destroyed by hand. Shand set out for Edmonton.

S HAND sold his big gun when he reached Edmonton. Then he began looking for a job. He had spent nearly a year in looking around – ranching in the south, farming in the Vegreville country and homesteading at Edison. Now he decided to go west. That way lay the mountains. He was now ready to answer the call of the remote passes towards which the railways were headed. To do this he had to get a job with one of the survey parties.

In the decade after 1900, railways practically sprouted out of Edmonton's ears. All through the hundred years before that, Fort Edmonton had been the great depot serving the West's only industry, the fur trade. In all of the West there had been only three key posts: Fort Garry, later to become Winnipeg; Fort Vancouver, the ocean gateway on the Columbia River, later to be practically absorbed in Portland, Oregon; and Fort Edmonton, the focal point for the trade of Montana, Alberta, eastern British Columbia and the Northwest Territories as far as the Yukon. Fort Edmonton was the central depot on the Saskatchewan River highway – until 1885 the only east-west highway across Canada. From it radiated trails and water routes to all points north and south.

To Edmonton, therefore, in the 1870's had come the first generation of railroad builders – Sandford Fleming, McLeod, Lucas, Ruttan. They proposed to build the first transcontinental, the CPR, from Winnipeg through Edmonton and the Yellowhead Pass to a seaport on the Pacific – a new Vancouver, as yet unnamed and even unconceived, but destined to be one of the world's great ports. Following the surveyors came preliminary railway locations slashed out of the forests and accompanied by a telegraph line that, for the first time in history, gave the West and Edmonton easy communication with the East.

Perhaps the greatest of the CPR surveyors was Walter Moberly. In 1872, he had been informed officially that the Yellowhead Pass had been selected by the head office and he was instructed to make a reconnaissance survey through it. Approaching from British Columbia, he came through the pass and, by going down the Miette, came to Henry House – the one near the junction of the Miette and Athabasca Rivers. The old post had entirely disappeared, with the exception of a hole that represented the former cellar, and a pile of stones that had once been a chimney.

Moberly had been told that Sandford Fleming, the Engineer-in-Chief of the CPR, was expected to pass through the Yellowhead Pass on his way from eastern Canada to the Coast. As he was going down the Athabasca he met Fleming's party. It had been an interesting trip from Fort Edmonton to the Yellowhead Pass. About a week before meeting Moberly, they had camped on a stream which, from Grant's description, was most likely Hardisty Creek. There, "while hacking with his axe at brush on the camping ground, just where our heads would lie, Brown struck something metallic that blunted the edge of the axe. Feeling with his hand, he drew out from near the root of a young spruce tree an ancient sword bayonet, the brazen hilt and steel blade in excellent preservation, but the leather scabbard half eaten as if by the teeth of some animal."

While Fleming continued towards the Coast, Moberly, working his way down the Athabasca, spent some weeks in the Jasper valley. He arranged to have a camp built on the west side of the Athabasca River about a mile and a half below Henry House – that is, about that far below Cottonwood Creek. This he named the Athabasca Depot. This depot, which consisted of a large building for the men's quarters, a store house and a barn, was apparently on the flat on the west side of the Athabasca directly across from the mouth of the Maligne River. It is difficult now to locate this depot and the old Henry Houses and the other early buildings in this area.

While the Athabasca Depot was being built, Moberly worked his way down the valley and by Christmas was camped at Fiddle Creek. He has left an interesting description of his fare in Jasper on Christmas Day:

I paid a visit on Christmas Eve to the survey camp, to have a talk and smoke with the staff, some of whom were bewailing the loss of a dinner on the following day, so I invited them down to partake of the luxuries in my camp, about two miles away. My stores consisted at that time of some pemmican, flour, and tea, without sugar. I had several courses prepared, the first being pemmican raw, the second pemmican boiled, and in due season the dessert, which was pemmican fried; and my guests looked somewhat disappointed when I informed them they saw all the luxuries before them, and the only thing we could do was to have a good smoke, as I had plenty of tobacco, and try to keep warm.

By January 2 the survey was completed from the west to Fiddle Creek. There Moberly built a depot in which to winter his party, meanwhile sending the pack horses to winter on the favourable pasture along Solomon Creek at the lower end of Brulé Lake. He was still in need of the supplies which had been left high up the Whirlpool River in the old Athabasca Pass of the fur traders. The snow was too deep to use horses to bring the supplies, so Moberly sent a message to Chief Factor Hardisty two hundred miles away at Edmonton, requesting him to send dog teams to assist in fetching these goods. In due time the dogs arrived and accomplished their mission. From Fiddle Creek camp Moberly decided to carry a reconnaissance survey further east. He describes one of his further adventures :

We took two dog-sleighs, but, there being no snow on the flat and side of the hill beyond Fiddle River, Louis, one of the Iroquois hunters, sent back for his two daughters to pack the loads to the top of the ridge. One of the girls, who was a tall and very powerful young woman, took an enormous load without any difficulty, and, on the party crossing the ridge, we came to a large pond some two hundred yards in width and a long way round. There was about six inches of water on the ice, so telling the Indians and half-breeds to camp in the woods on the opposite side, as night was coming on, I sat down, thinking, that as I must get wet feet, I might as well have a smoke and get to camp by the time the fire was burning and the supper cooked. I saw the huge woman wading back, and wondered why she was returning, but soon found out, for she told me her father had sent her to pack me over the ice. I had travelled by every known mode, but to be packed by a woman was a novelty, so I protested; but she insisted, saying that I was much lighter than the load she had just packed over, and if she did not take me her father would be very angry so I resigned myself to my fate, and was ignominiously packed over. Louis was very proud of the girl's strength, and that evening, as we were smoking a pipe, he pointed out the great advantages in having such a powerful girl, and, as he wished to get a horse I had, he made me an offer to make an exchange – I to give him the horse and a few other things, and take the girl instead, to which she did not object; but as I had nó idea of becoming a permanent resident of that country, and hardly liked the idea of presenting her in the civilized world, I was obliged to decline what might have turned out a troublesome investment in the end.

This was Walter Moberly, and he appears to have remained aloof from domestic entanglements while in the Jasper area. His younger brother Henry J., an employee of the Hudson's Bay Company in charge of Jasper House from 1855 to 1861, was the patriarch from whom all the present-day Moberlys in that area are descended.

While Walter Moberly eschewed domestic bliss, the desire for it was strong in one of his young West Coast Indian employees. One night about a week after Moberly had been carried through the water, as they were camped on Hardisty Creek, which flows through the new town of Hinton, the young Indian "told me he wished to be paid off, and get a horse, a gun, ammunition, and some provisions, &c., instead of money. This was decidedly very inconvenient, as he had been with me a long time, was a capital cook, packer, hunter, and fisherman. On pressing him for his reasons he told me he wanted to marry the 'big woman' for whom I would not trade the horse. I refused his request, and he was very sulky. The next day, Sunday, only Louis and the young Indian being with me, the former complained of being sick, and I took my rifle and strolled along the river until the evening. On my return, I found that Louis had left in an excessively bad humour. They had evidently made up their minds as to the marriage, &c., and for having at first refused the female property myself, and afterwards prevented my servant from obtaining it, or rather her, my sins were now being visited upon me."

The Indian Louis was undoubtedly a member of a small band of Iroquois. Since about 1820 this band has regarded the area from Grande Prairie south along the edge of the mountains to Jasper as its homeland. When Louis left Moberly to return to his people on the headwaters of the Smoky River, he would probably be going to the rendezvous which today we call Grande Cache. This native village is near the Smoky River some sixty miles practically straight north of Mount Robson.

In spite of hard feelings over the love affairs of his young Indian, Moberly persisted in his reconnaissance towards Edmonton. Eventually the line was continued to the west bank of the McLeod. From there Moberly sent a train of horses to Fort Edmonton, requesting the Hudson's Bay Company to send him some supplies, including a few gallons of whisky and some beef cattle on the hoof. In due course these arrived, but it was not long after that that Moberly severed his connection with the CPR and made his way back to Victoria, British Columbia. He had concluded that the best route for a railway lay along the north shores of Jasper and Brulé Lakes, and subsequent studies during 1875 and 1876 confirmed this.

One of these studies was carried out during the winter of 1874–1875 by E. W. Jarvis, a surveyor, accompanied by C. F. Hanington and a few Indians. Jarvis started at Fort George (Prince George), ascended the McGregor River to the Continental Divide, and descended by the Kakwa River, one of the major tributaries of the Smoky. The snow was so deep in the pass that they had to put four men ahead to make the road, the other four dividing the six dog trains. In descending one steep place, says Jarvis, "one of the sleds broke away from the driver, and coming in violent contact with a log in its downward career, made a sandwich of the unfortunate dog nearest the sled, and broke the 'nose' (or turned-up bow) into a dozen pieces, besides damaging the harness. This was our first serious calamity, but, the dog excepted, everything was set straight in a couple of hours – the poor animal was past all care when the sled struck. A trivial incident like the death of a dog (and especially such mongrel curs as some of ours were) would not affect one seriously in a civilized community; but it cast quite a gloom over our little party, and even the dogs looked at one another, as who should say, 'It may be our turn next.' "

After travelling down the Kakwa for some distance, Jarvis decided to strike out across the foothill country in the hope of reaching the Athabasca River before everyone in the party starved. The men suffered considerably, but the dogs had the worst of it. "The frequent 'ups and downs' were hard on the poor dogs, who were very weak, and fell exhausted daily; in order to spare them any more suffering, the stragglers received a *coup de grâce* from one of our revolvers, and the others, 'closing up,' continued the march, only howling a requiem over their dead companions round the camp at night."

Finally, after strenuous days working south up and down the ridges of the high foothill country, "Alec caught sight of a, to him, well-known feature in the landscape, the 'Roche à Miette,' whose peculiar and distinct profile was plainly visible about twenty-five miles south of us. This mountain is opposite Jasper House, at the eastern end of the Yellow Head Pass, and the sight of it was an immense relief to the minds of the leaders of the party, since it was from the Hudson's Bay Company's post there that we expected shelter and supplies, the latter having now reached very small proportions."

Then, after sitting down for a rest, the party continued and soon struck the Chain of Lakes, of which the most southerly is now known as Jarvis Lake. Next morning they "found themselves on the benches overlooking the long-sought river, and it became a perfect scamper who should reach it first – *mal de raquette* was forgotten (though it is generally a pretty attentive companion) and the half-starved dogs staggering along after us joined in the enthusiasm with the most feeble of barks. But the effort was too much for them, and one more faithful servant dropped in his traces a few yards from the river bank. Ascending the river a couple of miles we came to the 'Lac à Brulé' where the ice was almost glare, the snow being blown off by the furious winds that rush down through the Pass like a funnel; and we travelled without snowshoes the first time for three and a half months. The eight miles up this lake was soon got over, and arriving at the Fiddle River depot (built by Mr Moberly) we were cordially received by the Iroquois Indians camped there. An immense dish of boiled rabbits set before us disappeared in quick order, and after this good meal we were more reconciled to hear the Company's post at Jasper House was abandoned."

While survey work on the CPR was carried on in various parts of the West up to 1874, the line was actually located from the east to the vicinity of Edmonton by 1875. During 1875 and 1876 a great deal of careful survey work was put in locating a definite route from there to Jasper. Hundreds of miles of trial lines had been run by the end of 1876, and a location was chosen which crossed the Saskatchewan River west of Leduc, continued around the south side of Lake Wabamun and then crossed the Pembina near Entwistle. The line then continued west essentially along the route which was later followed by the Canadian Northern to Brulé Lake.

A study of the records of this survey serves to show the sketchy nature of the trails in existence at that time from Edmonton to Jasper and the tremendous difficulty inherent in transporting supplies to survey parties. Up to that time there had been little reason for white men to venture west of Edmonton. The old transcontinental highway of the fur trade, which was in constant use from 1824 to 1885, had skirted the worst of this country by a seventy-mile portage north and west from Edmonton to Fort Assiniboine and thence proceeded up the Athabasca River. Not until 1857, when Henry Moberly took the first white man's train of pack horses to Jasper House, had any white man made a serious attempt to travel straight west of Edmonton.

Since the trails for hundreds of miles east of Edmonton were sketchy and the one west was almost non-existent, the problem of provisioning the survey parties of 1875–1876 was a hurdle hard to overcome. It was a problem difficult enough in 1906 when Edmonton was a city of about ten thousand people, but the Edmonton of 1875 contained possibly less than five hundred, and access to it was limited indeed. The first steamboat ever to ply the upper Saskatchewan arrived at Edmonton on July 22, 1875. The telegraph line, which the CPR built along its proposed route solely to serve the needs of the railway construction, was not extended right into Edmonton until 1879. A cart trail had long been in use along the old fur trade trail to Fort Garry and another sloshed its way along the newly located right-of-way. The trail to the newly established North West Mounted Police post at Fort Saskatchewan was fairly well defined, as was the Victoria Trail. Finally there was another trail turning off at St Albert to go on west to Lac Ste Anne. These, then, were the cart trails and the steamer route by means of which it was proposed to provision the survey parties between Edmonton and Tête Jaune Cache. At that time H. A. F. McLeod had two parties, about seventy men in all, working under Messrs Lucas and Ruttan, along this part of the proposed railway. From Ottawa in April 1876, via the United States, he had wired the company's purveyor in British Columbia to send three months' provisions for these two parties to the Athabasca Depot in the Jasper valley. He hoped that they would be delivered from Kamloops by July.

When McLeod reached Battleford about the end of July, he received a telegram informing him that the supply of provisions at Edmonton was very small. Moreover, the Hudson's Bay Company did not have any, and the last news from Lucas and Ruttan was that they were entirely out of food and still without news from British Columbia. McLeod also met two men of Ruttan's party who were returning to the East because the scurvy they had contracted in the Athabasca Valley made them unfit to work.

In spite of requisitioning supplies from Fort Carlton, some four hundred miles east of Edmonton, McLeod had to permit the Lucas and Ruttan parties to leave the Yellowhead but assigned them to work on the right-of-way well east of Edmonton, where presumably he hoped they might augment their supplies by buffalo and pemmican. Then at Sandstone Creek, near present-day Pedley, as McLeod was proceeding west, he met the party which had been sent from Kamloops with the provisions. They reported that they had cached these at the Athabasca Depot and were taking twenty-four horses and twenty-one cattle to Edmonton for the winter.

Mr McLeod arrived at Athabasca Depot on the 24th of September and found the cargo of provisions stored there; another train load was expected to arrive daily. Mr Trapp took charge of the stores for the winter.

Near the first crossing of the Miette he met the expected train, with supplies from Tête Jaune Cache. The train went on to the depot and discharged. This load made the supply stored to be about twenty thousand pounds, mostly of flour.

After spending some time in the valley at Jasper, McLeod returned to Edmonton, but at little Whitemud Lake (where the Marlboro cement plant was later built) he encountered a heavy gale which filled the trail through the burnt country with fallen timber, and caused endless trouble till they got to Root (Carrot) River. In many places the trail was so full of timber that they were unable to make any headway through it and were forced to make extensive detours.

When McLeod reached Edmonton he found that a large extent of the country about Edmonton had recently been on fire, and that a large quantity of cut hay had been destroyed. It was consequently difficult to keep the stock together, and the supply of hay would probably be short before the next spring. He wrote:

"I therefore decided to send all the horses and mules to Bow River for the winter, in charge of some men from British Columbia, who could not be sent back at that season of the year. There was sufficient hay secured to keep the cattle at Edmonton, and I put Mr McGinn, who accompanied me from Winnipeg, in charge of the cattle and Government stores at that place. My horses were not in a condition to proceed further, and the other horses could not be found just then, on account of the fires."

So much for the problem of supplying the railway surveyors in the years around 1875. By 1906, when Shand began to consider the problem, Edmonton was supplied by rail, but from the city west everything had to be carried by pack horses.

All of the work done by Moberly and by McLeod and his parties was done in vain. One day, a few years later, Edmonton's telegraph key clicked out the message that the route by way of the old fort had been abandoned. It was decreed that the CPR was to go through the Kicking Horse Pass. The moving key had writ, and having writ moved on to messages more mundane, leaving Edmontonians to welter in their gloomy backwater, while two hundred miles to the south, on a gravelly flat surrounding a Mounted Police detachment called Calgary, a new city was born. But soon Edmonton burst into renewed activity as freighters plied the new two-hundred-mile wagon road from Calgary.

When the CPR in 1891 laid its tracks beside this road, the freighters transferred their activity to new wagon roads cut through the bush to points like Athabasca Landing and Lac Ste Anne.

After 1885, when the CPR was built through Calgary, the old fur trade route to the Coast via Jasper fell into disuse. Once household words, the old fur trade passes – Athabasca Pass, Yellowhead (Tête Jaune) Pass, the Leather Pass and the Committee's Punch Bowl – now became far-off unknown places somewhere in the mountains three hundred miles to the west. Except for Indians and half-breeds coming in to Lac Ste Anne to worship or to trade furs, the old pack trails were deserted. The era of canoes and pack trains sounded far off.

THEN about 1905 the old names of Tête Jaune, Jasper and Roche Miette came back into focus. Once more Edmonton was to be on the route to the Coast. Calgary could boast of only one transcontinental railroad, but Edmonton was now deemed worthy of two. There was great rivalry between the Canadian Northern Railway, which ambled into Edmonton in 1905, and the Grand Trunk Pacific Railway, which was striding across the plains from Winnipeg. Both were to go to the Coast, and both planned to use the Yellowhead Pass. In 1906 the Canadian Northern pushed its rails on to Stony Plain, the plain of the Assiniboines or Stonies, and sent survey parties west towards Lake Wabamun. The Grand Trunk leapfrogged its surveyors ahead and sent them out to secure the best route through the narrow defiles of the Yellowhead Pass. It slapped an injunction on the Canadian Northern, not only preventing that company from building west from Stony Plain but causing it to abandon the track already built. The competition between the two companies to obtain the best route through the pass was also extended to building branch lines radiating out from Edmonton. Every available man and pack horse in Edmonton was caught up in the mad scramble to survey competing routes.

In the fall of 1906, when Shand returned to Edmonton, he was anxious to get work on any survey parties heading west towards the mountains. With all the talk of railways – main lines from the East, branch lines to St Albert, Morinville and Camrose – his prospects seemed good. But branch lines did not interest him for, like all Edmontonians, his eyes were focused on the two new transcontinentals and the Yellowhead Pass.

While thirty years earlier the CPR surveyors had been supplied only with the utmost difficulty by ox carts from the East, now the Canadian Northern and the Grand Trunk could bring in their men, materials and supplies by rail. The problems inherent in provisioning the survey parties working west of Edmonton, however, were no less rigorous than they had been thirty years earlier. Though the terrain across the prairies to Edmonton had made railroad construction easy, that from Edmonton to the Coast made it difficult. East of Edmonton, freighting teams carrying men, materials and supplies could travel almost anywhere. West of Edmonton the story was vastly different. Much of the two hundred miles to the mountains was muskeg. From Jasper west for hundreds of miles the unyielding mountains dictated the terms upon which they would permit railroad tracks to run and over which of their precarious rocky ledges the freight wagons might crawl. West of Edmonton, pack horses came into their own.

A pack horse could go nearly anywhere a man might be able to lead or follow him, and he could carry two hundred pounds of freight. From Edmonton west, pack horses took in the many surveying parties and tended them during their arduous work. Usually these parties left the city early in the spring and travelled one, two or three hundred miles to the point where they were to begin their operations. From that point, day by day, they carried their surveys forward until the snows of late fall found them a further hundred miles into the mountains. Pack horses carried them and their gear to the starting point, and then, day by day, attended upon them, moving the camp and the cook and his pots forward every few days to a new location cleared out amongst the pines. As a rule there were about twenty men in the survey parties and their pack train consisted of possibly thirty horses and three packers. Moving camp two or three times a week provided work for part of the packers and horses, while the rest of them returned again and again to central caches to bring more food back to the cook tent. Then in the late fall, when the work was finished, the surveyors, packers and horses started the long return trip to Edmonton. If they were lucky, they reached it by Christmas.

Shand wanted to join one of these survey parties, but he found that he would have to wait until the following spring, because that was the time of year when the parties set out along the trails leading west. He could have taken work with Mackenzie and Mann, who were putting the finishing touches to the Canadian Northern grade to Stony Plain, but any survey parties were all away in the foothills, busy with their summer's work. In the end he got a few days' work with a freighter taking goods out to Lac Ste Anne. Since this was the jumping-off place for all parties going west, he was anxious to see it.

Bright and early one August morning, with the freighter leading the way with his team, Shand set out driving the second one. The road as far as St Albert was familiar. Shortly after leaving that point, they passed the junction of the Egg Lake Trail, and a few miles further on for the second time chose the trail to the left. The other one, the old Klondike Trail, led off to the right to Riviere Qui Barre near at hand and ultimately to Fort Assiniboine. The country west of St Albert, through the established communities of Rae and St Pierre (later Villeneuve), was rapidly being cleared up and presented a tidy, orderly appearance. Almost imperceptibly, however, the trail slipped by the last farm and entered the Calihoo Indian Reserve.

Eventually the freighters arrived at Dan Noyes' hotel or stopping place, located at what is still known as Noyes' Crossing of the Sturgeon. There they put up for the night, and Dan entertained them with tales of his adventures. As a young man some fifty years before, he had left the New England states to fight in the Civil War. Then he had travelled all over the West and for many years had lived at Edmonton. In 1897, when the gold rush to the Klondike was getting under way, he had organized the Alaska Mining and Transportation Company. Amongst other things, this company planned to establish a stage route by way of Whitecourt and Sturgeon Lake and then on to Fort St John and the Yukon. He had planned to build stopping places at several strategic points, but before he got too far involved in the project, the rush to the Klondike by the overland route from Edmonton had died out.

Shand liked old Dan and wondered at the audacity of his scheme.

"How far is it from Edmonton to the Klondike?" he queried.

"Oh, about fifteen hundred miles."

"Wasn't that quite an undertaking?" asked Shand. "Working out a stage route over half a continent?"

"Well, yes, but if the rush had held on I coulda been set up in a big way. But this hotel and my sawmill over there were as far as I got. Didn't make no money by my plans, but didn't lose none neither."

"Weren't there several routes to the Yukon?"

"That was the trouble. There were at least four routes out of Edmonton. Most of the Klondikers went by boat down from Athabasca Landing, and eventually down the Mackenzie. Some went sort of overland by way of Peace River Crossing. Others followed the old Fort Assiniboine Trail through St Albert – when they reached the Athabasca River, they went through the Swan Hills. The government sent a man by the name of Chalmers, who cut out a road from Fort Assiniboine through the hills to Lesser Slave Lake. I planned to follow the old Indian route from Lac Ste Anne to the Grande Prairie by way of Whitecourt, but the government didn't spend no money on that route. Some day, though, they'll build a road that way – after the railway goes through."

"Is the railway going that way?"

"Well, they've already surveyed as far as Sagitawa."

"Sagitawa?" said Shand.

"Yah, Indian word, means the mouth of a river – where the McLeod runs into the Athabasca." (The present-day Whitecourt.)

"Which railroad is going that way?"

"The Grand Trunk. About three years ago they ran a line along the Fort Assiniboine Trail to Belvedere, and from there they went pretty well straight west to Sagitawa and then kept on towards Sturgeon Lake."

"But," said Shand, "the Grand Trunk is fighting the CNR right now and wants to go straight west of Edmonton to Stony Plain and Lake Wabamun."

"Yah, I know," said Dan. "Them railroad fellers is the biggest liars there is – good fellers, them surveyors, and smart too and cute as all get out – always pulling the wool over someone's eyes, especially the other company's men. John Callahan was head of that survey, and he had Alexis Bellecourt and Mooswa working for him."

"Mooswa the runner? I saw him run at Edmonton," said Shand.

"Yes, that boy can sure run. That summer John Callahan came

to the big muskeg out Eagle Creek way and wanted to change the route of the line, so he sent Mooswa in to Edmonton to send off a telegram to the head boss and to bring back an answer. Was about a hundred miles away and Mooswa was back with the answer in two days. That Mooswa, when he runs he sure reaches for more land."

Shand, noting the large garden and the relatively large fields of timothy and oats, commented upon the snug appearance of Dan's farm.

"Yes," said Dan, "with these new settlers coming in this last year or so, I do a fair business selling oats and hay. Couldn't haul it out and sell it, but with so many travellers along the trail I can sell all I can grow. Most times they pay me cash – sometimes they can't. Most of these homesteaders don't know a thing about the country or about farming. Half of them will pull out in a year or so. The rest will have a pretty hard time before they learn their way around – and the country will change too when it gets settled up. I've seen it happen all the way across the Western states, and each time I've moved on. But now I don't aim to move no more." Then, with a shake of his grey head, "This place'll do right by me for the rest of my days."

"I suppose it's getting so there's no place to move on to," said Shand.

"Oh no, a feller could go farther back – up into the foothills and mountains where it freezes so early in the fall that the farmers won't follow you."

"What would you live on?"

"Don't take much to live on – to keep a man and his kin. A feller could do a little trapping, a little trading now and then, and catch a job guiding some of these survey parties or packing for them. And you could always grow a few oats for your horses and some spuds for yourself."

"Well, are there many squatters from here west?"

"Oh, not many, maybe eight or ten from here to the mountains. From Lac Ste Anne west there are no homesteaders except the Yates boys eight or ten miles out. There are three young fellers in on that deal – grazing cattle. Their brand is a Lazy 3."

"What's a Lazy 3?"

"One that lies on its back, like this," said Dan, sketching a ω lying flat.

"What a fascinating implication," exclaimed Shand.

"Huh?" said Dan. "Come again?"

"Well, I mean –" spluttered Shand.

"Oh yah, I see. Well, you're right. Them boys ain't really lazy, 'cept maybe that all of us out here don't bust our britches working too hard. So they call themselves the Lazy Three, and them and all of us call it the Hobo Ranch."

"What about the other squatters?"

"Well, beyond them, on the old Jasper Trail, there's Pierre Gris, some people call him Peter Gray, at Lake Isle. Then there's Ben Berthoux at the Big Eddy and Jack Gregg at Prairie Creek, and right in the mountains is Lewis Swift at Henry House. Of course," he said, "there's the Hudson's Bay store at Whitemud Creek near the Big Eddy and one at Sagitawa – been there since '97. And then there's Charlie Williams who went in to Sagitawa two years ago. Some people call it McLeod Flats.

"All you need is a creek or a lake where there's plenty of fish and some meadows along the creek to pasture your stock. You can get meat, moose and elk, back in the bush, and a bear or two, and you're all set up for keeps. You can pick up a little cash by trading with the Indians."

"Are there many Indians?"

"Not really many of them, and they're sort of mixed up. Crees, Stonies, and a few Chippewas – and even a few Iroquois."

"Iroquois?" asked Shand. "Aren't they eastern Indians – Ontario and New York State – the fierce story-book Indians? How did they turn up here?"

"It's a long story," said Dan. "Used to hear about them when I was a boy in Massachusetts and was surprised to find them out here. Came out to work for the Hudson's Bay Company, I reckon."

"Do the Indians just wander around all over the country?"

"Well, yes, an Indian and his teepee can get along anywhere, but there are two or three spots they like best, where there's good pasture for their ponies. Some of them live mainly at Grande Cache, others live in the valley at Jasper House, and some live up Sagitawa way."

"Are they any bother to the white men? I don't mean do they scalp people – I mean how are they as neighbours?"

"Best there is," said Dan. "Best there is, if they like you and trust you. Guess maybe they need white friends. If an Indian is your friend, you can't ask for a better one. 'Course they're lots different from us, and it takes a long time for a white man and an Indian to allow for each other's funny ways. You're going to Lac Ste Anne just at the right time to meet up with them," he continued. "Every year about the end of July they make a pilgrimage to the mission there – from miles and miles away."

Next day when Shand reached Lac Ste Anne, the ground around the mission and along the lake shore was covered by tents and teepees. The hamlet of Lac Ste Anne consisted of the mission buildings near the shore, with the Hudson's Bay Post and other assorted buildings and shacks farther west. The smoke from dozens of evening cooking fires spread a soft blue smudge over tents and mission alike and drifted lazily out over the lake. Around the fires, tending kettles hung from sticks driven slantingly into the ground, were groups of squaws, chattering and laughing. Children were playing hither and yon throughout the camp. And fighting, gambolling or merely lying watching were as many mongrel dogs as there were men, women and children. In little groups away from the fires sat the men renewing friendships and exchanging the news from different parts of the country. For these men, Indian and half-breed – and it was hard to draw a clear-cut line between one and the other – had come from all points of the compass and from as far as three hundred miles away.

A few wagons stood beside the tents of some of the Indians from the reserves south and east of Edmonton. But most of this large gathering had come in by pack trains, and from time to time other groups with their strings of horses emerged from the bush along the trail from the west – from Jasper, Grande Cache, Prairie Creek, Sturgeon Lake, Flying Shot Lake, Tête Jaune Cache and Lesser Slave Lake. Some had been weeks on the way, travelling leisurely along the rarely used and ill-defined pack routes converging on Lac Ste Anne, religious and temporal capital of the vast west country.

Lac Ste Anne was an old settlement in the Canadian West.

Shortly after 1812, when Fort Edmonton settled down permanently within what are now the city limits, the lake became an important source of the fort's food supply. Dr Hector of the Palliser Expedition reported the situation there in 1859:

The Fort at Edmonton contains about 40 men, 30 women and 80 children almost entirely supported on buffalo meat, the hauling of which for sometimes upwards of 250 miles across the plains, is a source of great and most fruitless expense. Indeed the labour and difficulty of providing for a consumption of 700 pounds of buffalo meat daily and from so great a distance would become precarious, were it not for an abundant supply of fish from Lac Ste Anne, about 50 miles west of the Fort. . . . These are fine wholesome whitefish, averaging 4 pounds weight each. . . . Two years ago the quantity caught and stored by being frozen at commencement of winter was 40,000 and these were caught in five days.

First a Métis settlement grew up around the old fishing station. Then in 1842 Father Thibault, the first priest to take up residence in Alberta, came to Fort Edmonton and made a trip to visit the Métis settled even then on the west end of what was then known as Devil's Lake. In 1844 he sent an assistant, Father Thibert, to build a shack on the lake. Later that summer he and Father Bourassa arrived to complete their house and moved into it in September. The Indians, impressed by the size and beauty of the lake, had called it Manitou Sakahigan – lake of the spirits or of the Manitou, lake of the Gods.

The first white men, in their ignorance and intolerance, sneered at the Indians' Manitou as one inspired by the devil, and the lake became Devil's Lake. Father Thibault – perhaps nearer in spirit to both God and the Indians – rechristened it and once more dedicated it to God through his patron, Ste Anne de Beaupré.

To this mission in 1852 came the great Father Lacombe. And in 1859 Sister Superior Emery and Sisters Lamy and Alphonse of the Grey Nuns came to teach, nurse and minister to the Indians and Métis, who looked upon Lac Ste Anne as their spiritual headquarters.

By July 1906 this frontier hamlet was taking on the semblance of a white man's town. It was beginning to feel the first ripples of the wave of settlers, and the impact of railway construction was seen in new log buildings and in an expectant air of bustle. A post office had been established in 1903 in the old post, with Bessie Gunn as postmistress. A pool room did a flourishing business. Billy Connors owned a hotel which had been built in 1905 by Dr N. Steele. The school was taught by John McConnell, who also owned a store which he had set up in opposition to the Hudson's Bay Company; while his brother Frank, who had come out in 1902 to teach school, owned a livery barn. Constable Geoff Tyler was the lone representative of the Royal North West Mounted Police.

The Hudson's Bay Post, with its two stories and eight rooms – four with clay fireplaces – was the most imposing building. July was the slack season at the post, as in the town. The pack trains were all away with various survey parties. No furs were traded then and little freighting was being done, because whenever possible this was done on sleighs in the winter, when the mud holes were frozen solid. Even the meadows around the lake and in the forests south of town were still unmolested, awaiting haying time two or three weeks hence.

Father Lizé at the mission was the only white man with much to do, and he had his hands full. The main ceremonies of the pilgrimage lasted for two days as the hundreds of supplicants came to the shrine, some to prove their devotion to this new religion, some to make confession, others bringing with them their crippled, blind and ailing, expecting and hoping that Ste Anne would intercede for them.

In the camp grounds there was none of the regularity and order of a white man's military camp. Similarly the religious procession lacked apparent organization. Amongst the hundreds in this heterogeneous group there was no levity and no sadness, no uproar and yet no silence, no excitement but yet good discipline. As the priest led the devout into the lake and blessed them, the women filled an assortment of vessels with the lake water. Whisky jugs and bottles, jam pails, syrup and lard pails would be treasured throughout the ensuing year with their supply of blessed water. For it would be used on cuts and wounds and in cases of illness, to protect the members of the family from the dark evils that might befall them far back in the valleys of the remote foothills.

On the last night of the pilgrimage Shand went to watch the solemnity of hundreds of worshippers holding lighted candles as they took part in the Way of the Cross and knelt in the open air.

That night and the next day the camp hummed with activity. Old friends visited, old tales were related, and amongst the young people new alliances were contracted. A little trading too was done at the stores, to lay in supplies for the months ahead. Far into the second night the camp fires burned.

Next morning, after a late breakfast, Shand wandered over this way, and found the camp grounds empty and bare, while on numerous unmarked trails radiating west and north, little companionable groups of these self-reliant people returned to the remote valleys peopled by the spirits of their sturdy ancestors.

He strolled over to talk to Father Lizé, who had served the Indians and Métis here for twenty years. Like so many of the early missionaries, Father Lizé loved and understood his primitive charges.

"They are all on their way home today," he said. "Out there, living by themselves in small groups, they are happy, strong and self-reliant men." He shook his head. "Whenever they come into contact with white men, they are mere children – afraid, uncertain, almost ashamed. That's why they are sullen at times, and that's why they drink. When they drink they forget, and for a while in their maudlin drunkenness they are confident once more and the equal of the white man."

"These Indians – are they really Christians?" Shand asked.

"Not absolutely," replied the Father. "They try to grasp the meaning of Christianity and we try to impart it to them, and we are slowly making some progress. Some of them, perhaps most of them, keep a foot in both camps. It's obvious to them that we have some powerful 'medicine' and they feel that in this world of spirits – sometimes malicious spirits – some of our medicine may aid in combating them. In times of crises they revert to their pagan customs."

"This annual pilgrimage," said Shand, "must meet a great spiritual need."

"Oh, a great need. Ye cannot live by bread alone."

"How long has it been going on?"

"Since 1889, when Father Lestanc conceived the idea. I was here then."

"And it is held on the feast day of Ste Anne?"

"The feast day is July 26th – it is held on the Wednesday closest that date."

"I've heard that 1889 was a very dry summer and that many medicine men prayed for rain in vain, and then immediately after the ceremonies here it poured for about three days."

"That was a dry year, and it did rain as they have told you," said Father Lizé cautiously.

"What difference did rain make to the Crees? Why should Indians living on fish at Sturgeon Lake or half-breeds from Jasper, shooting mountain sheep on the cliffs, be concerned about rain?"

"Our Métis at Ste Anne and at Lac La Biche had their little oat fields. By then the buffalo were gone, and we tried to show these people how to farm and they became dependent on rain."

"Do you remember the buffalo?"

"Well, I really don't, but all the older priests do. And most of the Métis here remember the great annual hunts, where everyone went off into the prairies a hundred miles or so. They often look back to those good old days."

"What were the hunts like?"

"Oh, for that you should ask the old people. Go to Alex Belcourt or to John Calihoo. They have great tales to tell, and true ones. A year ago we buried old Sam Letendre – he was over a hundred years old. I used to enjoy his stories of the prairies. By the way, the Belcourts and the L'Hirondelles are two of the earliest Métis families to settle here. They came some time before 1840."

"When was the last buffalo hunt?"

"The last large hunt was about 1877. Some years earlier smallpox struck the camp at Tail Creek. That was a sad time, but most of the old hunts were a time of celebration and happiness, and always a priest went along. On those hunts the Métis and Indians from far and near congregated at Edmonton and at Tail Creek. Friends and families, separated for a year, all met once more. It was a time of rejoicing – many marriages were performed – it was a time of fête."

"Then, after the buffalo were gone, these great friendly gatherings died away?"

"Yes."

"To some extent, then," Shand said, "this pilgrimage must have filled the need for these friendly celebrations?"

"Only a few of the world's thinkers and philosophers have been able to live lonely, aloof lives," sighed Father Lizé. "Métis are like the rest of us – they need to get together, to celebrate. They are so friendly, so gregarious. Their lives in the bush are lonely and hard.

"You should be here about Christmas," he continued. "Then your English and Scottish and American boys come in from their long trips with pack horses after spending all summer in the wilds. And they go to the hotel and for a few days they – they raise hell till their money is gone. They, too, love to congregate and celebrate. But they do not come to me to try to guide their celebrations, nor do they invite the young Methodist missionary who sometimes holds services here. You see, there's little difference between the white man and those whose skins are blackened by the smoke of the teepees."

Shand picked up a few days' work here and there, and several times during his brief stay went over to talk to Peter Gunn, the Hudson's Bay Company trader, the other outstanding man in the settlement. Gunn was one of the progressive fur traders who was able to move with the times. As a young man in 1883 he had come out from Scotland to the Hudson's Bay post at Dunvegan. When he was transferred to Lac Ste Anne in 1900, he was well acquainted with the fur trade and with many of the Indians who lived in the borderland between that post and the Peace River country. While he looked forward to the future of Alberta as a province rich in resources, he could reach far back into the fur trade days.

"Lac Ste Anne has been important to the Company for over a hundred years," Gunn told Shand. "It supplied the fish needed to keep Fort Edmonton going. But it was not until 1861 that Colin Fraser started the first Company trading post here."

"Colin Fraser?" Shand said. "Last spring I went over to see the furs brought in from Chipewyan by a Colin Fraser."

"Ah, that's his son. The first Colin Fraser spent much of his life in this country west of Edmonton. He came out to work for the Company in 1827, and in 1828, when Sir George Simpson made one of his famous and furious canoe trips to the West Coast, Colin went along as his piper. As the party approached each post, Colin, dressed in full Highland costume, started up his pipes, and when the canoe touched the bank, he piped the Governor into the post. Nothing impressed the Indians more than the dignity of the Governor's procession into the fort and the skirl of Colin's pipes.

"Colin died suddenly here in the spring of '67 and was buried at Edmonton. Nancy, his wife, died in Edmonton in the spring of 1900, the year I took over here. Before he settled down here, Colin had been regularly married to Nancy Chantelaine, of mixed French and Indian blood. They had a large family and most of them played quite a part in the story of the West. The Colin you met was one of the eleven children. Unlike some of the traders, Colin was a good family man who remained faithful to Nancy all his life and did a good job of bringing up his large family."

Peter Gunn then went on to explain that once Lac Ste Anne post was established, Jasper House became less important. For many years it was occupied only on a seasonal basis, with some-one making a brief visit there each year to take the Indians' furs in trade. At this time the Iroquois band from the Jasper area began trading at Lac Ste Anne.

"Why didn't the Company build a post here till 1861? If it wasn't needed before that, why was it needed then?" asked Shand.

"Well, it's a long story," said Peter. "As they say in the Bible, 'in the beginning' the Hudson's Bay Company and the North West Company had forts in the vicinity of Edmonton. After 1811 various posts were operated in the wide valley at Jasper. The most recent was Jasper House, which was moved to the north end of Jasper Lake about 1829. After 1824 the route from Edmonton to Jasper House was by the road Sir George Simpson ordered cut out from Edmonton to Fort Assiniboine. Pack horses were used on that part of the trip. From there on, everyone had to go up the Athabasca in boats or by pack trails. That was a tough piece of river to travel, but for some twenty-five years it was the only way to Jasper. Edmonton, Fort Assiniboine and Jasper House, then, were the only inhabited posts in all of this part of Alberta – until Father Thibault got his mission built here in 1844."

"And he built it because there were Métis here?" asked Shand.

"Yes – but he was looking for a place to locate a mission where the Crees and the Thickwood Indians would be safe from visits of the Blackfoot. Edmonton wasn't safe, because the Blackfoot also traded there and many a Cree scalp they took back across the river with them. But here the mission was far enough away from the beaten track, so that the Crees would be safe. After the mission became established, it seemed a good idea to start a post here. Once the mission was started, the priests cut this trail through east to join the Fort Assiniboine Trail just this side of St Albert."

One whole evening Peter Gunn and Shand discussed the opening up of the trails into the country west of Lac Ste Anne. Gunn explained that after the mission had been started, Indians and Métis, including the Iroquois from Jasper, began converging on it. But the trail left by their sporadic pack trains made little more impression on the country than a wandering coyote or the wraith of a morning mist. The white man, thinking of trails as capable of carrying heavily loaded vehicles from one point to another, is apt to read far more into the mention of Indian trails than is justified.

When Henry Moberly became in 1857 the first recorded white man to take a train of pack horses through to Jasper, he had to follow Indian trails where he could find them, and at other places had to strike out in a generally westerly direction. Some of the first white men to use the trail pioneered by Moberly's pack train were the famous travellers who have written books of their experiences. Lord Southesk, on his way west to the McLeod River and thence south towards the country at the headwaters of the Saskatchewan, passed through Lac Ste Anne in 1859.

The Overlanders of '62, en route across Canada to the famous Cariboo Gold Fields, were the first large party to travel the crude pack trail. On August 1, 1862, Hunniford, one of the party, wrote down his impressions of the road between St Albert and Lac Ste Anne:

Travelled through woods and mud to the knees, arrived at St Anns mission at 10 o'clock, camped, got new potatoes for dinner. St Ann is a settlement on the Banks of a Large Lake. The inhabitants is half breeds.

Awoke early by a beautiful sound of a church Bell calling the settlers forth to their devotions . . . it made me think of those our friends many many miles away & the happy moments spent with them . . . little did I think that such charming sounds could come from an old bell. . . .

Our way for the remainder of our journey was totally different from what we had before passed through; for, instead of the hard and level roads with which we had been favoured in the first part of our journey, swamps and hills and streams alternated; and dense forests, where we were obliged to keep a gang of men ahead of the train to chop out the brush and fallen timber, were substituted for open prairies.

In June 1863 Colin Fraser entertained Dr Cheadle and Lord Milton at Lac Ste Anne on their way towards the Yellowhead Pass. They found the travelling hard: "When we left Lake St Ann's the track led us immediately into the densest forest, where the ground was boggy and rotten, thickly covered with fallen timber. The horses sank in up to their girths, and every few yards were obliged to jump over the obstructions in the path."

The old trail west from Ste Anne, although used by a few expeditions going to the mountains, was merely an ill defined trail wandering around deadfalls, plunging through muskegs and plagued by fallen trees.

At Lac Ste Anne, Shand bought a team and buggy and began taking new settlers out to look for land. He became well acquainted with the primitive trails and the wagon roads cut out by the homesteaders. That fall he spent many a night at pioneer stopping places. Some of these offered poor accommodation, but most of them were clean and provided meals of good quality, with no skimping on the quantity. The usual charges were a dollar a night for a bed, 25 or 35 cents for a meal. Hay for a team cost 25 cents, while oats were 35 cents extra.

It was not long before he had his first experience with bed bugs and lice. Even the cleanest proprietor sometimes found his place temporarily infested. One evening while visiting Peter Gunn the talk turned to stopping places, and Shand mentioned the cleanliness of Dan Noyes' place.

"Yes," Gunn agreed. "Good place – no permanent residents in Mrs Noyes' beds."

"Old Dan's a rough diamond," said Shand.

"Yes – good-hearted, but a bit hard-bitten."

"Guess you've got to be hard to come through the Civil War and the early American West as he has," volunteered Shand.

"Yes – and old Dan's not very long-suffering with greenhorns. I was having supper at his place a year or so ago and the only other traveller was a young, smart-alecky bachelor, who didn't know any more than he should have. He did enjoy Mrs Noyes' cooking, however, and really stuffed himself. Like every other settler, he'd eaten rabbits for weeks on end. I gathered that on some previous occasion old Dan had pulled his leg unmercifully and had recommended coyote meat as a pleasant change from rabbits.

" 'Say,' said the greenhorn, 'about a month ago I cooked a part of a coyote. The smell of it made me sick. Had to throw it out. You told me it was good, said it was nearly as good as chicken.'

" 'Well, so it is,' said Dan. 'Maybe you didn't get a good coyote,' he added. 'But probably you didn't cook it right!' "

They sat watching the fire, and Shand said, "I can't say that I know any of the half-breeds very well yet, but they don't impress one, do they? I suppose some of them are all right, if you get to know them."

"Well, in their own way of life they are nearly all very fine people. If they get to like you, they'll do anything for you. You've got to be loyal to them too. You can't bluff. But if they feel you respect them, they'll stick with you."

"Guess it's pretty hard to make the transition they've had to make in a generation or two."

"They've got so much to learn," said Peter. "Take a simple thing like money. Out here in the early days a white man could spend his whole life and never see or need money. All payments to the Indians were made by barter – so much fur for this and so much for that. Then about thirty years ago, when some of the Indians took treaty, they began getting annual payments in money. It took them a long time to understand its value. One time I stopped an Indian from trading a worn five-dollar bill for a crisp new dollar bill."

One day Shand took a settler to the Narrows, some five miles beyond the mission. A year or so previously a wagon trail had been cut through to that point, where a primitive ferry carried horses and wagons across the narrow part of the lake. The ferry was owned by a Stoney Indian with the name of Peter Painted Stone, known to everyone as "Wee Zaw." He had stretched a rope across the narrows and fastened it firmly at each end. It passed through eyes on the ferry and kept it on its appointed route. The ferry itself was made up of a few wooden barrels with planking nailed to them, and it would carry a load of about a ton. When a team and wagon wanted to cross, old Wee Zaw made two trips, taking the wagon on the first one and the team on the second. The fare for the whole operation was twenty-five cents.

Wee Zaw lived in a teepee on the north shore of the lake, and made his money more by his organizing ability than by his labour, for that was done by an indeterminate number of squaws. When a team approached the ferry, Wee Zaw set up a hullabaloo which aroused three or four squaws who took their station on the ferry. When the load was aboard they seized the rope and by a hand over hand operation soon pulled the ferry to the other side of the Narrows. Meanwhile, Wee Zaw bustled about pocketing the fare and piloting the craft by exhorting the squaws to exert themselves. While Shand had undertaken only to deliver his passenger at the ferry, he nevertheless paid his fare for the chance to ride back and forth.

Three or four miles before reaching the ferry, Shand had over-taken two men heading west with about forty fine range horses. The owner, a man by the name of Perry, explained that he had decided to leave Cardston because the country around his ranch was becoming thickly settled. He had sold everything except two hundred horses with which he set out for the Grande Prairie country. There he hoped to use some Boer War scrip to acquire land, and planned to lease still more. He had heard glowing reports of the feed on the Grande Prairie. On the way up from the south he had sold most of his horses at a good profit to new settlers. Now he was taking the remaining forty, his best breeding stock, with him.

"You'll be late reaching Grande Prairie this fall, won't you?"

"Oh, maybe, but if I don't get there I can always find some good meadows along the way where I can pasture the horses until spring. Then I'll go on again."

Perry did not attempt to cross his range horses on the ferry. He went a little farther west to another narrow part of the lake surrounding Horse Island, where he planned to swim his horses across. Most travellers with pack horses did this, which was how the island got its name.

When fall came on, Shand decided to stay in Edmonton and to get some work for his horses. He rented a desk in Herbert Grainger's real estate office, and he and John Graham hired a driver and put their two teams on to handle light delivery work around the city.

Shand's first winter in Edmonton had been a mild one, but his second, that of 1906–1907, was a real rip-snorter. With excessive snow and long spells of extremely cold weather, it established a record of severity that has not been surpassed in over half a century. Early in January Shand bought a "jumper" for his driving team and made trips out to various parts of the country. F. B. Smith, a mining engineer, was getting ready to open up the Cardiff Coal Mines, and Shand took him out there several times. Perhaps his most interesting trip was out to Burton's Stopping Place, some fifty miles west along the Saskatchewan River, in the locality we know today as Burtonsville.

Great stands of spruce covered many square miles on both sides of the river here in the timber berths owned by John Walter and D. R. Fraser. Along the river near Burton's place, men were busily engaged in an old-time logging operation – cutting the majestic trees, hauling them on wide-bunked sleighs along the skid roads and piling them at the edge of the river bank. In spring, as soon as the ice went out, the logs would be dumped helter-skelter into the river, to be swept downstream to Edmonton. There they would be herded into booms awaiting the day when each would be yanked out of the water and sent to its doom on the whirling saw.

The previous fall a fire had swept through this timber. The

October rains and the early winter had put it out, except in one spot where it had set fire to the exposed face of the Coal Arch and from which it was feared it would spread back into the timber when spring came. Since this was no longer a forest fire, the timber men called in Smith, the mining engineer, to cope with it. So he and Shand, equipped with dynamite and drilling equipment, set out.

The Coal Arch is an unusual phenomenon. At this point the Saskatchewan River meanders through channels between gravel bars and islands in a valley some two miles wide. In a bend where the main stream of the river cuts sharply into the high cliff-like bank, the Coal Arch stands out sharply. Some fifty feet below the surface of all the surrounding country lies a thick seam of coal. Earth-building pressures have squeezed the flat seam so much that at this point it is folded up into an arch almost like those of a Gothic cathedral. Here at the bend of the river, where this arch nearly a hundred feet high is exposed by the erosive action of the stream, the black coal stands out clearly against the grey clay of the sheer bank. The fire had caught in the coal of the exposed face.

Smith soon sized up the job and set lumbermen to work drilling holes behind the fire and loading these with dynamite. After this had been done, and after Shand had returned to the north bank to watch his team and await the spectacle, Smith waved his arm and set off the dynamite. Suddenly the face of the arch was blasted outward, black streaks of powdered coal burst out in all directions, and tons of coal rained on the thick snow of the river. The roar of the explosion nearly deafened Shand. When it died away, the fire was out, except for some chunks of burning coal sizzling their life out in the choking snow. The operation was a complete success.

Some time after Shand returned to Edmonton he had his first and only brush with the law. Even at this early period Edmonton had its parking problems. In front of each store were hitching posts and rails, and along many stretches of the street rings had been bolted to the sidewalk; to one or other of these contrivances everyone was expected to tie his horse or his team. Now Shand had a saddle pony which had been taught the proper etiquette of the range. Once Shand dismounted and dropped the reins over its head so that they touched the ground, his horse would remain in that one spot just as resolutely as if it had been tethered.

The law, however, specified that horses, whether single or in teams, whether obedient or not, should be securely tied. The minion of the law must have been in a bad humour, for he sought out Shand, who was seeking solace in the hotel bar, and hauled him off before the magistrate, who fined him for this breach of the regulations.

While there were many blooded horses in the Edmonton area, Shand's pony was just one of the sturdy, nondescript horses of the frontier. Most of these were small, scrubby-looking animals, but they were hardy, adaptable and sure-footed, and they could scrounge a living off snow-covered meadows where their more aristocratic cousins would have perished from cold and hunger.

Horses deserve a monument to commemorate their contribution to the opening up of the West. Not a statue of a paunchy percheron or a prancing polo pony, but a gaunt-ribbed pioneer pony pulling his heart out, or humbly following the lead mare in a string of pack horses to pioneer a path into the wilds.

When the rush of railway surveying was on, not enough horses were raised locally to supply both the needs of the railway and of the new settlers. Ranchers and horse traders from the south brought in carloads to sell, but the railway companies shipped in most of the horses they needed. One very cold day, just before Christmas 1906, Shand stopped to watch a pack train. He had delivered some express to Malcolm Groat's place, where Allen Stewart was then wintering well over a hundred Grand Trunk horses all marked with the Company's brand G_P. As he was leaving Groat's place, a string of frost-coated horses and frost-bitten men rode in single file along the trail to complete the season's survey by delivering horses and goods to the compound there. Montana Pete was in charge of the train, of which thirty-seven horses had been lost in returning from the mountains in the bitter December weather. Rod McCrimmon, one of the packers, recalls that when this train reached St Albert the previous evening the thermometer at the hotel there registered fifty-eight below.

For weeks after, as various men of this survey party relaxed in the comforts of civilization, Shand listened to tales of their trip.

At times he fell in with Rod McCrimmon – just turned seventeen, but a full-fledged packer in that party.

One night as I sat in Shand's cabin, listening to his reminiscences, he said, "Up to that time I had not been out with a pack train, but I had heard many of the tales of Montana Pete, Allen Stewart and Pete Talbot. Why don't you go and see Rod McCrimmon? He's still hale and hearty. Ask him to tell you about some of the tricks and antics of pack horses and the hardships of the men who built the railways from Edmonton to Tête Jaune Cache."

So, following in Shand's steps over fifty years later, I sought out Rod McCrimmon. And I spent many a happy evening listening to his tales of the great days of railway building.

ROD McCRIMMON had been reared on railroad construction. His father, Malcolm, had long been one of the major contractors working for Mackenzie and Mann, the financiers and builders of the Canadian Northern. From the time he was big enough to carry a water bucket, he had advanced across the prairies with the grade. While the Canadian Northern laid its tracks to Stony Plain, Rod was ahead with the surveyors picking out a route towards Lake Wabamun.

In this region he spent a glorious summer, of which his most lasting memory is wild strawberries. They seemed to be everywhere, covering the ground of the park-like areas with their white blossoms and red fruit. The Indians who lived on the reserve near Lake Wabamun picked and sold them to the camp cooks. Rod took advantage of this state of plenty and bought berries for his mother, paying a dollar for a fifty-pound lard pail full. As he recalls it, that summer his mother canned 250 quarts of wild strawberries.

Rod's adventures with the Canadian Northern were stopped when legal intervention on the part of the Grand Trunk called a halt to the westward advance of the Canadian Northern through Stony Plain. Perhaps because of the extreme care with which it chose its alignment and built its excellent grade, the Grand Trunk had approached Edmonton more slowly than its rival. When it reached the outskirts of the city in 1908, it laid out its yards and created the hamlet of Calder. From there it too headed for Stony Plain and built a duplicate grade. The building of this second rail line for this distance was a rare piece of folly, but the Grand Trunk had the law on its side. It claimed that it had filed prior location plans on the route west via Stony Plain. The Canadian Northern was forced to throw up its hands and seek another route. Today, if you watch carefully as you drive west on Highway 16, you will see a fringe of trees growing south of the road and starting off towards Stony Plain from a point about two miles east of the new overpass over the modern railway. That fringe of trees and two rows of grain elevators in Stony Plain are all that mark the location of a railway that was wasted in northern Alberta, which for long cried out for other lines that were needed.

While the Canadian Northern was also starting another railway north to Athabasca Landing, and while Rod's father was a major contractor on it, Rod decided to strike out on his own. He was sixteen now, knew his way around, and was already well acquainted with all phases of railway construction. One day he went over to Malcolm Groat's place to look over the hundred or so horses recently shipped in by rail. These had been bought in the east or in the United States and had recently been branded with the Grand Trunk mark.

At Groat's he found Montana Pete, who was looking for a bell-boy or third packer. Rod asked for the job and was rather surprised to be taken on. Montana Pete was to be in charge of a pack train assigned to supply the needs of Oscar Englund, who was going out to locate the final line for the Grand Trunk grade from the Big Eddy west into the mountains as far as Tête Jaune Cache. Besides Englund, the survey party consisted of Lincoln Ellsworth, later to become an outstanding explorer and flier in the far north, Emerson Bell, a leveller, one cook and fourteen men who were to serve as chainmen, rodmen and axemen.

The three packers, Montana Pete, Tommy Groat, of mixed blood, and young Rod, were to handle the twenty-five horses needed to take the surveyors and their instruments and provisions out to the point where the survey was to begin. Once that work was started, they were to serve the instrument men and move their camp forward every two or three days. While they carried some supplies with them, a large cache had to be made at Prairie Creek, and from time to time the packers were to replenish the party's stores from this point.

These food caches were an essential part of the complex organization that went into the building of a railway. Before making surveys, pack trains had to be sent out to provide caches of supplies at strategic places. A sturdy, windowless log building was built and equipped with a door that, when it swung at all, swung out, so that inquisitive bears could not easily push it in. The supplies were then deposited there, to be left possibly for months, until the surveyors needed them.

So, early in April 1906, Rod and his associates set out on the trip that was to take them nearly nine months – a trip that was to give Rod his first sight of the Rocky Mountains and his first insight into the problems of working a pack train into the very heart of them. As far as Lac Ste Anne the party could follow the wagon road, but a few miles west of there they were on their own. Then they followed an old pack trail seldom used by white men and rarely traversed even by wandering Indians. This trail skirted Lake Isle, near its east end passed the Yates ranch, and farther along the shore passed Pierre Gris' place, the western edge of settlement. After leaving this point, the party saw not another human being until many weeks later they reached Prairie Creek, some three or four miles west of modern Hinton.

By the time the horses got to Lac Ste Anne they were well acquainted with each other and had established amongst themselves the order of their going. Horses, like duchesses, have diverse dispositions. These two horses can't stand each other, those two are always together. This one of dominating character takes the lead, while that one has every horse's hoof against him, and brings up the rear. It takes a few days for a new group of horses to work out its order of precedence, but having done so, woe betide any packer who tries to alter it! He is bound to have trouble until he yields to the will of the horses. On the march, a train of twenty-five horses gets strung out for several hundred yards along the vaguely defined route, as some horses pause to nibble here and there. One horse does not necessarily follow in the footsteps of the one ahead of him; but he is free to pass to the right of an obstruction which the previous horse, in his judgement, went around on the left. The pack trail west of Lac Ste Anne was in no sense of the word a beaten path in which every horse could tread. A previous train might have swung to the left for half a mile around a slough, while some other struck out around its right shore. Only in the sense that its general direction was always the same, and that usually the fording places of the various rivers and creeks were common to all pack trains, was it what we think of as a trail.

As an illustration of this, the old pack trail first worked out by Moberly in 1857 followed essentially the route of the modern highway from Styal to Jasper. An alternative route from Wildwood swung around the north side of Chip Lake, crossed the McLeod north of present-day Peers and went on to Edson. Then, after the CPR survey was run in the Seventies, many of the pack trains used the route cut out by the surveyors. From about Wildwood, this ran on the higher ground some six miles south of the modern road until it crossed the McLeod River at the Big Eddy.

Pack horses were expected to forage for themselves, and at the end of a day's trip were turned loose to graze. The packers had to govern the length of their day's trip so as to stop at some meadow or creek bottom where the horses could find good grass. Next morning they had to get out and round up the horses, and often this took considerable time. Then each animal had to be loaded each morning. During the first days of a long trip, when the horses were fresh, one or other was constantly darting away from the main route or bumping into other horses or trees along the way. The packs shifted and the ropes slackened, and delays occurred while the loads were tightened or repacked. Finally the pack train settled down, and then the packers got time to draw a free breath, to roll a cigarette, or light a pipe.

Rod, as third packer, had to lead the first horse of the procession consisting of twenty-one men, usually all walking, and twenty-five horses laden with various goods. The lead mare, "Badger," carried the survey instruments, which had to be handled more carefully than the bulk of the loads, and so Rod had a special responsibility. Not only must he make sure that this mare never bolted, but use his judgement, combined with that of the animal, to lead the train by trying to follow the tracks of any previous party. At times this was baffling. Since the passage of the last pack train, several trees had fallen across the way, and Rod and his mare had to decide whether to try to jump over them, go under, or swing around the obstacle. Usually the next horse would do what Badger did. The animals were adept at getting over a log too high to step over. For a moment they would stand still facing the log and then, lifting both front legs up, would leap over with a sort of rocking motion. When too many trees had fallen across the way, the party halted while a new way was chopped through or around the deadfall.

Everything went well with Rod and Badger until they had to decide whether or not to pass under a fallen tree that was leaning across the trail. It was mid-afternoon, the horses were getting along well together and there was little to break the silence of the forest. Badger decided to go under, and so did the next horse. So, for that matter, did Comanche, the third horse, but he did not succeed. His load was too high, for on top of cases of canned goods he carried the telescoping Sibly stoves. The noise they made when they hit the tree was bad enough, but when Comanche lurched ahead and they broke loose, the clatter scared him out of his wits, and he bolted, scattering stoves and canned goods along the way. The other horses, startled and not unwilling to share in some action that would break the monotony, broke for the forest in all directions, banging their packs against trees and stumps.

Badger broke into a run, dragging Rod along with her. For a while it was a grim tussle as the horse tried to shake Rod, while he, conscious of his responsibility and of the precious load in his charge, hung on for dear life.

"She dragged me half a mile over logs and stumps before I got her stopped – well, anyway, it seemed like half a mile, and a long one at that."

Having won the tussle, Rod led Badger back to survey the damage. The horses were scattered, as he says, "from hell to breakfast." Tommy Groat was in a rage, blaming the incident on Rod and swearing that he would have him fired. Some of the men started to make camp while others went out to search for the horses and for the loads that were liberally sprinkled over the floor of the forest. When it got dark, three of the horses were still missing. The Grand Trunk always instructed its packers that no horses with the Company's brand should remain at large. Such a horse had to be caught or shot. While this seems unusually harsh, the reason behind it was simple. If one of their branded horses were legitimately found by someone else and added to his string, he could honestly claim that he had found it. But a dishonest man might steal a Grand Trunk horse and also claim to have found it. If all strays were killed, then it would be certain that anyone found with one of the Company's horses had stolen it. On this occasion, Montana Pete recaptured one horse but had to shoot the other two. Young Rod felt that he was in great danger of being fired, but Montana Pete refused to fire him.

Next day the party set out again. Rod, properly cautious, swung north around Round Lake, and heading for the Pembina River, was again in the lead. Now at times pack horses are hard to keep going. The usual procedure was for the head packer, in this case Montana Pete, to take up a position about the middle of the train. From there he could urge along the horses ahead of him. The second packer, Tommy Groat, brought up the rear, and before long they reached the deep valley of the Pembina River.

In the spring, when rivers were high, the Pembina was a risky one to cross, especially downstream from present-day Entwistle. This first crossing was another test for Rod's inexperience. It was hard to tell just where to start across. He looked over the stream for signs of a trail emerging from the water on the other side, but could not see any. He knew that the best ford is often indicated by a ripple. Fortunately the water was not so high as to drown out all ripples; after working upstream about three-quarters of a mile, he found one. The horses crossed without difficulty and came out where a well marked trail went up the bank. This, the first crossing for which he was responsible, turned out well and Rod could tuck another experience under his belt.

The train climbed to the high land west of the river and north of the mouth of Lobstick River. Before long Rod had to lead it across this stream, which, while difficult, was much smaller than the Pembina. Then, once on the south side of it, about a mile east of present-day Wildwood, the trail headed for the famous muskegs south and west of Chip Lake. He had heard packers talk about muskeg – a peat bog always saturated with water, always unstable and at times quaking under foot. On the prairies east of Edmonton there had been no muskegs. Near Edmonton and out Lac Ste Anne way occasional small patches occurred but could usually be detoured. Here, west of the Pembina, the muskegs were so widespread that the pack trains had to strike across them. Rod found that it was customary to tie one horse to the tail of the one ahead, but this presented difficulties : when one horse stopped, the next one lay down, and so on back along the string. The silence of the muskegs was broken by the curses of Tommy Groat and the continuous swearing of Montana Pete, who, even among packers, was rated high for his artistic profanity. Finally, by the utmost exertion of the poor horses and of all the men of the party, and with Montana Pete performing at his best pitch, the train would get across each stretch of muskeg – only to be confronted with another after a short distance.

Eventually, sometimes after spending hours getting across some muskegs or chopping a way through deadfall, the party crossed the McLeod River straight south of the site of the future town of Edson. Six or seven miles farther west they came to the Big Eddy.

At the time, there were only two white men living in all this area. One of them, Ben Berthoux, operated a small trading post at the mouth of Sundance Creek, on the high bank overlooking the Big Eddy. When Rod's party passed it, Ben was away on some expedition. Similarly, when the surveyors reached the vicinity of present-day Marlboro, ten miles west of the Big Eddy, the man in charge of the Hudson's Bay Company outpost at the mouth of Whitemud Creek was temporarily absent.

At this point the survey started. The instruments were unpacked and the real business of staking out the centre line of the proposed railway began. For Rod and the other packers life became a little easier now that the days of constant and strenuous travelling were behind. From here on for many weeks, their duties were to move camp every two or three days as the survey progressed, and once in a while to make trips to the main cache to bring back food and supplies.

The men of the party had sorted themselves out into different groups as their likes and dislikes dictated. Some became lifelong friends, while others avoided each other. In the same way, the horses began to stand out as individuals, and a few, because of their strength, willingness or temperament, became general favourites. Rod's horse, Badger, still nervous because of some illtreatment in the past, was apt to be excitable. Because of his strength, Hudson Bay Brownie, a large bay who could consistently carry 250 pounds, stood out for his sturdiness and reliability. And Sappo, a small, mischievous rascal, became a general favourite around camp and profited greatly by a mutual attachment he formed with Jimmy, the cook's flunkey.

Everyone put in long hours each day in the sunshine of early summer. On mornings when camp was to be moved, the surveyors would strike out west, while the cooks cleaned up after breakfast. Then the packers took over and moved the camp on past the surveyors and axemen and set it up at some point farther on, so that in the evening the instrument men would come to it from the east. Rod was up at four every morning, so that before dark he, like everyone else, was glad to roll in for the night. The chief surveyors had bed-rolls and blankets, but the packers had to use saddle blankets. Three or four of them crowded into one tent to sleep.

To Rod, who was sixteen, the hard work and exposure were a small price to pay for the camaraderie of the camp and the freedom and fresh air enjoyed by the survey party approaching the foothills. On Saturday nights everyone sat around for a prolonged pow-wow. On Sundays, socks and other garments were patched and washed, and for those who felt like it, the McLeod and its tributary streams provided excellent trout fishing.

One Saturday night, near present-day Medicine Lodge, the camp was pitched in a little open spot. Stories of other surveys passed around the pow-wow as men recalled humorous or tragic adventures with fire, flood or wild animals. Invariably the talk ran to encounters with black or grizzly bears. Rod was tired and soon made his way across the moonlit clearing and stepped into the tent he shared with three other men. In the pitch dark he groped his way, feeling for his own saddle blanket. Finding it, he sat down and, as he leaned back, his hand sank into a mass of warm hair. In an instant he was on his feet again and out in the moonlight, streaking across to the pow-wow, afraid to look back to see whether he was pursued by one bear or by a group of them emerging from his tent.

Montana Pete went back with him, and instead of entering the tent, went around behind it and shook the canvas while Rod stood well out of the way of any bears that might come out. Instead of bears, four black and white animals strolled sedately out into the moonlight – a mother skunk and three well grown kittens. Rod and Montana Pete stood by most respectfully until the unhurried procession of skunks crossed the clearing and were lost in the shadows of the bush beyond. Next morning they found that this clearing was a favourite rendezvous for skunks and they counted some thirty of them; but by a mutual and strictly observed tolerance on both sides, nothing untoward happened.

This year the main cache of supplies for the use of the three survey parties under Oscar Englund, Betts and Featherstonhaugh, who was working west of Tête Jaune Cache, had been made at Prairie Creek. Fred Young, Allen Stewart and the Yates brothers from Lac Ste Anne had packed the goods in. Pete Talbot remained in charge of the supplies, and when called upon, issued goods to the various parties.

For some weeks Rod was kept busy making trips back and forth from the camp to the cache. On his arrival there on his first trip, Pete Talbot was the first stranger he or any of his party had seen since leaving Donald McDonald's place at Lake Isle. At Prairie Creek (three miles west of old Hinton) Rod found an impressive settlement. Besides the Company's cachekeeper, there were the ranchers Jack Gregg and N. H. "One-Eyed" Jock, who some years previously had been attracted to the rich pasture on the creek flats and were grazing a herd of horses. A few Métis also lived and pastured their horses in the valley. The Cree name for the creek, Maskuta, meant prairie or a creek along which the original forest had long since been burned and had been replaced by small poplars and willows and abundant grass. Today much of this area has grown up to timber, but in 1906 several hundred acres were mainly open grassland.

While Rod was making trips to Prairie Creek, the survey advanced daily and eventually moved on to work out a route from Fiddle Creek to the site of the present-day town of Jasper, then known as Henry House. This was the territory which thirty years previously Walter Moberly had studied so carefully for the CPR, but his notes were not available and this work had to be done anew.

The entrance to the mountains did not present major difficulties to the railway surveyors, yet there were some knotty problems. The Athabasca River flows north through Jasper town and some fifteen miles downstream spreads out to the width of a mile to form Jasper Lake, which extends some six miles in a northeasterly direction. Leaving it, the river twists and turns for another ten miles before spreading out into another sheet of water of similar size called Brulé Lake, through which the river flows in a northerly direction. The lake had been given that name because at one time all the surrounding area had been burned over. After leaving Brulé Lake, the river flows in a deep narrow valley for some miles to the northeast. The difficult part for the railway surveyors was the twenty miles from the lower end of Brulé Lake upstream to the upper end of Jasper Lake. In this stretch two major tributaries enter the Athabasca, the Snake Indian River from the west and the Rocky River from the east. And towering above the Athabasca, barring the way with bastions jutting into the water, stand the mighty guardians of the gate, Bedson Ridge on the west, and on the east the famous Roche Miette.

For three months Oscar Englund and his men sought a practical route through this, the entrance to the mountains. First the east side of the pass seemed the easier one, even though near the Rocky River it was most difficult for a railway to creep around the spur where Roche Miette jutted into the swirling Athabasca. The old pack train route had been stopped here, and to overcome this obstacle had climbed hundreds of feet over a shoulder of Roche Miette and had then descended its west side. Only the numerous mountain sheep which cavorted up and down the crags could cope with this spur. Englund, however, was persistent and laid out a route where one rail of the track was nicked into the cliff, while the waters of the lake lapped at the other.

In a couple of miles a second obstacle barred the way. This time it was not rugged rocks which the horny-fisted builders could fight, but sand – shifting, sifting sand that moved and writhed under their feet, burying their survey stakes one day and undermining them the next. No practical railroad, Englund concluded, could be built through these creeping dunes. So, abandoning the east route, he turned back to the beginning of the gateway and picked out a new one, crossing the Athabasca below Brulé Lake and following along its west side.

For a few miles this route looked promising. But then a jutting spur of the Bedson Ridge made it impossible to bend his rails enough to creep around it. The only possibility for a railway was to blast a long expensive tunnel through the flinty rock. The west side of the gateway had also thwarted him. Reluctantly, he once more turned to the east side, and this time tried to avoid the sand by looking for a route around the Fishing Lakes (Talbot). When this also proved impractical, he was forced to fight his way through the sand dunes.

Three months altogether were spent before a satisfactory route was selected and staked. Meanwhile Rod, busy from dawn to dusk, enjoyed each day's bracing sunshine in the magnificent valley of the Athabasca. With the surveyors inching their way along precarious toeholds in the vertical crags, the packers did not have to move camp so often, although they were kept busy bringing up enough food from the Prairie Creek cache.

The pack trail, well marked now by their frequent comings and goings, presented no unusual difficulties except where it had to climb hundreds of feet over the spur of Roche Miette. This precarious mile, the dread of every packer, taxed every man's courage and exacted its toll of horses. The way up one side and down the other was difficult, but the real danger spot was a few square yards at the top where the smooth rocks, polished to a glassy surface by the winds of centuries, appeared level. In reality they sloped, gradually at first, then more steeply till finally they became almost vertical where, hundreds of feet below, they plunged into the rushing river. A horse straining up the steep path to gain the top invariably stopped on this level space to blow. The next horse and the next invariably crowded up beside him, until finally the pressure of horses behind pushed the leading horses off balance and set them sliding along the smooth sloping surface, slipping faster and faster as they inevitably hurtled to their doom. Because of the many horses lost here, today's maps call this mountain spur "Disaster Point."

Experienced packers who had been over Roche Miette before tried to prevent disaster at the summit by arranging that not more than two, or at most three, horses were between each man and the next. In this way, not more than three horses were on the treacherous rocks at one time, and the packers saw to it that they started on their way down the other side before the next group came up.

One pack horse has achieved immortality in the memories of all packers and old-timers of the foothills as the Grand Trunk Cheese Horse. He was loaded with three large, flat Cheddar cheeses. He was jostled at the summit, lost his footing and went sprawling down the slope. Rod, who was in the party, ran over in time to see him carom off one tree and come to rest wedged behind another about a hundred feet down. When the horse hit the first tree, the cheeses came loose and rolled, bounced and then flew down the mountainside. One smashed against a rock a few feet down and could be salvaged. Each of the others rolled and bounced, smashing to pieces and smearing cheese down the mountainside until the last remnants splashed into the river far below.

Rod dashed down the rocky hillside and was the first to reach the horse. Although winded and utterly unable to free itself, by some miracle it did not have any broken bones. It took several men with ropes and slings to get it back on the trail again, but in a few days it appeared as good as ever. Meanwhile someone else retrieved the one badly broken cheese, but for many a day the fragments of the other two must have provided tempting morsels for all the mice of Roche Miette.

Rod was young and strong and, because of a variety of escapades on the mountainside, was nicknamed the mountain goat. All summer he wore moccasins, which he found ideal footwear for clinging to the rocks. He got them by trading salt pork to the Indian women of the valley. Much pork must have changed hands, for he declares that that summer he wore out over fifty pairs of moccasins.

In the Jasper valley Rod first met the Moberlys – half-breeds of high integrity and intelligence, descendants of Henry John Moberly who spent six years at Jasper House in the 1850's. Tommy Groat, who some years later was to marry a daughter of Ewan Moberly and up to this point had been the party's second packer, left the crew here, and Rod was promoted to fill his place, with a jump in salary from $40 to $85 a month. At the same time one of the legendary natives of the Athabasca valley, Dolphus Moberly, was added to the crew. He was already famous as a packer and guide and was highly respected for his knowledge of the ways of the mountains. From him Rod learned much.

Shortly after Dolphus joined the party, Oscar Englund decided to study the west side of the pass, so that camp had to be moved across Brulé Lake. The move was accomplished without much fuss, but fording a mountain river or rafting over a mountain lake always presents problems. Some of the pack horses were loaded and made to swim across the lower end of the lake. Pete, a horse who swam high in the water, was packed with boxes of dishes and got carried into an eddy. Each time he came within a few feet of the bank the water swirled him out and farther downstream. Finally, just as Rod felt that Pete was getting exhausted and would never make it, he put on an extra spurt, and the men managed to get hold of him and help him out of the water.

Rod and Urquhart made a raft and took a large load across the lake, but the eddy likewise caught it, and it too was in danger of being carried down and dashed to pieces in the rapids of the river. Fortunately Urquhart was a strong man and a good swimmer, for he jumped off the raft, holding the end of a seventy-foot rope in his mouth, and swam upstream for shore. The strong current, the icy water and the rope nearly proved too much for even his strength, and Rod was afraid that he could never gain the shore. Just in the nick of time Urquhart ran up the bank and snubbed the rope around a tree, saving Rod from a ducking in the rapids below, at the very least, and the raft from breaking up and losing all its load.

A few days later Rod chose a calm spot in the lake and went for a swim to celebrate his seventeenth birthday. That evening, since the party was divided and there would only be a few for supper, the cook was in no hurry. Just as he should have been starting the meal, he spotted a bear on the hillside and, grabbing a rifle, rushed in pursuit, expecting to return soon with fresh bear meat. As it turned out, he never caught up with the bear, but was away a long time hunting for him. Rod, who was left to tend camp, decided to help out by cooking the bannock, so that it would be ready when the hungry men came in. For months he had watched the cooks at this and had been silently critical of their method of cooking as compared with his mother's at home.

He had put the frying pans on to warm and was soon literally up to his ears mixing the bannock dough. His mother had often explained, when baking bread, that the more the dough was kneaded the lighter it would be. Rod poured in the water and mixed until he judged that the amount of dough in the mess before him – added to that which stuck to his hands like toffee

and that which he planned to scrape off his clothes and face –
would make the right amount of bannock. The cook was still
away by the time he had reunited the various streamers of dough
into one pile on the table, so he decided to apply his mother's
teaching. But alas, bannock, unlike bread, should never be
kneaded. Quite unaware that a practice that should make delect-
able bread might make diabolical bannock, he kneaded with a
will, looking forward to the cook's discomfiture when the men
praised Rod's light, fluffy bannock. As he set the bannock to bake,
the cook and the other men returned together. Smirking to himself, he waited for the men to sample his cooking.

"What the hell's this stuff?" said the first man to bite into it.

"Good God!" said the second one.

All swore that never in their whole lives, on survey or pack
trail, had they tried to tear pieces out of such leathery bannock.
For a few moments the air was full of curses and slabs of bannock
aimed at Rod.

Bill, one of the axemen, did not throw away his share; he
reserved it for Rod's further humiliation. After supper Bill shot
eight or ten ·22 bullets into a soft pine log and then Rod helped
him split the log to recover the lead pellets, which although a bit
flattened on the end, were essentially undamaged. Bill pocketed
the bullets without explanation or comment.

Next day at noon, Rod found the explanation when he, Oscar
Englund and Montana Pete came in for lunch. For there, nailed to
two handy trees, were two of his bannocks which Bill said the
boys had been using for target practice. As evidence of the dur-
ability of Rod's culinary efforts and grouped close to the black
bull's-eye which had been smeared on each, were four or five ·22
bullets, which although flattened a bit on the end, had failed to
penetrate far into Rod's tough bannock.

While the party was still on the west side of Brulé Lake, Rod
came to know and admire Dolphus Moberly. His knowledge of
pack horses and of the wildlife in his mountain homeland amazed
the younger man. One evening when the men were in the cookhouse devoting all their attention to supper, Dolphus jumped up
and listened. The others looked up but could hear nothing out of
the ordinary.

"Sick horse," said the mountain man, as he strode out with Rod at his heels. Sure enough, one of the horses grazing in the meadow by the creek had evidently eaten wild parsnip and was bloated and in agony. Dolphus sent Rod running back to the cookhouse to melt a pail of lard. With this and other medicine which he poured down the horse's throat, the animal was well by morning.

Another evening as Rod lay back listening while the native packer told tales of the hills, Dolphus suddenly rolled over, seized his gun and disappeared out the tent door. As Rod scrambled to his feet and ran outside, he saw Dolphus disappear into the trees, and after a long interval heard one shot. Says Rod, "He killed a bear – and it must have been a quarter of a mile away. I never could make out how he knew it was near. He couldn't have seen it. I doubt if he heard it – certainly I didn't. He must have smelled it – he had the sharpest senses of any man I ever knew."

Meanwhile Oscar Englund, after many a huddle with Emerson Bell and Lincoln Ellsworth, his instrument men, decided that the drifting sands were preferable to a tunnel, and moved his camp back to the east side of the lake. Those sands, where today's highway follows the long abandoned railroad grade along the east side of Jasper Lake, were a major problem. When Emerson Bell resumed his levelling south along them, he found most of his old stakes buried, and in one place the drifted surface was twenty feet above the stakes he had pounded in some weeks before. The sand swirled and sifted in, under, over and through everything. The axemen who chopped the trees along the line complained that somehow the very wood was impregnated with it and dulled their axes. It blew into the men's noses and ears. Their faces smarted as it whipped into them, and at times they dared not open their eyes. One day in crossing the camp, Rod solved this problem by inverting a water pail over his head and picking his way along. Lincoln Ellsworth, the transit man, was bitter in his denunciation of the eternal wind and the drifting sand.

Fall was beginning to close in, and Ellsworth, ever an adventurer, had to leave the party so as to keep an appointment in New York with members of another expedition bound for some far-off place. Now Rod, like the other packers, had neither bed-roll nor blankets, and slept in horse blankets. When Ellsworth left, Rod bought his packsack and bed-roll, but since all the men had no use for money on the trip and were to be paid when they returned to Edmonton, he wrote a note to his mother, asking her to pay Ellsworth as he passed through Edmonton. His note, scribbled on a corner torn from a piece of brown wrapping paper, said:

Dear Mother: Please pay to Lincoln Ellsworth the sum of $6.00 for bed-roll and packsack. Your loving son,

Rod McCrimmon.

He wrote it hurriedly, forgot about it, and was grateful for the bed-roll.

Throughout the long, glorious fall, the survey continued, crossing over to the west side of the Athabasca and making good time in the flat terrain through Swift's farm in the shadow of the Palisades. Soon the site of present-day Jasper was reached. Across the river from it lay the ruins of the second Henry House. Here the line left the Athabasca for good and turned west to ascend the Miette River to the Yellowhead Pass. Next year it would be continued to Moose Lake, Tête Jaune Cache, the Fraser River, on to Prince George, and ultimately to Prince Rupert on the coast.

In the dry fall, the breezes ever blowing down the valley rustled the ripened grasses. The poplar and balm trees turned golden and glowed against the dark of spruce and pine. Higher up, the blue of the mountains deepened, while far above fresh snow fell to cover the old ice of the glaciers and the nakedness of limestone crags. Every few days a fresh fall brought the snow-line farther down the mountains. Over all, the sun shone in a brilliant blue sky. The days spent tramping back and forth in the magnificent valley were one long joyous holiday for Rod, but at night ice formed over pools and on the water buckets. The cosiness of the campfire was doubled now that its heat was as welcome as its cheery glow.

These glorious days led on imperceptibly to late fall with its chilling, soaking rains, and then one morning the valley was covered with snow. Winter had begun, but the survey had to go on, until late in November Oscar Englund packed up and turned the train homeward. As well as the twenty-five horses of their own party, they started back to Edmonton with thirty beasts belonging to the Featherstonhaugh party, which had been working west of Tête Jaune Cache.

It was not a day too soon, for this was the beginning of the terrible winter of 1906–1907. Ice was forming wide margins on the rivers and floating in the channels. Snow swirled about the mountains and coulees and drifted over the still meadows, covering the rich native grasses. The crossing of the Athabasca was dangerous and they lost a horse or two. This was just a foretaste of what was in store for them, for snow fell day after day, and daily the temperature dropped. The party had plenty of food, but the horses were expected to forage for themselves.

At Prairie Creek they left some goods in the cache and took on further provisions, while they rested their horses and allowed them to graze for a day. At Obed they floundered through snow four feet deep. At the Big Eddy they stopped for another day and turned their horses loose. Here the men were taken in and welcomed by Ben Berthoux, the storekeeper, and by Alex Sinclair, who had just built a shack and planned to winter with a young man by the name of Ansell. Some of the men went over to visit a new arrival in the country, a man named Hornbeck, who a few days before had arrived with eighteen fine percheron horses. He had intended taking them on to Prairie Creek to winter, but with the onset of heavy snow, had turned them loose on what we now know as Hornbeck Creek. Then he and his friend, Harry Neergard, a young Norwegian, built a shack for themselves. The men met with a warm welcome and came away admiring the fine percherons.

Next day the pack train resumed its way towards Lac Ste Anne. Progress was slow, and almost daily one or more horses died from lack of feed or fatigue. Those that remained were pitifully thin and weak, all except little Sappo, who early in the season had formed an alliance with Sandy Potts, the bull-cook. Sappo's hide was still sleek and his ribs barely discernible. His friendship with the cook was paying off, and each evening he would slink around to get a double handful of rolled oats and then slip away to the other horses. But as the trip dragged along, making two or three miles a day, even the men's food began to run low. It was then that Sappo's greed was his downfall. One evening Sandy was busy when Sappo called, so he nosed into the tent, caught the sack of oats in his teeth and, dropping it behind the tent, soon made short work of it. Potts rushed out just as the last of the oats vanished. With sticks and curses he belaboured poor Sappo, who on further visits to the cook tent was turned coldly away.

It was a weakened pack train that staggered into Lac Ste Anne late in December. Of some sixty horses that started east from Jasper, thirty-seven had died on the way. For a day or so the remainder were fed good hay and oats and then made their way to St Albert, where the next morning the first thermometer Rod had seen since the spring registered fifty-eight below. The following day the party reached the horse pound at Groat's, where Shand Harvey was on hand to see the gaunt horses and frostbitten men conclude their nine months' trip.

Rod hastened home to a warm welcome from his mother, but a strange coolness from his father. All he said was: "I want to see you in my office at ten in the morning."

Wondering what was in the wind, Rod showed up at ten, to be confronted by a wrathful man who read him a stern lecture on the disgrace of forging his father's name to a cheque. Rod, quite unable to understand what he was talking about, swore his innocence. This further enraged his father, who reached into a drawer, produced a scrap of torn wrapping paper and waved it in his son's face.

Here was the note Rod had sent to his mother, asking her to pay Lincoln Ellsworth six dollars for the bed-roll, but now it was all covered with rubber stamps and endorsements. Ellsworth had evidently carried the note with him to his home in New York. There he had turned it in to the First National Bank of Manhattan to be cashed. Via Montreal and Winnipeg, as the rubber stamps attested, it had eventually been presented to Malcolm McCrimmon's bank in Edmonton, where, in spite of carrying Rod's "Your loving son, Rod McCrimmon," it had been cashed.

The older man was mollified when he heard the explanation and examined the wrapping paper note more carefully, but by this time Rod, whose temper was as hasty as his dad's, reached for the paper and tore it to shreds.

"Lad," said his father, "till your dying day you'll be sorry you tore that up. You should have kept it as a souvenir."

So ended one season's survey work. For many miles, over rock and coulee, shifting sands and muskeg, it had laid out a line of stakes curving through the forest. Along this line, after the labours of many more years, giant locomotives would carry the nation's commerce into the distant echoing passes of the Rocky Mountains. But at this stage much more surveying had still to be done.

IN the spring of 1907 Shand finally gratified his
urge to start out for the mountains. During the winter months he
kept his driving team well employed, and for relaxation sought
out Montana Pete, Rod McCrimmon and many another man who
had travelled west into the mountain area. That spring he got a
job on the party that was going out to extend the survey of the
14th Base Line all the way to the mountains.

For some twenty blocks west of First Street, Jasper Avenue
followed the north boundary of Township 52, which was also
the 14th Base Line. At its west end where it curved to avoid
running into the river bank, a cut-line continued over the Groat
Ravine and finally was lost to sight in the hazy west. This cut-
line, too, was the 14th Base Line, and Shand knew that over hill
and dale, muskeg and meadow, it swept on and on till it lost itself
in Lake Wabamun, at what was later to be the summer resort
of Kapasiwin – the old "camping ground" of the Crees and
Stonies. Many a time as he walked or drove west on Jasper
Avenue his eyes followed this line as far as it could be seen, and
then in his mind's eye he followed it farther through lake and
forest to the very summit of the continent, where north of Mount
Robson it crossed the boundary line into British Columbia.

During 1906 this line had been carried west to a point some
four miles beyond the Pembina River. The fact that a new railway
was heading towards the Yellowhead Pass made it necessary for
the federal government to extend this survey west to the mountains, so that the railway could tie its right-of-way in with it.

The 14th Base Line thus passed through Edmonton. The 5th
Meridian ran north and south through the hamlet of Stony Plain.
Far to the west – some 160 miles west of Stony Plain – the 6th
Meridian had yet to be marked on the ground by pits, mounds,
stakes and cairns. When it was finally located, it was found to

pass some thirty miles east of the present site of the City of Grande Prairie and to continue south until it lay three miles east of Jasper. Shand was to be at work on the 14th Base Line, while another party was to start near Grande Prairie and run the 6th Meridian until the two lines intersected.

One day early in May, when snow still lay in the shady places, Shand heard that Archie Ponton, DLS, had arrived at Strathcona with three carloads of pack horses, so he hurried over to see if he could get a job. Each carload was intended for a different party. One surveyor by the name of Hawkins was to take a load of twenty head to lay out the 15th Base Line, which ran west from Morinville. Arthur St Cyr, DLS, was to take his horses – or rather have his horses take him and his party – to the vicinity of the Grande Prairie where he was to start running the 6th Meridian south. Somewhere near Jasper, if all went well, he would meet the third crew working west along the 14th Base Line.

The third party was headed by George Ross, DLS. Shand soon met Tommy Thompson who was to be in charge of its horses and who hired him as a packer. In short order the twenty horses, all of them from the Blood Indian Reserve and branded with a ∞, were unloaded. Shand helped to take them across the river to a feed barn near the Edmonton Market Square, hard by Frank Good's Imperial Hotel. While the packers took care of the horses, George Ross hired wagons to convey the supplies, tents and bedding, as well as all the party except the packers, out along the road to Lac Ste Anne. Early the third day they reached the Hudson's Bay Company's post there.

Since they could not carry enough supplies with them to last till Christmas, another pack train was due to leave Lac Ste Anne in July to take the remainder, which was to be cached at Jack Gregg's place at Prairie Creek. Part of this train's load was to be winter clothing and stoves. Tommy Thompson and Shand spent a few busy days making up their packs. Everything that the men of the party would eat, wear or use during the next several months had to be packed on twenty horses. Tents, axes, stoves, flour, bacon and beans had to be made into packs, which every morning would be lashed to pack saddles, and every evening would be unloaded. Making up the packs at the beginning of the trip had to be done with the utmost forethought and care. Any mistakes made now could not be rectified later at a general store, for the party would not see a store again until they emerged eight months later from the pack trail to re-enter Lac Ste Anne.

Shand's evenings at Lac Ste Anne were spent visiting his friends Father Lizé and Peter Gunn.

"It's been a terrible winter," said Father Lizé. "Very heavy snow in November and long spells of bitter cold weather. My Métis here tried hard to save their horses. Many a day they spent breaking a trail through the deep snow by travelling back and forth, back and forth, on their snowshoes from slough to slough so that the horses – poor skeletons – could follow and scrape for feed. It's an odd thing, though, that the deep snow kept the ground from freezing and it wasn't safe to drive on the ice of the lake until spring. But the poor horses – so many of them died."

Shand was to hear from Peter Gunn more tales of horses and of the bitter winter. His company had always maintained a reputation for selling good liquor, and Hudson's Bay Company whisky was a favourite brand of the early settlers. Gunn's competitors, however, were not always so scrupulous.

"This last year or so some of my Métis friends have been buying their whisky across the way, but since the winter most of them have come back to trade with me," said Peter. "Along in January Dan Noyes came in here grinning and told me that a few nights earlier Alexis and Pierre and a couple of other freighters had put their horses into his barn and then sat around his stove thawing out and cursing. They had left here in the morning – and a bitter morning it was – and had bought a bottle across the way. By noon they were nearly frozen and stopped to light a fire to thaw out while they chopped off some frozen beans to fry. While the fire was blazing up, Alexis turned around to one of the sleighs and reached for the bottle, and then set up a howl. Not only had it frozen solid, but it had cracked the glass. They dumped ice and glass and all into a pot, but a lot of it had dropped on to the snow. It's damned poor whisky that'll freeze even in a winter like this. Dan said they were still cursing that night as they sat around his stove."

"Well, they'll learn," said Shand. Then, after a pause, "Bad winter for horses?"

"Worst yet. Fellow named Perry from the south somewhere lost about forty head up Whitecourt way."

"Did he go through here last fall heading for Grande Prairie?" asked Shand.

"Yes."

"Met him up near the Narrows. He lost them, did he?"

"Yes. He didn't get very far on his way after you saw him. It seems that early in November, when the heavy snowfall came, he quit travelling after he crossed the Athabasca and turned his horses out to winter on the big meadows on Eagle Creek [Sakatamau]. The winter was very cold and the snow three feet deep in most places, and on top of that we had a few chinook winds. To most people these warm winds are a blessing, but this winter they killed off a lot of horses. They thawed the snow just enough to put a good firm crust on it and then the horses couldn't paw through it to get at the feed underneath.

"The Métis at Hash Lake [Iosogun] – Alexis Bellcourt, Narcisse Coutrais and Dan Letendre – lost every one of their horses, even though they had some hay put up. So Perry's horses didn't have a chance. I imagine now that spring has come and the grizzlies are out again, they'll have a grand feed on the carcasses."

"Losing all those fine horses is enough to break a man's heart," said Shand.

"That's just what it did to a man named Hornbeck up near the Big Eddy," Peter said. "Last fall he went through here, heading for Prairie Creek to Jasper, with eighteen fine percherons. Think he was planning to keep them up there for a year or so and make a killing selling them for railway construction. Had a young Norwegian lad named Harry Neergard with him.

"In February word came to the Mountie here that Hornbeck had gone crazy. Evidently the horses, one by one, became too weak to carry on and young Harry shot them until Hornbeck's favourite saddle pony was the only one left. Then one evening Harry had to shoot her. This was the final blow that sent Hornbeck off his head. They tell me that he heard the shot, and when young Harry came in he asked, 'Did you shoot her, Harry?' 'Yes, I did.' 'Well, God help you if she isn't alive in the morning. I'll shoot you.' With that, Harry went over to Ben's store and in the morning all hell broke loose. But these stories get so mixed up.

You'll be passing through the Big Eddy in a week or so and you can get the story straight when you get there."

In a few days the survey party's preparations were completed, and the horses brought in and loaded, though some of them resisted. Then they had to be watched to see that they didn't lie down to try to dislodge pack and saddle alike. Finally Tommy Thompson gave the order to start, and before long Shand found himself crossing the Pembina, and soon the train was up the west bank and turning south to cross the Lobstick. After a few more miles the party made its first camp near the west bank of the Pembina and beside the line it had come to cleave through the forest. The horses were turned out to graze in a small meadow, and all hands set to putting up tents and stowing provisions. The surveyors unpacked their instruments and chronometers in preparation for an evening's work observing the stars to check the latitude of this, the beginning of the line they were to project westward.

After supper Shand walked east to look over the river from the brink of the precipitous clay and sandstone cliff rising three hundred feet above the rapid stream. For a long time he looked across the deep valley to the other bank half a mile away, fascinated by last year's cut-line. This stark gash in the forest ascended the steep slope for a mile or so and then, where the otherwise unbroken sweep of forest formed the horizon, this narrow slit let the distant blue of the sky peek past the roots of the trees. Beyond this gap, unseen from here but falling away on the far side of the hill, flowing east to Edmonton over marsh and meadow, headland and hollow, eight feet wide and sixty miles long, marched the slash of the 14th Base Line. From here west, Shand and his colleagues were to clear a similar strip eight feet wide and some 120 miles long. At the moment, this line was only theoretical, its position as inexorable as the laws of spherical geometry, but George Ross and his party were to mark it by a narrow swath through the forest. At the end of each mile they were to dig four pits, erect a mound and drive in an iron stake, so that men for all time to come could see and know exactly where it ran. The implications of such a line were far-reaching. Shand was amazed at the audacity of men – of men so physically puny yet so prodigious of purpose as to girdle the globe by scratching out lines, so mighty of mind as to claim this vast wilderness with mystic mounds and monuments. On and ever on, as this line penetrated the forest, what secret nooks would it discover? Somewhere ahead would it invade the midnight lair of lynx or wolf? On some creek bank deep in the woods would it expose the door to a bear's den? Finally, a hundred miles west, up among the high peaks, would it cross the lambing shelter of the bighorn ewe, scramble over the craggy lookout of the woolly goat, or enter the eyrie of the far-seeing eagle?

Unlike a railway survey, which sought to find a practical grade for rails by avoiding obstacles such as lakes and cliffs, this base line survey had to go forward irresistibly, overcoming all obstacles. If a lake lay in its way, the line went across it; if a cliff intervened, the line was laid out up one steep side and down the other. For this line had to follow a definite parallel of latitude, and at all points had to be equally distant from the North Pole.

Shand enjoyed his part in the survey. Most of his work consisted of ranging the country for two or three miles on each side of the line, making a rough map of its hills, its valleys, creeks and other natural features. Each day the line advanced, and with each day came new signs of spring. It was a very late spring, with little evidence of new leaves till the beginning of June, and then, all of a sudden, winter yielded to summer. The weather warmed up. Birds nested in every thicket. Ducks, two by two, and water birds in pairs, abounded on every little slough. Frogs rejoiced, and the woods, redolent with the fresh smells of spring, resounded to their croaking. For much of the country along the line was marshy.

This muskeg made the work unpleasant, for all day long the men floundered in water and raised clouds of mosquitoes and sandflies. The horses suffered too, but on the whole they were lucky, because only one of them contracted hoof-rot. Fortunately Tommy Thompson, an experienced packer, was watching for this and caught it in time; he was able to cure it by putting hot bacon grease around the coronets of the horse's hoofs. This section of the pack trail from Chip Lake to the McLeod River was noted for being infested with hoof-rot. Undoubtedly the extensive muskeg was a contributing factor.

The land was not all muskeg, however, and Shand, when he

was out taking topography on either side of the line, often encountered splendid areas of timber. One of these occupying several square miles was on what came to be called Blueberry Hill, a slight elevation some six miles south and east of present-day Wildwood. Most of this hill was covered with a stand of fine lodgepole pine. Here also in cathedral groves majestic spruce trees two and three feet through stood motionless and silent. The breeze far above rustled in their tops, but underfoot the thick pile of the forest's carpet hushed all sound : it was moss, ankle-deep, ages old and infinitely trim. Even the spruce cones shelled by squirrels had been heaped into tidy piles. Here and there a yellow or red toadstool stood on tiptoe. Bunchberry plants, with their four white petals and dark shiny leaves, provided the bolder pattern of the carpet, while draping the rotted trunks of forest giants fallen long ago were the tiny pink bells of the twinflower or the shy head-hanging wintergreen.

Shand rejoiced in the cool silence of these woods. The botanists, he thought, called this the boreal forest, but even so, as June and July came on, a multitude of flowers bordered his walk. In the open glades shone violets, blue and white, and amidst the purple of the vetches the ground was carpeted with snowy strawberry blossoms. Even the muskegs were interesting, with cotton grass, Labrador tea and golden acres of marsh marigolds, the earliest, gladdest flowers of the year.

And in the fresh greenery, hidden to casual eyes, the hermit thrush poured out his evening song, while at intervals the white-throated sparrow, with his *Ah – dear – Canada – Canada – Canada*, expressed for Shand and all other sentient beings the ecstasy of spring. Surely, thought he, in no other land could spring mean so much. In one day its sudden, almost violent return, cast off winter and ushered in summer. All at once and together every living plant or animal, even the very brooks, rejoiced. Through the six long wearying months of winter each of the living, flowering, silent or singing beings had endured, each in its own manner. The plants had introverted to dull sticks and straws, the hibernating beasts had hidden in holes and dens, the migratory song-birds and water-fowl had deserted to softer climates. Only the sturdy of soul had remained to face the biting blizzard, the smothering snow and the searing cold.

While all rejoiced now in the sunshine and the scents and songs of spring, Shand felt a new respect for the weasel and the wolf, the moose and the deer, the partridge and the chickadee, the rabbit and the whiskyjack. These had not run away, but in their courage had faced up to winter, shrugged off its fury, borne its length, and now in the balm of spring were reaping the reward of their steadfastness.

What a bitter battle it must have been, thought Shand. Through poplar forest, willow meadow and muskeg, one sign of one phase of this grim battle showed on every hand. Over large areas the bark of every willow and poplar had been gnawed off by rabbits seeking sustenance. Not just a nibble here and there – for acres, up to five feet from the ground, every tree and bush had been stripped of its bark. Obviously, as the snow had deepened, the rabbits had been able to reach higher and higher. Even broken trees that had not fallen flat, but lay inclined as their upper branches had caught on other trees, had been stripped of their bark as the rabbits had climbed shakily ever further aloft. Here and there through the forest swung a carcass of a rabbit whose luck had not held. For he, having slipped off such a leaning tree, had not fallen clear to the cushion of snow below, but by mischance had caught his neck in the fork of two branches and dangled there until strangulation stopped his struggles.

Shand had plenty of time to observe and reflect, as all day long he walked or rode through the forest on either side of the line. Often on returning in the evening, he would find the camp had been moved farther west. So, daily, the slash through the forest moved ever farther west, and before long reached the area some six miles south of Chip Lake. Here it approached the Jasper Trail, and from here on the party camped in the regular camping places along that trail. More and more Grand Trunk pack trains, bound westward with survey parties or passing to and fro taking supplies out to the caches, were using the old trail.

In July the line reached the meandering McLeod River, its canyon-like walls deeply incised into clay and sandstone cliffs. The pack trail crossed it some three and one-half miles straight south of the present-day Edson station, but the line intersected it a mile farther downstream. The horses of course had to swim, but George Ross had brought along a canvas boat which enabled the men to keep dry when their work made them cross and re-cross the large, swiftly flowing river. For the next thirty miles the line was rarely more than a mile from the McLeod, and actually intersected it twice more. The last crossing was a mile upstream from the Big Eddy.

At the Big Eddy the McLeod makes a spectacular hairpin bend, and right at that point the waters of Sundance Creek charge in from the west to clash head-on with the rushing stream. The resulting whirl of the angry waters seethes as it swirls off down the other leg of the hairpin. Far above, the dense forest virtually overhangs as it looks down the two-hundred-foot cliff to the eddying waters. The Big Eddy was to cause many a headache for the builders of the Grand Trunk and the Canadian Northern, whose lines had to cross each other and the wide valley of Sundance Creek by stupendous curving trestles. But when Shand first looked down at these swirling waters, the Grand Trunk line was a mere slash in the forest, and the problems faced by the Canadian Northern engineers were still some years in the future.

The Big Eddy was then merely one of the far-flung flecks of civilization that sparsely dotted the map of this vast wilderness – Lac Ste Anne, the Big Eddy, Prairie Creek and Jasper. But it was a strategic point along the old pack trail, which swung along a few feet back from the brink of the canyon and brought a few white travellers and many natives on their way to trade furs for supplies. Moreover, the old trail from the area we now know as the Coal Branch crossed here on its way down the valley of the Embarrass and McLeod Rivers, and then took off up the Sundance, heading north and west. The flats along the Sundance Creek provided good pasture for passing pack horses. In the spring of 1907 the Grand Trunk had set up a cache there in charge of Pete Talbot, who had spent the previous year at Prairie Creek.

A year or so before Shand's visit, Ben Berthoux, a slight, grey-haired old Frenchman who at one time had been a chef in CPR hotels, had started his little trading post on the high bank over-looking the Big Eddy. In the fall of 1906, Alex Sinclair, a trapper, had built a little shack below this point and was wintering there with a young man by the name of Ansell. Then a month or so later, to add to the congestion, Hornbeck had arrived with his horses and a young Scandinavian companion by the name of

Harry Neergard. Hornbeck had intended taking his horses on to the meadows of Prairie Creek, but when, early in November, by repeated falls of deep snow the severity of the winter of 1906–1907 began to make itself felt, he had been forced to camp along the Sundance. He turned his horses out to pasture and built a shack a mile or so up the creek from Ben Berthoux. On his way through Lac Ste Anne Hornbeck, who appeared to have plenty of money, had bought a good grubstake. As the temperature dropped and the snow deepened, his horses, turned loose on strange range, fared poorly. Then a cold snap after the February thaw froze a deep crust on the snow, and one by one the horses starved, until of them all only Hornbeck's favourite saddle pony remained.

Hornbeck had been used to the activity and sociability of ranching on the prairies near Calgary. The inactivity and solitude of the long winter bore heavily on him. His loss and frustration, as one by one his horses died, made a heavier load than he could carry. Finally, to save his favourite mare from further suffering, she too had to be shot. As the rifle bullet crashed through her skull, something in Hornbeck's brain snapped.

Neergard, expecting such an outcome, fled to the safety of Alex Sinclair's and all through the night Hornbeck was left alone with his thoughts, his rifle and his well filled cartridge belt.

Next morning Ben Berthoux was aroused from sleep by a maniac brandishing a well oiled rifle. With soft words Ben fended him off long enough to get his clothes on, and then, making his escape from the store, rushed down the hill to the Sinclair cabin.

All day long Hornbeck stayed in the store and did not show himself outside. As the day wore on, the others, huddled in the Sinclair shack watching the smoke rise from the stovepipe, realized that Hornbeck intended to remain in possession of the store. Next morning they saw him emerge from it and they hurriedly threw themselves to the floor as some of his rifle shots smacked into the logs, while another tore through the stovepipe. Hornbeck, though a good shot, soon tired of shooting and went back into the store.

After dark, Harry Neergard set out on snowshoes for Lac Ste Anne to fetch the Mounted Police. The men in the cabin knew that it would be many days before he could travel the hundred miles of unbroken trail and return with the police. At daylight next morning Hornbeck sent three or four more shots smacking into the logs of their cabin. Then he went back in the store, but reappeared a moment later carrying a sack of flour and brandishing a knife. He ripped the sack to shreds, scattering the flour over the snow in all directions. A sack of beans received similar treatment, and then he re-entered the store and was not seen for the rest of the day. On the next two or three days he repeated this performance – lobbing a few bullets at their shack and destroying more food.

Now nothing is more sacred to all men who live in the winter solitude of the forest than food. Any man is welcome to eat of it, but only a madman wantonly destroys it. Its loss means hardship and even starvation to those dependent upon it. Any man who destroys food must himself be destroyed. By the glow of the heater, Ben Berthoux, Alex Sinclair and Ansell made their decision. It might be many days before the Mountie arrived. When he did, a battle would ensue, undoubtedly ending in the death of Hornbeck and possibly in that of the Mountie or others. Meanwhile, they were in constant danger from the gunfire. Before daylight next morning they crawled up to the shoulder of the hill to a spot where, when the sun came up, the door of the store would be visible.

At daybreak Hornbeck stepped out carrying his gun, and the two men, concealed by the brow of the hill, glanced at Sinclair. He nodded, and three shots rang out. Hornbeck crumpled into the flour-littered snow.

When the policeman arrived, with Donald MacDonald as guide and a flat sled on which to tie the madman for his return to Lac Ste Anne, he had three peaceable men to arrest. They shut up their cabin and the store, helped him lash the corpse to the sled, and set out for civilization to face trial for manslaughter. In due course they were acquitted on grounds of self-defence.

Such was the story of the Hornbeck killing as Shand heard it when he reached the Big Eddy in July. The front logs of Alex Sinclair's cabin were filled with bullets, the stovepipe was riddled, and in front of Berthoux's store patches of flour lay white and soggy in the new grass. Shand wandered up the Sundance valley looking at the skeletons of the horses and peering into the deserted cabin on the bank of the little stream which today we call Hornbeck Creek.

The line continued west, and Shand fought mosquitoes and sandflies as he waded through the muskegs near Sundance Creek, while the surveyors had to triangulate around Octopus Lake. A few miles farther on, the line and the pack trail both crossed Whitemud Creek, a stone's throw upstream from the little Hudson's Bay Company's outpost where some years previously Dan Noyes had bought furs. In later years, Edmonton businessmen were to take note of the white mud, or marl, in the little lake a mile to the north, and were to build there the great Marlboro cement works.

A mile west of that creek the line crossed the survey of the Grand Trunk, and from then on it played tag with the railroaders' stakes, crossing them six times in the next twenty miles. Much of the land west of Whitemud Creek was muskeg. Here and for some miles east the snow fell to a greater depth in winter than it did in the rest of the province, and here too the summers were rainier. Most of the summer had been fair and dry, but now Shand had a solid week of steady cold rain. Day after day it dripped from the leaves and spattered into pools. Every night the tents steamed in a fog of drying clothes. Everyone was miserable.

Then one morning a wind from the west swept the rains away. The sun shone clearly, warming up the forest and bringing out with double strength the invigorating scent of balm trees. Shand caught his horse and set out once more on his survey of the land on either side of the line. To have a look around he urged his horse up a small hill, and there before him, shining blue and white, rose the great wall of the Rocky Mountains, the very backbone of the continent. Here were the mountains he had set out to see, a vast expanse of them, fifty miles away but so clear and sharply defined that he felt that he could ride to them in half a day. This was his first never-to-be-forgotten view of the mountains of the Jasper area, the highest mountains wholly within Canada.

Before long the line had advanced to a point called "The Leavings" near modern Hargwen, where the Jasper Trail left the McLeod River and began the slight climb to the summit of the divide between that river and the Athabasca. Here at the summit, on August 17, as Shand remembers it, the party endured one of the worst and coldest August storms he has ever experienced. Without warning the weather turned so cold that a foot and a half of snow fell. Totally unprepared for this freak weather, the party were caught without any stoves for their tents, and as Shand says, "We survived around a big open fire, which even the horses were glad to share."

West of Obed Lake the line crossed the Grand Trunk survey for the last time. Here the railway survey and the Jasper Trail turned south and west to run within a mile or so of the Athabasca River to the entrance of the mountains. Towards the end of September, with the mountains shining blue in the distance, the party made its last camp along the old trail. Amongst the maze of mountains, stretching like an endless blue wall across the party's front, one stood out boldly – a great square block, flat on top and rising two thousand feet sheer above the pass.

"Roche Miette," said Tommy Thompson, and there was an unusual reverence in his tone. "Gateway to the pass – the Athabasca flows at its foot. It's the main landmark in all this area."

At last Shand was approaching the far-off places, Roche Miette, the Yellowhead Pass and Tête Jaune Cache. For days this mighty blue bastion was in sight, towering over the pass. Shand, too, came to regard Roche Miette with an inexplicable reverence.

After crossing the Athabasca, only twenty-five miles stood between them and the end of the year's work. The country was higher and less marshy, and the timber was mainly pine and less difficult to get through. It was autumn, the most beautiful time of the year. The weather was clear, and the sun, shining brilliantly in an unclouded sky, brought out with startling clarity the details of the massive snow-covered mountains. The intervening ridges of the foothills rose one behind another, each a deeper blue, as increased distance thickened the haze of mystery that beckoned. Every leaf of the millions upon millions of aspens had turned a bright golden yellow, and interspersed and contrasting with these masses of trees were pines, green in the foreground but appearing black in the distance. The floor of the forest was generally open and easy to walk through, while such bushes as there were had turned red. The bearberry vines, such a shining green all summer, now glowed with a reddish tint.

Even the swampy plants of the muskegs were crimson. The combination of golden hillsides, the crimson underbrush and the brilliant blue sky, added to the fresh nip of the fall air, were as bubbling wine to Shand. Here amidst this blazing beauty, in this bracing air, no day was too long, no daybreak too early. Never had any part of the world appealed in its every aspect as this did. Surely, of all the world, this would be the place to live.

Perhaps wealth was to be won in steaming jungles, riches wrested from teeming cities, but here in the silent blue of the golden foothills was wealth beyond measure by dollars or millions. Here surely was the wealth which could bestow health and freedom and a contentment that made a man glad to welcome each day. During the long fall days working on the base line survey, Shand made up his mind. This country of blue foothills and shining mountains was to be his country.

The men had speculated about the progress made by the other party in running the 6th Meridian south from the Grande Prairie, and all wondered which of the two parties would be first to reach the point of intersection of the two lines. One day a shout from the axemen indicated that, in a thick grove of lodgepole pines on a steep hillside, the base line had broken through into the cut-line left by the other group on its way south. By the look of the freshly cut stumps, Shand's party was about a week behind.

George Ross spent a few extra days here taking additional observations on the meridian. His men had slashed a line for 120 miles west through the vast forest. The meridian party had driven a line 120 miles south through similar forest, and here, out on a wilderness hillside, the two lines intersected with an error of only a few links – a remarkably accurate achievement.

The end of November was near, and the packers made short work of returning to Gregg Lake and of following the old Indian pack trail south along the chain of lakes to reach the Athabasca at the good crossing place at the mouth of Prairie Creek. At the little settlement there George Ross hired two Indians, who brought along enough extra saddle horses so that everyone of the party could ride across the creeks and rivers and keep dry. Nearly three weeks later they re-entered Lac Ste Anne, cached their goods and turned the horses over to the Hudson's Bay Company to winter, rejoicing that on this trip of nine months no man had been seriously injured and none of the horses had been lost.

Then, having left everything shipshape at Lac Ste Anne, the men hired two teamsters with sleighs to take them to Edmonton in style. At dusk on Christmas Eve they arrived, and with Seagram's "83" at a dollar a quart, they celebrated the festive season in the manner of men who for nine months in the wilderness have hungered for the bright lights and the belles of the city.

CHAPTER
EIGHT

Shand spent his third winter, that of 1907–1908, in Edmonton, with plenty of time to think over the last two and a half years and to try to set a course for the future. Edmonton was indeed the land of opportunity. In the city itself and radiating out from it in all directions, a civilization was to be set up in an area which a scant ten years before had been a land empty and unexploited. On every hand lay undeveloped wealth: land, timber and coal. Every day more men came to turn their hands to developing it. Homesteaders by the thousands, labourers by the hundreds, merchants by scores and promoters by dozens, each according to his energy or enterprise, planned to produce or profit. This was reflected in the motto on the seal of the young City of Edmonton – "Industry, Energy, Enterprise."

This business of enterprise, thought Shand, could be carried too far. During his stay in Alberta he had found it easy to earn enough to pay his way, and after partaking of some of the pleasures of the wide-open city, to put by a little for a rainy day. By exerting himself more, he too might play more part in this "Enterprise." His many acquaintances amongst the businessmen were doing just that, and visions of riches danced before their eyes or were actually within their grasp. Many of them were in the real estate business, operated sawmills or planned to open mines, and undoubtedly would become rich. But nearly all of them took life very seriously, working with intense and continuous grimness. Some struck Shand as devoting themselves to an unrelaxing campaign of money-making. To some indeed the criterion seemed to be "Is there anything in it for me?"

"Maybe," thought Shand, "I'm not ambitious enough – maybe I have spent too many years at school – but 'what shall it profit a man if he shall gain the whole world and lose his own soul?'"

As the winter wore along, the urge to escape from the crowds and the ordered ugliness of the city deepened. Shand's mind went back to the foothills and the mountains. Out there lay the Athabasca, swift and purposeful, lapping against its jagged rock walls, taking tribute from rivers and rills that reached back up the most remote valleys. Out there lay the golden hillsides, the little green lakes and the deep blue of the distant mountains, the white of fresh snowfalls far up on the peaks, and the vast blue sky. Out there lay the tinkle of little brooks, the rustle of the wind in the spruce branches, the bugling of the elk far up in the open forests, the ozone of the pine trees and the faint perfume of willow smoke from the teepee fires, welcome flickerings of light from the lake shore far below.

"What shall a man give in exchange for his soul?"

Shand resolved that he would take the first opportunity to get back out to the land of the silent foothills. Though an occasional white man had travelled through parts of this vast unsettled region west and north of Edmonton, it was largely unexplored. In one direction it extended one hundred and fifty miles from the Wapiti River and Lesser Slave Lake south to the Brazeau River, and in the other from Lac Ste Anne west two hundred miles to the summit of Mount Robson. Over this area of 30,000 square miles the soil was marginal, and its western half was subject to early frosts, and it seemed unlikely that farmers would penetrate it to any extent. There was little reason to think that in Shand's lifetime civilization would spread into this area and overwhelm it. It would be left alone to its few natives and to such white men as himself who would love it all the more because of its remoteness.

On the base line the previous summer, Shand had entered this realm of pine trees, sunshine, silence and mountains. That trip had given him a peek into the way of life of the people who called this land their home. Given some food and a pack horse, access to any part of this widespread timbered area was assured. Given a gun and some traps, a man could procure his food, while the natural meadows would provide forage for his horse.

Now that at least one railway was to penetrate this country and provide a way of carrying its riches to distant markets, many men were eager to study its stands of timber and its outcrops of coal. These men needed packers to take them out to the remote valleys and they were willing to pay well. Here, then, was a way Shand could earn a livelihood whilst enjoying the privilege of exploring every nook and corner of this area and the pleasure of spending day after day in the open air.

Money, with reasonable luck, he might amass by remaining in Edmonton in the comfort of a warm, dry office. Yet here already many men toiled for months to save enough to pay for a holiday at a lakeshore or on a fishing trip. For fifty weeks a year they worked, so that for two weeks they might be free to live as they liked. For Shand, last summer's trip with the pack train had been one long holiday of nine months' duration. The days on the pack trip had been far from a bed of roses, but to compensate for a spell of blizzard or a week of cold rain were many weeks of sunshine, when waves lapped softly on the shores of little lakes and at night on the moss-girt brook bank the murmur of running water seduced slumber.

As the winter wore slowly away, Shand, in his eagerness to escape from the city, took the first chance that turned up. Maurice Kimp planned to lay out a townsite at Medicine Lodge. Interest in the Peace River country was high, and some settlers were flocking in there. In a year or so, thought Kimp, the Grand Trunk would reach his new townsite. He hoped that then it would become a divisional point and would also be a jumping-off place for a rush of settlers bound for the Grande Prairie. So, before the spring breakup, Shand was off again towards the mountains with a pack train, taking Maurice Kimp and Justus Willson west. With them went Barney Belcourt as head packer and Jackie Hornby, who twenty years later was to win renown and a slow death in the Barren Lands.

When the future streets and avenues were indicated by cut-lines through the timber on the high bank of the McLeod River, Justus Willson — like many of the early surveyors a veteran of the Riel Rebellion — set out up the McLeod River to run a timber survey for Calder and Gilliland. Shand was to take part in the actual survey. The trip out was uneventful, and before long a large stand of good timber was mapped out in what we know today as the Coal Branch country. The return trip, though short, was far from uneventful. Barney Belcourt and the rest of the party went over the pass to Jack Gregg's place, but Shand and

Justus Willson decided to raft down the McLeod River. The spring freshets were on and the river sizzled and swirled along, whipping the raft against overhanging logs and whirling it in amongst large cakes of grinding ice. In no time at all they had descended twenty or thirty miles of river, whisking around headlands and hairpin bends. Shand says, "As the raft bumped and swirled around bend after bend, while we hung on for dear life fending off trees and roots, I kept expecting to meet ourselves coming back."

The ride was soon over. Suddenly the raft struck a sweeper, upended, and threw the men into the icy water. They managed to clamber ashore, but their goods slid off and bobbed merrily down the stream, and in a moment the raft righted itself and followed, leaving the drenched men shivering in the rotting snow. Fortunately Shand did not lose his Stetson hat. He had been in the habit of carrying a few matches stuck in its band, as well as a few yards of fishing line coiled around it. Now five of the matches were still dry enough to light. The two men quickly built a fire and spent the rest of the afternoon drying their clothes. That night, with snares made of the fishing line, they got two rabbits. And next morning they set out afoot, well fed, to face the thirty-mile walk back to Medicine Lodge, with their two remaining matches. The bright sunshine bothered their eyes and made the long trek back to camp unpleasant.

Meanwhile the men who had remained in Kimp's camp had not fared well. Moving downstream, one man by the name of Greenlees broke through a weak spot in some ice that remained in the river and was drowned. Allen Kilgour became snow-blind and for a few days suffered intensely. Jack Hornby, unsocial at times to the point of being eccentric, quarrelled with Kimp and left the party at the mouth of the Embarrass. With only his light pack, he set out afoot and alone on the hundred-mile trip to Lac Ste Anne, through melting snow and across rivers that were now breaking up. In a couple of weeks Kimp's party also started back to Lac Ste Anne, which they reached about the end of May.

This trip had perhaps produced more hardship than pleasure, but Shand counted it as all part of the day's work. He had seen some new country and had learned some new lessons.

In June he was off again, this time with C. C. Fairchild, DLS, to subdivide timber berths in a sector of the forest he had not yet seen. This trip took up all of the summer and fall, and Shand went from Lac Ste Anne to the Athabasca River at Fort Assiniboine, and from there up the Freeman River to McLeod Lake far up in the recesses of the Swan Hills. At one time or another that summer Shand ranged the vast, silent forests on both sides of the Athabasca River, from the ferry operated by Holmes at Holmes' Crossing on the old Klondike Trail up the Athabasca to the mouth of the McLeod.

When winter came on, Shand divided his time between Edmonton and Lac Ste Anne. This old hamlet was the first spot of civilization reached by the packers returning from a summer in the field. Most parties concluded their season's work about the same time and as a rule reached there within a few days of each other. Money was of no use to them in the bush, so they drew their pay at Lac Ste Anne. Most of them left it where they drew it – transferring it perhaps from the Hudson's Bay store, where they received it, to the hotel. The packers' pay was usually higher than that of ordinary labourers, so that when they returned to the lake they were what the local residents called "stake bound" and ready for a big celebration. Many of the townfolk, of course, looked forward to their return and aided and abetted their festivities.

While the packers' money was making the rounds, the town was *en fête*, or perhaps we should say on a spree. Every packer had a drink and a cigar on every other one. Then, as the party grew merry, someone would set out to outdo the others by buying all the liquor and cigars in stock. The purchaser and the hotel proprietor made a deal, whereupon the buyer took his place behind the bar and dispensed free drinks until the supply was drained. The thirsty from all the surrounding countryside flocked in to participate.

Meanwhile the hotel proprietor, always a man of good and generous spirit, would have sent out to Edmonton for another stock, which by some miracle would always arrive just in the nick of time. Then one of the other packers, not to be outdone, would buy out the house and set up as bartender. As each man went broke, another stepped in, until most of the season's pay had been spent. By then the inevitable hangovers, and in some cases remorse, would take over. But generally the men from the far places felt that they had had good value for their money.

Sunday, when it came, was a welcome respite after an arduous week. The half-breed packers were mostly Roman Catholics, but all the packers, Catholic or Protestant, trooped off to attend Father Lizé's church, for he was a man loved equally by Catholic, Protestant or atheist. Even when things were dull in the town – when the packers were far afield – nearly everyone went to Father Lizé's church.

The packers who made Lac Ste Anne their headquarters had plenty of chances to use their horses and their knowledge of the country and of how to get about it. Supplying the railway survey parties provided them with as much work as they could handle. Now that the country was on the point of being opened up by the two railways, there was a further demand for their services, as adventurous men, backed by capital from Great Britain or eastern Canada, came rushing in to explore and to acquire timber berths and coal leases.

The Indians and a few of the earlier explorers had known that coal outcropped on many a river bank in that vast stretch of foothills wilderness extending for one hundred and fifty miles north from the Brazeau River. With the coming of the railways this coal became of economic importance. The Indians had regarded it as an interesting stone which they could rub on their arms as a black paint, but they had never burned it as fuel. Whether or not they even knew it would burn, Shand does not know. "For their small fires," he says, "wood was sufficient, and since it ignited so readily it served their needs." The railway engineers realized the true importance of our great deposits of bituminous coal. It would provide their locomotives with the proper fuel, and hauling it to the East or to the Pacific Coast would provide them with a much needed payload.

According to Shand, R. W. (Bob) Jones, one of the famous divisional engineers whose energy found a way for the railway through rock and muskeg, was the first to put his finger on this coal. He bridged the gap between the white man's capital and the Indians' detailed knowledge of the secrets of the wild water courses. Jones asked Jack Gregg, who was ranching at Prairie Creek, if he knew of any good seams of coal. Now Jack's wife

Mary was a Stoney half-breed girl by the name of Cardinal, whose ancestry, renowned for its faithful voyageurs and guides, stretched far back into the annals of the fur trade.

"Coal?" said Jack Gregg. "Well, I ain't paid much attention to it. There's a lot where the trail crosses the Pembina out Edmonton way."

"Yes, I know that," answered Jones, "but I was looking for better stuff."

"Well," continued Jack, "there's the odd piece comes afloatin' down the McLeod – you can see it here and there in the river gravel."

"I've seen that too. But do you know where it comes from?"

"Let's ask Mary," suggested Jack, "she knows all the country up the McLeod River." The question took some explaining, but at last with a smile and a vigorous nod the young woman declared that she knew where to find some of the soft black rock.

"It's away up the McLeod River and then you cross over to where the Pembina starts, about four or five days' travel from here," she said, pointing to the southeast and explaining to her husband the particular creek she had in mind.

In the summer of 1907 Jones rode to the creek with Jack and Mary. When they reached it, Mary rode ahead, watching for old landmarks, and finally dismounted.

"I think it's in there, beyond that point of trees," she said. "Wait and I'll go in and look."

In two or three minutes she returned, holding her hands behind her. When she held out her hands they were moist and black where she had rubbed them on the exposed face of the seam – and she playfully clasped Jack Gregg's face between them and blackened it with the coal. Thus the first commercial discovery of coal in the famous Coal Branch came about by the simple process of asking a native woman where to find it.

Both Jones and Gregg staked leases at Lovett; in a very short time Mr Seebolt laid out claims at Mountain Park and at Luscar, and the rush to the Coal Branch was on. Under the forests lay a vast field of coal, the seams twisted and distorted by the forces that had pushed up the foothills. The coalfield was proved to be large enough to warrant building some eighty miles of railway to haul it out, and the Grand Trunk made plans to do so.

Capital for developing the mines came from eastern Canada, the United States, Great Britain, and even France. Early in the spring of 1909, Shand undertook to pack in supplies for a party going in to test coal claims for the Pacific Pass Coal Company, owned by the French capitalists Barra and de Bernice. His destination was the Pembina Forks, later known as Lovett.

Actually the Hudson's Bay Company at Lac Ste Anne provided the pack train. Shand was to take charge of it and to supply four horses. With him went Dan Letendre as guide and packer, and another Indian. By the time the party left, the snow was nearly all gone, but on account of the scarcity of feed the horses had a hard time. The pack train went west to the construction town of Wolf Creek, where it picked up its loads and then struck off into the wilderness. Its route lay up the creek to Wolf Lake, which was near the height of land between the waters draining into the McLeod and those flowing into the Pembina. In one of the muskegs near Wolf Lake, which Shand decided to corduroy, one of his horses slipped off the logs into the sucking mud. All their efforts to pull it out were unavailing, so Shand put it out of its misery by a rifle shot and then distributed its saddle and pack amongst the other horses. Some of the material to be packed in, especially the dynamite and caps and some long steel rods, was awkward and dangerous, but Shand and his horses delivered it. After taking the party in, the pack train returned the seventy miles to Wolf Creek for another load of supplies. These were delivered at Pembina Forks without incident, and about a month later Shand and his horses rode into Lac Ste Anne once more.

By now Shand was well acquainted with most of the Indians and half-breeds in the area west of Lac Ste Anne. His recent trip with Dan Letendre had increased his respect and liking for them. Already he realized that it was impossible to draw a hard and fast line between half-breed and Indian. In this large area, with rare exceptions, there were no full-blooded Indians.

This region had been inhabited by small bands of various tribes whose ancestral lands overflowed into it : Beavers in the north and Assiniboines (Stonies) along the east and south sides, and Snakes and Shuswaps in the Jasper valley, which they had entered by pushing east through the Yellowhead Pass. The influence of the white man had first manifested itself by an invasion of Crees from the east and northeast. These virile Indians were the first to come in contact with white men along the shores of Hudson's Bay. Soon, by trading with the white strangers, they acquired firearms and started out on an era of militant expansion. They drove the other tribes before them and became the dominant tribe as far west as Lac Ste Anne, Lesser Slave Lake and Sturgeon Lake. Soon there were more Crees in this area than all other tribal stocks put together. The Beavers withdrew, and the Snakes and Shuswaps returned through the mountain passes, leaving only a handful of their people in the Jasper valley.

Then into the area came infusions of the blood of two other tribes, the Chippewa and the Iroquois. No one is certain how the small band of Chippewa came into the region. One of the earliest references to the Iroquois, however, is in Thompson's Journal, where he tells of passing through the valley at Jasper in the last days of 1810 with "Thomas, the Iroquois." These Indians were imported by the North West Company before 1810, and by 1818, if not before, the Hudson's Bay Company was using them as company trappers and voyageurs. When Colin Robertson of the Hudson's Bay Company came out to the Peace River country in 1819 his canoe was manned by seven Iroquois and a guide. Robertson says: "I have frequently heard the Canadian and Iroquois voyageurs disputed as regards their merits, perhaps the former may be more hardy or undergo more fatigue, but in either a rapid or a traverse, give me the latter, from their calmness and presence of mind which never forsakes them in the greatest danger."

The Hudson's Bay Company used Iroquois as trappers also, and in 1820 Robertson speaks of several of them going up to the source of the Smoky and at times he distinguishes between his company's Iroquois and those of the North West Company. After their period of service with the fur trade companies expired, several of them became so-called free trappers and remained in the area between the Peace and Athabasca Rivers. Many also became trappers and packers for the Hudson's Bay Company in the old Oregon country. Today the greatest distinguishable concentration of their descendants is in the Athabasca-Smoky River country, and includes the families of Plante,

Wanyandi, Caraconté, Joachim, Gauthier, Findlay and Callihoo. Victoria Callihoo, who in 1960 celebrated her hundredth birthday, was the wife of Louis, a grandson of the Callihoo who came west before 1820 to work for the Hudson's Bay Company. She believes that he and some of the other Indians were married before coming west and brought their wives with them. The Iroquois were taller and finer featured than the Crees, and amongst the people in the area today it is sometimes possible to pick out the Iroquois strain by the large stature of their descendants. The Iroquois people were the natives most highly regarded by the fur traders, trappers and forest rangers who came to know them.

In the vast friendly wilderness of the Smoky River area many remnants of the ancient tribes thus dwelt together in peace – an honest, hospitable, kindly people. As a result of the influx of the Crees, their language became universal within the area. Until some forty years before Shand's time, Indian blood had predominated and it was possible to find rare cases of full-blooded Indians. But gradually this had been diluted, always by the same route – white fathers, who spent a year or so in the country, and Indian mothers, who took their fair-skinned offspring back to the teepees to be raised in the native ways.

Then about 1870, after the troubles in Manitoba, came an influx of Métis from the Red River Settlement seeking to escape from the white man's civilization. Colonies of Métis moved in with their native kinsmen around the main fishing lakes: Sturgeon, Lesser Slave Lake, Lac La Biche, Lac Ste Anne and Lac La Nonne. With them came many more of the French names so long familiar in the fur trade – Letendre, Belcourt, L'Hyrondelle, Chalifoux, Cardinal, Berland, Belrose, Delorme, and many others. They were of the Catholic faith, and many of them congregated around the missions.

About the same time, a line was drawn between Indian and Métis when, by treaty, those who said they were Indians settled on reserves. By the terms of the treaty each Indian man, woman and child got some cash and the promise of five dollars each year to them and their children forever. One square mile of land was also allotted to each family, and they could choose whether they wished to select an isolated plot of land of this size or to go together in bands and have their holdings all in one block on a reserve. They were given some clothes and farm implements, if they wished to farm, or bulls and cows if they chose to raise cattle. If they chose to fish and hunt, they were given an allotment of ammunition and twine for fishing nets.

The government did not make treaty with the half-breeds or Métis, because it considered them white men; but since they had Indian blood and therefore had some claim to the soil, that claim was taken into account. If they wished, they could elect to throw in their lot with the Indians and thus make treaty, or else they could take scrip. Each half-breed was entitled to 160 acres. Unfortunately most of them sold this scrip to traders for a song. This was no fault of the government, which at first had insisted that this scrip was not to be negotiable, but eventually gave in to the pressure of the half-breeds and made it saleable.

"Many of the early businessmen of Edmonton made themselves a tidy fortune by buying this scrip from the half-breeds," said Shand as we were talking one sunny afternoon. "Several were able to obtain title to thousands of acres of unhomesteaded land. Of course they studied the country and picked out large blocks of the best soil they could find. As soon as the rush of settlers came in, they sold these quarters of land at many times what they had paid for them.

"Unthinking people," he continued, "are ready to condemn these men who made fortunes that way, but if a man had some money and all his business acquaintances were buying scrip, he would have been foolish if he had not done the same."

"Well," said Billy Magee, Shand's next-door neighbour, "it's the same as the recent sale of Alberta Gas Trunk shares at five dollars each. Each of us was entitled to buy so many shares, but many men got around the regulations by buying this many shares at say a dozen different places. Then, when overnight the price jumped from five to twenty dollars a share, as everyone expected it would, these men made a lot of money."

"Same idea," said Shand. "People don't change much. The shrewd amongst us do these things. The rest of us sit back and bellyache because we didn't get in on the bargain."

Shand went on to give details of these transactions in scrip to illustrate some of the things that happened. Several of the Edmonton businessmen went to greater lengths than this. One firm, for instance, got Shand's old friend Donald Macdonald from Lake Isle to round up half-breeds to come in and get scrip and then to sell it to this firm. Washy Joe, a Stoney who later lived in the Smoky River country and after whom Washy Joe Creek is named, was one of the half-breeds Donald cornered for the firm. His Stoney name was Sagapatura, "Long Hair." Donald sought him out and said, "Do you want to make five dollars, maybe more?"

"Why sure."

Then Donald explained what to do. He would take Sagapatura up to the treaty commissioner's office, and all Sagapatura had to do was to declare that he was a half-breed and ask for scrip. Donald and his principals would pay him five dollars and attend to the rest of the business.

"Remember," cautioned Donald, "you must say your father was a white man."

"But he wasn't," said Sagapatura.

"I know," replied Donald. "But the only way you can get five dollars is to say that he was."

"All right," said Sagapatura.

So they went up before the commission and asked for the scrip.

"What's your name?" asked the secretary.

"Joe."

"Joe what?"

"Joe Sagapatura."

"What was your father's name?"

"Little Bear," said Sagapatura.

"Yes," interjected Donald Macdonald hastily. "That's what the Stonies called him, but his real name was Atkins, Tom Atkins."

"I see," said the secretary, pointing to Sagapatura, "and his son here, what's his real name?"

"Joe," said Donald. "Joe Atkins."

So Joe Atkins was duly enrolled as a half-breed wanting his scrip.

Shand, who for many elections compiled the voters' lists, entered Joe Atkins on these lists. But the half-breeds could not pronounce Atkins, so whenever they referred to him by his official white man's name they called him Joe Agnes. Even this was hard to say, and in the course of time it was further changed to Washa, and before long to Washy Joe.

"Many of the Indians invented white fathers to get five dollars for the scrip which white paternity and anxious speculators would get for them. I remember another Sikanni Indian from Fort St John way who lived with the Iroquois. As near as I can remember, his name was Eneesjia, but at scrip time he was enrolled as Henry Kenny."

After the treaty there were Indians on the one hand, registered as such – irrespective of the amount of Indian blood in their veins – living on reserves and to some extent protected. On the other hand there were half-breeds who were considered as white men and could vote and, like white men, had to fend for themselves. But many a staunch Indian of the Stoney or Chippewa peoples refused to take treaty, preferring to maintain his primeval independence and freedom. And many a half-breed, especially if he lived well back in the foothills, whether or not he had taken scrip and sold it, continued the ways of his forebears in the haunts of his fathers.

These natives moved about through the seasons, depending upon where the best big game were at that time of year, so that there were trails known only to themselves, leading up every valley and over every pass – tracks no white man had ever seen. At times, to take their furs out to sell, to pay homage at the Ste Anne shrine, or just to visit their kin, they pitched off along the pack trails for a brief reunion. For they were a sociable folk. And as the years rolled along, the older folk died and the younger intermarried, until by Shand's time everyone was related to everyone else. During the intervals when he lived at Lac Ste Anne, he became acquainted with most of those who had chosen the settled life of the settlement. On the trail, and later on his incursions into the forest, he came to know, to respect and to like those of more independent ideas who chose the solitude of the woods. In general he preferred those who tramped in the wilderness the trails their mothers had trod.

"You see," said Shand one evening as Billy Magee and I sat talking to him, "the half-breeds have changed. So have the white people, but the main change has been in conditions and in the attitude of the two peoples to each other. Today, to most people, the term 'half-breed' conveys a suggestion of being second-rate. You will notice that I always use the term 'native' except in discussions like this. I remember these people as they were fifty years ago and there were none finer. While I do not regard the modern generation of natives as highly as I did their grandparents, still, having known these people for half a century, I can't think of them as second-rate either in intelligence, integrity or kindliness.

"Fifty years ago there were few white people out here and they were mainly engaged in dealing with the Indians or the half-breeds. These few were of a hardy, adventurous type. They had to be to like their work and to stay here. Their native customers were similarly hardy, and both white men and red men were equally competent and self-reliant in enduring the hardships of rapids, trails and blizzards. Generally speaking, a sincere respect existed between the two races. When a white man and a red man toil together on a trip and undergo hardships together, each is bound to respect the other and never sees the colour of his skin.

"If that relationship exists between white men and red men, it will certainly exist between a white man and a pleasant, obedient, reliant Indian woman. The result was that the white fur traders married Indian women. Soon their children of mixed blood grew to maturity and became the traders, packers and guides, all bound together by a love of this outdoor life and a mutual competence in facing the hardships of the frontier. A man, and for that matter a woman, was judged not by his skin pigment but, as in any other walk of life, by his integrity and his ability in his environment. Fifty years ago hardly anyone drew a line between white or half-breed.

"Take Mrs Swift. She was a Chalifoux, of good French stock, one-quarter Indian. She was fair-skinned and we all thought of her as white. Mrs Gregg – and there never was a finer woman – was half Indian, and looked it, but no one ever thought of her as being different. She was hospitable, pleasant and capable.

"Many Edmonton businessmen fifty years ago had some Indian blood. Everybody knew it, and never stopped to think about it. But their children and grandchildren today won't admit it, and instead of being properly proud of it they try to hide it. A change has come about in our thinking and it has become increasingly common to scorn the so-called half-breeds.

"On the half-breed's side, he was busy, happy and respected, with work to do, till about fifty years ago. With the changing of our civilization, he has seen most of that work disappear. His special skills are not needed in today's world, and he is no longer proud of the job he is doing or of the place he is filling. Consequently he has deteriorated. His old way of life is gone and so, naturally, is his pride. Such a change in environment is sad for the old people, but it is particularly hard on the new generation, which loses regard for its elders and the old ways without finding any substitute to respect. I'm sorry to see the lack of pride in themselves among the young half-breeds, but it seems inevitable, and I guess we must make the best of it.

"Fortunately, up till recently, their isolation has saved the natives in the Smoky River country from some of this experience. Long after many half-breeds in the rest of the country were slipping, my friends back in the bush were living their lives as they had always lived them, and consequently were needed and respected. But now that roads are opening that country up, I fear for them."

"Well, that's true," said Billy. "I haven't been here nearly as long as you, but most of the old people are pretty decent when they get to know you and trust you. But I'm not sold on the young ones."

"I'm sorry I talked so long," apologized Shand. "I'm not trying to be pedantic or 'holier than thou' or more tolerant than I really am or than you are, but I feel very strongly on the subject. What I'm trying to emphasize is that in the old days no one paid any attention to whether his neighbour was a half-breed or not. Don't get me wrong — we were not all equals — some of us were good, some indifferent and some even bad, but it wasn't the colour of your skin that put you in one class or the other."

"Yes, Shand," I said, "I see what you're getting at. I know it's true, because so many of the real old-timers have tried to tell me the same thing, only they haven't expressed it so clearly."

Shand got up and produced a bottle of Scotch out of a corner of his tidy cabin.

"Bill," I said, "it always amazes me. Shand can stow more stuff into this shack than I can get into my house."

"Yes," Billy grinned. "You wouldn't believe the number of things he can reach over and bring out without getting up off that stool."

"Well," Shand said with a laugh, "when you have to carry many months' supplies on a few pack horses, you learn to be tidy."

We sat quietly smoking and sipping, and then I turned the conversation back to the old days.

"Shand, you never actually worked at railway construction, did you?"

"No, I didn't, but at one time or other I packed a lot of supplies for the Grand Trunk. I kept on the move back and forth along the trail, tote road and grade, and I probably saw more of what was going on than some of the men who actually worked on construction.

"When I came out here there was just the first survey line. Then, month after month and year after year, I watched its progress – Stony Plain, the delay at Entwistle and the construction town there. Then it pushed on to Wolf Creek, and it was held up there because the two bridges had to be built within half a mile of each other. Then it went on – Edson, the Big Eddy, Bickerdike, Prairie Creek, Roche Miette, Jasper and Tête Jaune Cache. It was a wonderful experience to be sort of a bystander and to watch it from the sidelines and yet to feel proud of the progress it made."

Shand went on to illustrate his point by referring to his trip to Pembina Forks that he had told us about earlier in the evening. That trip let him mark the progress being made by the Grand Trunk. During 1908 the steel snaked its way past Stony Plain, past Wabamun and beyond, and met its first major obstacle, the canyon of the Pembina River, at Entwistle. Before the steel could go any farther the railway bridge, some 900 feet long and over 200 feet above the water, had to be erected. The delay caused by building this made Entwistle the end of steel for several months, and one of the first large railway construction towns grew up here. Entwistle became the starting place for pack trains, because goods could be brought the sixty-five miles from Edmonton and landed there by train.

Lac Ste Anne, however, did not wither on the vine. Many packers regarded it as their headquarters and stayed there. Moreover the hamlet looked forward to a railway of its own, for the third transcontinental road, the Canadian Northern, which had been forced to abandon its route via Stony Plain, was now surveying its main line through the old village.

Shand, who made his headquarters there, was dubious about the need for another railway. He had always been impressed by the Grand Trunk. It was not only the greatness of the conception of a second transcontinental railway nor the magnitude of the necessary financing that stirred his imagination, but also the way the construction of this gigantic undertaking was organized by the main contractors, Foley, Welsh and Stewart.

Shand had seen the survey parties and their pack trains, and gradually a line of stakes had come into being, marking the centre line of the future railway. A year or so later, hundreds of men with axes and crosscut saws had come in and cleared a swath a hundred feet wide. At the same time a tote road had been constructed, so that freight wagons could travel along the line with supplies for the thousands of men who were employed on the construction. The tote road itself was a costly undertaking, because not only was it necessary to grade down some hills and build up some fills, but the muskegs had to be corduroyed, the creeks bridged and ferries put in over the larger streams. As fast as the tote roads moved forward, a telephone line was strung to keep in touch with activities all along the grade.

Camps had to be set up about every two miles along the tote road. A clearing would be made in the dense bush beside the railway, and in many cases the trees cut down sufficed to provide the logs for the various buildings: cookhouse, bunkhouses and stores or caches, some roofed with shingles and others covered by canvas. The bunkhouses – long, low, log buildings fitted up along one side with two tiers each of two lumber bunks side by side – soon became lousy, bug-ridden, noisome places. Below the bunks were benches, stools, boxes and blocks of wood. During the rainy season the floor was covered with mud, while hanging from the ceiling were men's clothes, socks and boots drying. The place reeked with a steaming stench of cheap tobacco, wet clothes and socks.

The contractors had to bring in enormous quantities of food and supplies and they accomplished this by contracting the hauling to freighters. Around the official construction camps grew up a sprawling temporary and unofficial village of cafés, flop joints and barns to cater to the needs of the freighters and their beasts. Other institutions grew up too, for wherever there are hundreds or thousands of men, there will be liquor, gamblers and women.

By law, liquor was forbidden within many miles of the grade, and in Alberta the Royal North West Mounted Police did a remarkable job of keeping it out. But the stricter the regulations, the greater the reward that fell to those bootleggers ingenious and daring enough to smuggle in a supply. In spite of the vigilance of the few Mounties, much rotten bootleg liquor reached the camps. While the labourers earned a few dollars a week and the bootleggers were hard pressed to make a few dollars a day, the gamblers flourished, and from the numerous brothels housed in log shack or tent, women were constantly returning to Edmonton with $200 or $300 a week.

It was the freighters who were most akin to Shand. As he urged his pack train along the tote road, he was frequently jostled into the bush by their heavy wagons pulled by horses, oxen or mules. For freight was an individual affair. The contractor would pay a fixed amount for transporting a hundred pounds one mile, and everyone owning a wagon and a team of any kind was free to bid. From there on it was the freighter's responsibility to get his load through creek bottom, muskeg or mud hole as fast as he could. As the years went by, at each of the end-of-steel towns – Entwistle, Wolf Creek, Bickerdike and Prairie Creek – as many as a thousand freighters were constantly coming in empty, loading up, and pulling out for destinations many miles to the west. Their loads were as various as their destinations: cases of canned goods, bridge timbers, dynamite, sacks of flour, bacon, carcasses of beef and pork, light steel rails, oats and hay, rice and pork and beans – everything, in fact, needed to further the work of construction. And their destinations? The Big Eddy, Mile 108 (Wolf Creek), Mile 1 (the British

Columbia border), Mile 28 (Resplendent), Mile 53 (Tête Jaune Cache), Fiddle River, Henry House, Fitzhugh and Roche Miette.

Most of the freighting was done during the winter, when heavy loads could be drawn over the slick snowy trails to be deposited in great caches of supplies at the various advance camps, but much material also had to be moved forward during the summer. Except for the cold, which could be countered, winter hauling was easy on the drivers. But in the rainy season horses and drivers fought their way forward over slippery rock, through sticky muskeg or mud holes endlessly recurring every few hundred yards as some greater or lesser creek had to be crossed, the drivers cursing and straining to whip their beasts to extra effort. Often the extra effort was too much, and the horse dropped, never to pull again, or accident or injury led to the merciful shot that ended forever the exhausting struggle of a beast of burden. A logging chain around his neck, a flip of the lines to the other horses, and his carcass was pulled to the edge of the tote road out of the way of other teams, there to remain to taint the air for weeks. Many a fine horse and mule ended his days as a bleaching skeleton beside the tote road – a sacrifice to the westward course of empire.

In spite of hardships and mishaps, wretched stopping places and poor meals, most freighters made some money and enjoyed the life. They were a hard-bitten, determined lot of men, who come rain, shine or snow, kept their teams on the way, and when night came, camped beside their loads. For there was a fascination about it all – travelling in the open air, the rivalry of one team with another, and the camaraderie around the campfires. The regular freighters who had been at the game for years did their work in an orderly, systematic way, and in general knew its rewards and could cope with its risks and its hardships. Some would-be freighters looking for easy money soon fell by the way-side, but the bulk of them, hardy and resourceful, steady and reliable through good and bad, stayed with their work as the railroad pushed ever farther west into the dark mountain canyons.

Many other thousands of men were busy cutting through hills, filling up holes and building up a nearly level grade upon which trains might run. It seems strange now, with our giant dirt-moving monsters, to look back fifty years to the days of the Grand Trunk when muscles shovelled dirt and pushed wheelbarrows up planks to build a roadbed. Every foot of the thousands of miles of railway on the plains or in the mountains was placed in position by a sturdy race of sweating men – great golden-haired Swedes, swarthy Galicians, blond Ukrainians and dark Italians; American, Irish, Scots and Cornishmen, and English navvies with their clay pipes.

There were really three types of dirt-moving – station work, larger cuts and fills, and major cuttings and embankments – and these were done respectively by men, mules and machines. The general contractor for the line sublet smaller contracts to other organizations or individuals, and the smallest of these was the station. When the right-of-way had been cleared, the surveyors laid out the centre line of the grade by driving in wooden stakes, sometimes called stations, every hundred feet. When only a moderate amount of filling or cutting had to be done, one or more men might contract to build up the grade to the required specifications from one of these stakes to the next one. Because they undertook to complete the grade for one station, they became known as station men. This was piece work which was profitable alike to the contractor and to the station man, who with shovel and wheelbarrow built up the grade, was paid for it and moved on to do another station. For station after station, for miles and miles, men dug with a shovel and wheeled the dirt along a plank they had hewn from a tree, working fifteen or eighteen hours a day, as their thirst or ambition dictated.

The larger cuts and fills were done by mule power with a variety of carts, scrapers, slushers, graders and elevating graders, the latter often propelled by as many as eight horses pulling in front and eight more pushing from behind. Thousands of horses and mules pulled and sweated to build up the grade and to fill in the muskegs. Hundreds of them died from swamp fever or were shot when they broke their legs on the grade.

The major cuts were done by machines – great steam-shovels that puffed and groaned while they gnawed at loose rocks and dirt, and squealed as they swung and dropped them on the flatcars and carts, or dumped them over the side of the cliff. These and the locomotives and hoists were the only true machines on the whole job.

The hoists came into play when building trestles or bridges, and many a long trestle spanned a depression in the terrain. Trestles were considered as temporary measures to serve until such time in after years as they could be filled in by train-loads of dirt, but today many of them are still in use.

Finally, through the combined efforts of men, mules and machines, a stretch of many miles of grade would be built up to the level demanded for the finished railroad. Then the track-layer, a huge machine, spewing ties on to the grade from a conveyor on one side and rails from the other, was pushed along by an attendant locomotive and ministered to by over a hundred men. Some of these stood on the flatcars loading ties on to one endless conveyor, or lifting rails on to the other. Up in front many more men seized the ties as they were discharged and laid them in place, while others laid the rails and spiked them down temporarily so that in due course the machine could advance another rail's length. By the end of the day, these men had probably laid two miles of track – and they knew that they had done a day's work. Two miles of track meant six thousand heavy green pine ties put in place and over 500,000 pounds of steel rail spiked to them. Much still remained to be done after the track-layer had passed on; the rails had to be aligned and spiked solidly and the gravel ballast had to be hauled in and spread over the grade and tucked under the ties, but in the wake of the layer the line could be used.

The track-layer was the visible culmination of all the year's work. As it crept forward relentlessly, the sinuous double ribbon of steel crowded on and on over cut and fill, muskeg and mountainside, bridge and trestle, and a railway had come into being.

In 1909, as Shand travelled back and forth over the old Jasper Trail or the tote road, the railway took shape to Entwistle and beyond. From his frequent comings and goings, it appeared to be an endless belt, pouring horses, men, supplies and material ever westward into the bush. An endless belt loaded on its westward thrust, empty as it returned east. A centipede whose legs were men and mules scampering in frantic haste up and down the inequalities of the terrain, but whose body, by some mystic progression, was thrust forward ever farther into the hinterland, creeping slowly maybe – some sixty miles a year only – but steadily covering the three hundred miles from Edmonton to Tête Jaune Cache. A centipede with axemen and tote road at its head, followed by camps, wheelbarrows, track-layers and ballast trains, and leaving in its wake a railway.

CHAPTER
NINE

—◆{✳}◆—

"Howja' like to take a party of Englishmen up to Mount Robson and bring 'em back alive?" asked Shand's friend Gamblin, the new Hudson's Bay factor at Lac Ste Anne. He had been told to arrange transport for a mountain-climbing party, for the summer of 1909.

"Umm. After hearing what Johnny Yates had to say about the bunch he took up last year, I don't know," replied Shand.

"It's essentially the same bunch this year, and Johnny said they really weren't bad after you got used to them. Anyway, they'll be halter-broken this year."

"Well, see if Yates will do it again."

"Can't. He's away out west somewhere on the 15th Base Line."

"All right," said Shand. "But, as they say, 'I don't hanker after it.' Besides, I haven't enough horses."

"Neither has the company right here," declared Gamblin. "Guess we'll have to use all of our horses, all of yours, and then hire what we're short. The company will provide all equipment and supplies."

Shand was already busy planning. "There's no sense in 'em starting from here," he said. "Tell your Edmonton office to arrange to send their supplies by wagons over the tote road to Wolf Creek. Then when they reach Edmonton they can take an extra wagon or a democrat and accompany them. There's stopping places all along the right-of-way now, so they should be all right. At the proper time, I'll take the lightly loaded pack train and meet them at Wolf Creek. That will give the horses a chance to get used to each other."

Then after a pause, he added, "Wonder what the party will say when they see what will happen to their goods at Entwistle?"

"What d'ya mean?" asked Gamblin.

"I was thinking about the two chutes the freighters have on

the east bank of the canyon there where they unload the wagons and send everything slithering and banging three hundred feet down the chutes and then load up again and start off west."

In due course, at Wolf Creek in that summer of 1909, Shand met the party, headed by L. S. Amery, editor of the London *Times*, and including William Mumm of a famous London publishing firm, James Priestley, a young man recently from Eton College, Geoffrey Hastings and Moritz Inderbinen, a well-known Swiss guide. The previous year Mumm had approached Mount Robson by way of the Wildhay River in company with Dr Collie of London, so he at least knew something of pack horses, western packers and conditions generally. Moreover, Johnny Yates of the Hobo Ranch had been in charge of the party and had broken them in to western ways.

The English mountaineers, used to climbing the Alps and Himalayas, had been accustomed to subservience on the part of guides and porters. On their first day out the previous year they had insisted that at meal times they should eat first, followed by the Swiss guides and then the packers, an order of things which to them was routine. To Johnny Yates this meant cooking three batches of food and much inefficiency. He suffered this order of precedence for the first day, but on the second was forthright in his explanation that Canadian packers, even though of English birth like himself, were not used to this impractical way of eating. "From here on," he declared, "we eat together or we don't go on." After clearing the air in this way, excellent relations had prevailed – so much so that Johnny, even though he did not have proper climbing boots or equipment, was encouraged to climb with the sportsmen. The Englishmen, after all, were sportsmen in fact as well as in name.

Right at the beginning Shand, too, had problems with his employers. He wanted them to ride, but they insisted on walking because, they claimed, this would harden them for the strenuous mountaineering they hoped to do. So as to allow them to ride, he had taken thirty-five horses, including five which he had reserved to carry the climbers. The party had no difficulty crossing the McLeod River by the contractor's ferry, but after that they were on their own. When they came to the next small stream the climbers insisted on wading to add to their hardening process. In vain Shand protested that this was foolish, and they waded four or five more icy foothills streams, and had to press on in wet clothes. As Shand says, "They began to realize that water was wet and that in the mountain air wet clothes were most uncomfortable." After that the party made better progress, with everyone fording a stream on horseback and keeping dry. The larger streams were crossed by a canoe, if it was available, or by a raft made on the spot. For building rafts, Shand always carried an auger.

Shand formed some definite opinions of his employers, and Mr Amery too was not without his opinions of his packer. One evening as the group were enjoying their campfire, Mumm and Priestley, both former Etonians, sat discussing the recent death of a beloved old Eton master. Much to everyone's surprise, Shand spoke up. As Amery described the incident, "an ejaculation from one of our packers . . . the roughest diamond in our outfit, revealed the fact that he had once been that master's pupil." In the four action-filled years that Shand had spent in Canada, the influence of the West had gone far in transforming him from a scholar to a packer.

They made good progress for the way was well travelled. Every few miles wagon trails branched off the main one, and upon being asked where all of them went, Shand explained that they ended in hay meadows. At each of these, some enterprising pioneer was busy cutting and stacking hay, secure in the knowledge that by winter the contractors and freighters would be glad to pay at least twenty dollars a ton for it.

When Shand got to Jack Gregg's ranch at Prairie Creek, he was pleased to find that Johnny Yates had heard of the trip and had arranged with someone else to take his place on the survey, so that he too could go to Mount Robson. Yates put five of his horses in the string and this made lighter loads for the rest of the bunch. Shand had never been beyond Swift's ranch at Henry House and was glad that Yates could now guide the party the rest of the way.

Shand enjoyed the trip from Prairie Creek to Swift's ranch, located at what was then called by the generic name of Henry House to distinguish it from the locality of Jasper House several miles downstream. Hourly, as they drew closer to the mountains,

Roche Miette, with its 2000-foot vertical face, loomed ever larger, marking the north bastion of the rocky wall that guarded the pass opening into the secrets of the mountains. To Mumm and Amery, who had climbed in all parts of the world and were bent on scaling Mount Robson's 13,000-foot peak, Roche Miette's elevation of 7600 feet may have been insignificant. To Shand, however, this bold mass set squarely in the gateway never failed to appeal. To anyone living in sight of a sweeping view of the mountains, there is always one which grips the affections. To Shand, Roche Miette, pushing its bold, unscalable front out into the valley, became the symbol of the sturdiness and solitude of the Rocky Mountains.

After crossing the Fiddle River, the party met another pack train. This turned out to be Howard Douglas of the Parks Department at Ottawa, who, with his famous half-breed guide Albert Tate, was on his way to examine the Miette Hot Springs. The government had decided to create another national park, and to Douglas fell the task of determining what was to be included within its boundaries.

After leaving the camp of Douglas and Tate, the trail started its arduous climb over the shoulder of Roche Miette. No matter how this mountain appealed to Shand when he viewed it from afar, the pack trail over it, filled with risks for unwary horses, had no such appeal. As it zigzagged up the mountainside it was several hundred feet above the valley before the summit of the trail was reached. The summit presented glorious views of the Athabasca River and its encircling mountains. Laid out below were the two big lakes of the valley, connected by a tangled skein of channels and tributaries. Far below and across from the mouth of Rocky River, the remains of Jasper House were represented by one forlorn building. Farther upstream, above the end of Jasper Lake and out of sight from here, lay the ranches of John and Ewan Moberly, well-known and respected half-breeds whose residence in the valley went back fifty years. On the west side of the river, in the shadow of the Palisades, was the ranch of Lewis Swift.

The trip over the mountain and down the west side of Roche Miette was accomplished without accident to horses or men, but the crossing of the Rocky River was known to all packers as a likely spot for grizzly bears. As the train neared the river, the horses became uneasy, giving Shand his first intimation of the presence of one of these curious, fearless animals. Then, as they rounded a bend in the trail, about a hundred feet off to the side stood a great grizzly who had been listening to the noise and commotion made by the approaching train. Shand, expecting trouble, had his gun ready and with one shot killed the bear.

That night in camp, as they were drinking tea after supper, Mumm said, "I heard a shot as we were coming down the side of Roche Miette. What did you shoot at?"

"Shoot at?" said Shand. "What I shot at I hit and killed."

"What was it? Weren't you afraid of scaring the horses?"

"I was more afraid of scaring them if I didn't shoot and kill it – it was a grizzly."

"A grizzly! We didn't see it. Where was it?"

"About a hundred feet off the trail to the left."

"Why didn't you tell us – wait and show us?"

"We were behind time as it was," answered Shand, "and I wanted to get into camp here before dark."

Some hours after this incident, the party reached the crossing of the Athabasca near Ewan Moberly's. Here on his own shore of the river Moberly kept a dugout canoe hewn from a single balm log. Shand, grateful that the party could cross without having to swim or build a raft, fired two shots, the accustomed signal. Soon Moberly appeared, and by making three or four trips in the cranky canoe, the party crossed the broad river. The horses, of course, were driven into the water and had little difficulty swimming the strong current.

While Shand and his horses had crossed many a mountain stream, the varying manner in which different horses swam never failed to hold his interest. Some hesitated to take to the deep cold water and needed to be threatened and even beaten before they would venture across. Others, more enterprising or fatalistic, plunged in and took their chances. Some swam high in the water, while some almost submerged. On many a river crossing, Shand sat his horse and was carried across without difficulty. If the horse could walk most of the way and only had to swim a short distance, he usually stayed on its back. But if the swim promised to be difficult, he usually slipped off and, hanging on with one hand, swam too. When he did so, of course, he slid off on the upstream side, for most horses swimming any distance in strong water started out in an upright position, but as more effort was required rolled partly over and swam somewhat on their sides with their backs upstream.

At Moberly's the party met the Reverend G. B. Kinney and Donald "Curly" Phillips returning from what both believed to have been a successful assault on Mount Robson. As matter of fact, later knowledge of the mountain indicated that the summit scaled by Mr Kinney was lower by a matter of yards than a nearby peak. Until that came to light, however, he conscientiously believed that he had been the first man to stand on the summit of the great mountain. While disappointed that someone should have beat him to the top of the mountain, Amery, years later when writing of Kinney's climb, described it as "one of the most gallant performances in modern mountaineering history. After a series of attempts, in the course of which they consumed almost all their slender provisions and were forced to live mainly on marmots, gophers, and small birds, they finally managed in the course of two days of continuous climbing to reach the top of the northwestern rock ridge, if not, as they thought, the actual highest point of the mountain. So far as we were concerned, we could only congratulate them and push on in the hope of securing the credit of at any rate the second ascent."

Next day Shand's party went on about six miles and spent a day in the comfort of Lewis Swift's ranch, while the horses rested and the men looked around the valley. When they set out again, they travelled steadily making ten or fifteen miles a day up the Miette River and over the almost imperceptible summit of Yellowhead Pass. Then they descended the Fraser, passed Yellowhead Lake and finally came to the mouth of Moose River, a mile or so above Moose Lake. Here they left the Fraser and ascended the Moose, passed the splendid falls, and continued circling around the east side of the mountain mass till they crossed the height of land over to the headwaters of the Smoky. They planned to attempt to climb from the north – from the direction of Adolphus Lake, named after Dolphus Moberly, who had accompanied some of the party the year before, and of Mumm Peak, previously named after one of the leaders of the party. The packers made camp in the last patch of firewood at the northeast corner of the Robson Massive and remained there. The whole party stayed there for a welcome rest of one day before starting on the arduous climb ahead of them.

Unfortunately, the weather was most unfavourable, and although they tried several times, none of the party got beyond the 10,000-foot mark – some three thousand feet short of the summit. Eventually Amery and Mumm realized that the bad weather and the lateness of the season had defeated them for another year, and they returned to Edmonton. As Shand says: "The return trip to Lac Ste Anne was uneventful, packs were light and we made good time." And then expressing the typical thankfulness of all leaders of pack trains, he continued, "Horses all in good shape and no one had got sick or had been injured."

Having brought his mountain-climbing party home safely, Shand was free to turn his hand to anything else that suited him. For four months on that trip he had associated once more with men from his old way of life and men who, in their differing spheres, were destined to become prominent in the life of the British Empire. For four months these men had turned to the wilds and the mountains as the supreme holiday from a life of arduous mental effort. To them the wilderness had offered a temporary escape from the heavy loads and rigours of civilization. For four years now Shand had tasted of this life of freedom. At the same time, he had learned most of the skills needed by a man who would pit his resourcefulness against the simple physical hazards of life alone in the bush. And in spite of momentary physical discomforts, he had enjoyed every day of his four years on the frontier.

The uplift of freedom, which greeted him each new morning and which city people enjoyed so briefly for the few mornings of a holiday, would be his so long as he dwelt far from the roar of cities. In many ways this life was crude, lacking in intellectual stimuli and in many of the comforts of civilization. Yet this life was simple, yielding richly of warm friendships and of comforts and satisfactions unknown to civilization. Shand turned his face to the forest with no desire to retrace his steps. He said goodbye to his erstwhile employers and watched them leave for London, with no pangs at parting. Then once again he packed his ponies and herded them westward towards the rolling blue foot-hills and the silent mountains.

While Shand enjoyed his stay at Lac Ste Anne, he had been captivated by the attractions of Prairie Creek. Its extensive meadows would provide year-round feed for his horses. Its milder climate, with frequent chinook winds, would make the winters less onerous. Ever since first the mountains had opened out to his vision, since the sheer blue face of Roche Miette had hinted at inner mysteries beyond, since the autumn weeks spent in the clear air of the foothills, the green and gold hillsides had called. So he set out for Prairie Creek. He planned to live there, to hire out as a packer during the summer, and in winter to try his hand at trapping.

While he was getting his grubstake together and preparing to start, Mrs Lewis Swift arrived at Lac Ste Anne. Earlier in the fall, in the company of several Moberlys, she had come in from her husband's ranch at Jasper. The Moberlys had come to trade and to take back supplies for the winter, but Mrs Swift had been on her way to visit her mother, Mrs Chalifoux, who was ill at her home at Lac La Nonne. Now she had returned, and with her four pack horses was planning to start for Jasper. The prospect of the 200-mile trip to Jasper with her horses was not in her estima-tion anything remarkable. She was one of the breed of frontier women who took their places beside their husbands and carried their share, or even more, of the load.

"She was pleased when she found that I was also starting west," said Shand, "and suggested that we go together. She bought her 'grub' and about the middle of November we set out. The weather was cold but clear, and except that we had to cross rivers that were freezing over, the trip was uneventful. I left two of my horses to graze at Prairie Creek and cached my winter's grubstake there. Then Mrs Swift and I went on to cross the Atha-basca on the ice above the mouth of Stony River. Finally we reached Ewan Moberly's and spent the night with his family, and next day rode on to Swift's."

"Just a minute, Shand," I said. "How was it you didn't go over Roche Miette? Furthermore, which is the Stony River?"

"Oh. By being able to cross the river on the ice, we avoided the bad trail over Disaster Point by turning off just before reaching it."

"Ah, I see."

"Yes, and there's more to it than that. The best pack trail was the one which went over Roche Miette and then crossed the river to Ewan Moberly's. Disaster Point, of course, was troublesome, but we only needed to climb over it during the months of high water. Later on in the summer we could get around it by travelling in or fording one of the channels of the Athabasca. There was another trail that ran from Entrance to Solomon Creek and along the west side of Brulé and Jasper Lakes. It wasn't as good as the one on the other side, and it, too, had a spot similar to but not as bad as Disaster Point, where the horses had to climb over the spur of Bedson Ridge above what is now the railway tunnel.

"It's rather interesting looked at from the standpoint of a pack train. If you stay on the trail on the east side of the valley, you cross Roche Miette and Rocky River. If you take the trail on the west side, you cross the Bedson Range and the Stony River. A packer had to make a sort of Hobson's choice."

"Well, I've got that straight. Now clear me up on the river. Just now you spoke of the Stony River and I know you mean the one which present-day maps call the Snake Indian."

"I suppose the change has come about because there are apt to be too many Stony Rivers which would be called by that name whenever a pack trail crossed a river at an unusually stony place. 'Stony,' you know, could have two meanings. It could refer to the fact that it was full of stones, and in that case it would have the same meaning as its counterpart on the other side of the Athabasca – the Rocky River. I believe, however, that it was so named because its banks were inhabited by Assiniboines or Stonies.

"In an old sketch drawn by H. J. Moberly, which I saw long ago, it is called Assiniboine Creek. Actually it was on the flats at the right hand side of its mouth that the Assiniboines wiped out the last men of the Snake tribe. There seems to be some sort of ironic justice in the fact that modern maps call it the Snake Indian."

"Who were the Snake Indians?" I asked. "Were they a remnant of the large Snake tribe which lived in Montana? And what is the difference between them and the Snaring Indians after whom the river about five miles above Ewan Moberly's was named?"

"I doubt if the Snakes were the same tribe as those in the United States. I've never been able to straighten out the difference between the Snakes and the Snaring Indians. They could have been the same tribe. Some accounts speak of the massacre I mentioned as happening to the Snakes and some as happening to the Snaring Indians."

Then Shand went into the subject in detail, referring to the notes left by many of the early travellers, including Henry J. Moberly, who called them the Snakes in one place and later on called them the Snares.

"That may have been a lapse of memory in the case of a very old man," said Shand. "Until we have access to some of the Hudson's Bay Company's early Jasper House journals, we probably won't know – we may not know even then.

"According to Walter Moberly, however," he continued, "in the days before they had guns, the Snaring Indians caught mountain sheep, bear and buffalo by snaring them."

Shand took advantage of his trip with Mrs Swift to learn more of the lore of the forest and of the natives and to improve his knowledge of Cree. Soon he was quite proficient in it, and the fact that he had taken the trouble to learn their language cemented his friendship with the natives. One other factor contributing to the respect in which they held him was that, unlike most white men, he would never sell or trade liquor to them. Nearly all other white men gaining a livelihood in the area were not averse to making a little money by doing so. But even the importunities of the younger Indians failed to change Shand's stand on liquor, and it was not long before the elders of the race developed a deep respect for the one white layman who refused to profit by their thirst.

When Mrs Swift reached home she found that for some weeks her husband had been ill. In her absence things had not fared well with him or their small children. Food had run low at the ranch, which was obviously in need of a firm hand to guide it till Lewis Swift could be nursed back to strength. Shand set to work immediately, first of all hauling and cutting wood. Then Adam Joachim came over to help, and the two men butchered Swift's older bull. In short order some measure of comfort re-entered the Swift home. Then Adam and Shand set to work with flails to thresh the wheat which had been grown on the small field. The next move was to scour the hillsides for deer and moose and the mountaintops for sheep, and by Christmas the Swift larder was well stocked. Then, to celebrate the fact that things were on the mend, Shand broke out a gallon of rum, and as he says, "Christmas was well celebrated."

Lewis John Swift was a remarkable man, and his ranch was no less remarkable. He was of the breed of men known all over the Western States as "mountain men." A few of these men, knowing little and caring less about artificial boundary lines, wandered into Alberta – Jack Gregg at Prairie Creek, Livingstone, who finally settled in Calgary, Liver Eating Johnston, Dan Noyes and a handful of others. A pack horse or two, a few traps, a gold pan and the best gun of the day was all they needed to set out to explore the most remote valley. The civilization of cities stifled them. Once in a while – usually only when in need of supplies like salt, beans, tea, sugar, tobacco or painkiller – they appeared at some fur trade post. There they traded a few furs and maybe a nugget or two for a new grubstake and for a good drunk, and then, surfeited with society, rode off up the valley or over the hill towards more adventures and the solitude so necessary to them.

Somewhere in a remote valley, sheltered somewhat from the storms of winter and where their horses could pasture, they returned to an old cabin or built a new one before resuming their trapping or their search for gold. No mountain pass was too forbidding to cross and no mountain valley too remote to seek. Then, after many years had gone by, years that passed so quickly, the knees had a touch of stiffness in the mornings and the eyes watered a mite in a smart breeze; then the bed felt more cosy in the morning than it used to and more welcome in the evening; then it was time to seek a valley to abide in. Not that a man couldn't still climb a mountain all day or shoot just as straight – but a permanent cabin, maybe a hill or two of potatoes and some grain for flour . . . a fellow's ideas changed . . . and maybe one woman to live with. And so, finally, each mountain man settled down in his chosen spot and became a legend as the first settler dating from away back. Thus it came about that Lewis Swift settled in Jasper.

Born February 20, 1854, in Cleveland, Ohio, Swift set out for the mountains as a young man. He lived in many of the early mining camps in the Denver area, and spent some time in the Black Hills, including a spell as the driver of the stage from Bismarck to Deadwood. After years in the mountain states, he turned up in the embryo Calgary of 1888. But that city, springing up on the newly built Canadian Pacific Railway, was too crowded, so Swift moved north to the outpost village of Edmonton. There or at Lac Ste Anne he met many of the natives from the Jasper area and in 1890 travelled west with the Moberlys, till in the valley of the Athabasca he was once more in the shadow of the mountains. But he was still on the move, and before long passed west through the Yellowhead Pass to emerge in due course at Mission Creek in the Okanagan, where he appears to have spent the next two years.

In 1893 he turned his pack horses eastward again towards the solitude of the chinook-kissed valley at Jasper. This time he brought in a supply of trade goods and a six-inch grindstone. After looking over old Jasper House, which the Hudson's Bay Company abandoned in 1884, he repaired the only building still standing and lived in it for two years. Trading took little of his time, leaving him free to travel and to hunt and to think about the possibilities of this broad valley in the lowest pass through the Alberta Rockies. Many of the old CPR survey stakes left by Walter Moberly in 1872 were still visible, and visions of wealth entered Swift's ever practical head. He chose a piece of land in the area known then as Henry House Flats. He concluded that it would be the most desirable location for a railway divisional point some day in the future when a second transcontinental railway should cross Canada. From his observations of the rapid development in the Western states, he felt that this day was not far off and in 1895 he settled on this land. He quickly built a house on it and made sure to put himself in a position to get his title to it as soon as he could.

Assessing the prospects of his new homestead, Swift felt

doubly blessed. It was an oasis of farming land set in the majestic beauty of this mountain-girt valley. In summer it could be irrigated from a gravelly clear stream, and in winter from time to time the blessed chinook winds would come and overnight sweep it clear of snow. Here he could raise horses and cattle, wheat, oats and potatoes, while the surrounding valleys and crags delivered up a rich fare of moose and mountain sheep. Here he could enjoy all the freedom and solitude his heart could desire. And when the onrush of civilization intruded, as it would inevitably, it would come as a mixed blessing, bringing with it wealth from the sale of his land.

Swift set about to provide the essentials for a comfortable living. He continued to trade in a small way, he also drove in some cattle from Edmonton, and he carried in on his pack horses enough chickens to stock his ranch. In 1897 he married Suzette Chalifoux, a white-skinned girl whose resourcefulness stood shoulder to shoulder with his own. Before long, on the ten acres of land which he irrigated from his crystal-clear stream, he grew wheat, oats and barley. To grind his flour he fabricated an ingenious small waterwheel, so that the same stream that nourished his wheat also ground flour to nurture his growing brood. The wheel was small, but in the course of a day turned out one or two sacks of flour, so that Swift, when he operated it, consumed far more time than energy. But time in large measures was his chief commodity and his joy. For transportation around his tidy farmyard, time had aided him to fashion a one-horse cart, whose wheels were solid discs cut from a huge Douglas fir. His blacksmith work was done on an anvil which he unearthed while rummaging around the site of Moberly's Athabasca Depot, about two miles upstream from his house.

Swift's waterwheel had an interesting evolution. Stanley Washburn, in his *Trails, Trappers and Tenderfeet in Western Canada*, relates that while travelling in the area during 1909 he visited Swift and commented on its usefulness. The story he tells about its construction is essentially as follows:

"That must save you a lot of work," said Washburn, pointing to the wheel.

"Yah," replied Swift, "she does a lot of things, grinds grain, grinds coffee, sharpens axes and breaks down – mostly she breaks down.

"After I settled down here," he continued, "I decided to make a wheel to turn my six-inch grindstone. As you can see, I had to build her entirely of wood – no nails in her anywhere. Took me a long time to get her finished, and then I really sharpened up all my tools. Good job, too, for on the second day she broke down, and I had to make several new pieces.

"Next summer I was in Lac Ste Anne and saw a coffee grinder at Peter Gunn's store, so I brought it back here. I never did go in for coffee, likin' tea much better, but I calculated I'd better use coffee as bein' so handy to grind in my mill, and that's why I've used it ever since.

"But the coffee grinder was too small to do much barley, so by 'n by I got a larger one that can squeeze out about three bushel a day when I keep her agoin' steady. And there she is. 'Course, even now I can only drop in a few grains of barley at a time. But time don't mean much here."

"Guess not," said Washburn. "By the way, what's the latest news? Heard anything from the States lately?"

"Well, yes. I reckon I have got some news all right," Swift replied reflectively.

"Recent news?" inquired Washburn eagerly.

"Well, pretty recent I should say."

For a long time Swift ruminated, silently whittling away at a stick. At last he said, "Well, did you hear that Taft was elected?"

Washburn was set back for a moment. It was now July, and the election had been in November.

"Is that the last you've heard?"

The old man looked disappointed. "Well, I reckon it is," he said. "What's the matter with that? It only happened last fall, and there ain't been nobody through here since."

Swift had a comfortable house, a barn and a storehouse. As the years went by, he added to his possessions a wholesome brood of healthy children. With several cows and a bull, a bunch of sturdy mountain ponies and a percheron stallion, Swift's establishment was complete unto itself. Except for sugar, tea and tobacco, he was as nearly independent as a man could be.

When his farm duties palled, or his contemplation of the

changing hues of the mountainsides satiated his spirit, he could turn indoors to the comforts of his well run household, kept clean and orderly by Suzette. Copper kettles suspended from iron bars set into the wall above the open fireplace gave off the fragrance of meals cooking. On a shelf stood the various vessels made of birchbark sewn with fine roots and gummed – used as milk pans and containers. Hanging on walls and from the rafters were many roots, herbs and vegetables, bacon and hams, and swatches of dry sphagnum moss, so indispensable when cotton cloth was not available, so handy to line the baby's bed, to use as diapers, to scrub with and to wipe pots and pans.

For washing and scrubbing, Mrs Swift made soap from surplus fat and grease combined with the lye of wood ashes. A home-tied broom of willow twigs kept the floor spic and span. Swift's home was kept by a wife proud of her simple conveniences, of her skill and of her husband. Having little social life, she had time to spend at her needlework – a native art which with Suzette came to a rare perfection. Whenever store-bought cloth was available, she made it up into clothes for her family and occasionally into an intricately wrought dress for herself. Most of the clothing, however, consisted of artistic buckskin suits, ornamented with beads and embroidered with rich coloured silks – true works of art, designed and executed with infinite patience and pride.

Living on his own land, surrounded by these satisfactions of body and spirit, Swift was at peace with the present while he waited for the wealth of the future. In 1909, at the time of Shand's stay with him, his vision of future wealth was beginning to dim. The Grand Trunk had surveyed through the valley without indicating any interest in his land. "All right," thought Swift, "the other transcontinental, the Canadian Northern, is surveying towards Jasper, and surely it will need space for a future city and for its divisional point." But other clouds were drifting across the horizon of his vision. The Dominion government had decided in 1907 to set apart a vast area east of the summit of the Rockies as a national park, and had selected a headquarters in an area some six miles south of Swift's ranch. It was rumoured that all squatters and freeholders were to be moved out. Swift was not really disturbed. Though he had looked ahead without undue eagerness to the day when he would sell his land at a high price, he was nevertheless far from crossing the bridge of dispossession before he came to it. He would wait and see.

Meanwhile Shand had a chance to inspect this valley. Its history, as far as white men were concerned, had started about Christmas of 1810, when David Thompson had passed through it. A hundred years later this area in the shadow of the Palisades was known as Henry House Flats, but today no one knows for certain where William Henry, in the employ of David Thompson, built the first Henry House in 1811. It was succeeded by Henry's Winter House built by 1813 and later still by Henry House. This one was built by the Hudson's Bay Company about 1824 and the Company called it Rocky Mountain House. Since it was in the general locality of Henry's first and second houses, it was also referred to as Henry House. At one time or another the voyageur after whom the Miette River and Roche Miette were named lived in this house, so that sometimes it was also called Miette's House. While no one can be certain, it is probable that it was built on Cottonwood Creek.

While the natives had some hazy knowledge of these old posts, Shand found that their memories were very clear about the Jasper House on the left bank of the Athabasca, opposite the mouth of Rocky River. Its predecessor, at the north end of Brulé Lake, had been built by Jasper Hawse of the North West Company about 1813. Then in 1829 it was abandoned and succeeded by the Jasper House known to everyone, which in its turn had been abandoned by the Hudson's Bay Company in 1884.

Shand found the recent history of this broad Jasper valley peopled with the ghosts of small bands of Crees, Snakes, Stonies and Shuswaps. Iroquois, as well, had come to regard the Jasper valley as their home, although by Shand's time they were slightly mixed with Cree blood together with a trace of white. The most definite donor of white paternity had been the rugged trader Henry John Moberly, who was more or less steadily in charge of Jasper House from 1855 to 1861. His brother Walter, a Canadian Pacific Railway engineer who spent some months in this vicinity in 1872, seems to have been abashed even by the proximity of Indian beauty necessary to bear him across a lake, but Henry John, quite unabashed, seems to have partaken of the fruits of the valley with gay abandon. When he left the region he also left Ewan and John, two male heirs of his temporary union with Suzan, a Stoney woman.

Suzan was buried on the farm of her son Ewan in May 1905, and on a rude cross her name was carved as Suzan Cardinal. We do not know whether Cardinal was her maiden name or that of a husband to whom she was regularly wed after the departure of Henry John. Whichever it was, it was a name honourably borne and long known in the winding valley of the Athabasca.

Like so many names in the history of the fur trade, Cardinal was French. Along every river in the vast, lonely expanse of Canada's hinterland, some French voyageur has paddled his canoe. Down unnamed creeks leading to the Arctic Ocean some voyageur has urged his dog teams. Over the highest passes far up among the gnarled pines some voyageur has carried his traps. Along the most remote trails, winding day after day through the dense forests of pine and poplar, some voyageur has pushed his pack horses. Beside every lake, large or small, near or far from today's civilization, some voyageur has camped – often the first man with a tinge of white blood in his veins to do so. Rivers by the score and lakes by the hundreds, portages and passes, mountains and meadows, bear the name of some intrepid French voyageur. Sometimes with the passing of centuries little of the French blood remains, but always the French ancestry is there and often the French daring, the French thirst to see what is over the next blue hill or around the next forested headland.

The name Cardinal is amongst the most widespread. When in 1828 Ermatinger was going west to the Columbia, it was at the Campment de Cardinelle, a mile or so downstream from the later Athabasca Depot, that he camped. When Henry John Moberly was in charge of Jasper House in 1855, it was André Cardinal who was in charge of the transport of goods to that post. What would be more normal, then, than that Henry John for the duration of his stay at Jasper House should take to his bosom one Suzan of Stoney ancestry and of the Cardinal line to be the mother of a long chain of Moberlys? And what more normal than that these Moberlys should soon be absorbed into the predominant Iroquois band in the valley, and today, speaking only Cree and English, take pride in their white name and their Iroquois blood and physique? Many of them stand over six feet, broad-shouldered and erect, big men with aquiline noses and strong features, while the Crees are short in stature, with round faces and snub noses. The Iroquois who came west were select men. One of the originals to come to Jasper House, Dominick Karayinter (Caraconté?), was still going strong when Henry John Moberly reached there in 1855. Dominick was the last one alive of the band which had been sent out from Montreal by the North West Company and arrived in Jasper in 1814, the year after Jasper House was opened. He had fought with the British army in several of the battles of the War of 1812 – a sturdy character, whose descendants may well be proud of him.

Shand met the Moberlys and all of the Iroquois neighbours, the Findlays, Joachims, Caracontés, Gauthiers and Wanyandis, who, scattered along the valley, were faring well on farms similar to Swift's. About a hundred of them lived in the comparative security of a crude white man's type of civilization. Descended from canoe-men and snowshoe-men in the eastern forests, they were now horsemen and mountain climbers. Of them all, Ewan Moberly (pronounced Ee-wan, possibly a revamping on Indian tongues of the Scots name Ewen) was the leader. On the left bank of the river on the flat below Cobblestone Creek, he dwelt in a well constructed and comfortable house built about 1898 – today a landmark in the Park.

Shand and Adam Joachim took to each other immediately, and this liking grew into a deep friendship that lasted till Adam's death in April 1959 at the age of eighty-four. Of predominantly Iroquois ancestry, Adam was born in 1875 near Berland Lake on the river that was originally called Baptiste after Baptiste Berland, but which on modern maps is designated Berland. The original Iroquois name of the family has been lost, but some time before Adam's birth they were received into the Catholic faith and were given the name of the saint dear to the heart of the Oblate Fathers. Adam received his early education at the Roman Catholic mission at St Albert, and Father Lacombe, struck by the boy's brightness, his pious inclinations and his exceptional spiritual qualities, arranged for him to study for the priesthood at a Montreal seminary. There he became a scholar of exceptional promise, but a crisis in family affairs made it necessary for him to sacrifice his studies and return to the Smoky River Country.

In 1896 he returned and settled down near the Moberly homestead, devoting his education and his knowledge of the white man's ways to the service of his own people. A quiet, modest man, proud of his Iroquois ancestry, conversant with Latin and equally fluent in Cree, English and French, his colourful personality and fine mind made him not only the strong unofficial leader of his people but the friend of all white men who were so fortunate as to know him. Having returned to take up the way of life of his fathers, he did so wholeheartedly. As a trapper, prospector and guide, his endurance, his adaptability to the terrain and his thorough knowledge of wildlife, combined with his unmitigated honesty, made him an outstanding authority on the vast, friendly wilderness in which he spent his years.

After celebrating Christmas at Swift's, Shand returned to Prairie Creek early in January 1910. He soon set out a line of traps extending for some miles, and although his returns were not great, he did gain some useful experience in the ways of the fur-bearing animals.

Shand had met Jack Gregg on previous trips, but he came to know him well during his first winter at Prairie Creek. In his youth Jack had been a scout under General Custer and left his service before the Battle of the Little Big Horn in 1876. Later on, in the early Eighties, he fought against the Apaches under the famous Geronimo. Some time after 1894 he settled down on a choice piece of land along Prairie Creek. To add to his income he started a small store and traded with all who came along the old Jasper Trail. While he was a shrewd trader, he was well liked by all old-timers.

Jack's history prior to settling on Prairie Creek was swathed in some mystery. He gave varying explanations to account for his scars, but none could doubt the dozen bullet holes he could display. Shand says: "Well, maybe it wasn't a full dozen, but I saw them many times, and the number could not have been more than one or two short of that total."

Jack Gregg's wife, Mary Cardinal, was a fit partner for a pioneer of the pack trails. She was so well respected that a mountain stream has been named Mary Gregg River, while her husband's name has been perpetuated in that of both a river and a lake. By 1910 Gregg was well along the road to affluence. When eastern capital came in to develop coal mines, Jack staked a large claim and a year or so later sold it for a considerable sum, taking $3000 cash in advance.

Towards the end of January 1910, J. J. Maclaggan, a parks commissioner from Ottawa, arrived at Prairie Creek on his way to buy out the claims of squatters and other freeholders whose lands lay within the boundaries of the recently established Jasper National Park. These included Lewis Swift, the four Moberlys – Ewan, John, Dolphus and William – as well as Isador Findlay and Adam Joachim. Maclaggan had little difficulty in making a deal with almost all of them. The government proposed to pay cash for their buildings, corrals and other improvements. While they would have preferred to remain in the Jasper valley, they knew that without much effort they could locate somewhere else and that the cash they would receive all in one lump sum could go far towards buying new farm machinery and other necessities. The move would be profitable.

Swift refused to consider the possibility of moving, and being paid the cash value of his improvements did not appeal to him. For some years, and with good reason, he had hoped that when civilization reached the valley he could sell his land for enough money to make him financially independent. Maclaggan's attempts to deal with Swift failed, so he returned to Ottawa while Lewis Swift remained on his homestead. In 1935 Swift sold it to another private owner, and this 160 acres of land in the heart of Jasper Park has remained in private hands ever since – the only parcel of freehold land within its boundaries.

Even though the natives had a working knowledge of English, when they were dealing with Maclaggan they used the age-old protection of pretending not to understand, so he was forced to deal with them through an interpreter. As it turned out, it was fortunate for them that they did so. Tommy Groat was the official interpreter, although Adam Joachim, with his thorough knowledge of both languages, assisted.

Maclaggan called one meeting of the natives at Jasper and another at Jack Gregg's place, and explained the situation to them. Fortunately for the natives, as it turned out later, Shand attended the second meeting. The government wanted to be sole owner of all lands in the park. One of the purposes of the park was to protect wildlife, and it of course could not tolerate residents who lived by hunting. That being so, the government would pay them handsomely for any improvements they had made in the way of buildings and other work and then they would be free to settle *anywhere outside* the park boundaries. The natives agreed and promised to move as soon as the spring weather permitted. For a few months they would have to leave their horses to graze in the valley until they had found new locations. The necessary documents were signed, and before long the cash was paid over.

John and Ewan and the other heads of families made a trip to Edmonton, where they bought sleighs, wagons and ploughs before starting to build on the new land they had selected. In the spring John Moberly and his family moved out to Prairie Creek and filed on a quarter-section which to this day remains in the family's hands. Ewan Moberly and his sons and Adam Joachim went farther afield, to Grande Cache, long a favourite rendezvous of the Indians. This pleasant area on the upper waters of the Smoky River can be reached today by travelling some eighty miles along the forestry road from Entrance and then following a pack trail west for about twenty miles. Ewan Moberly and his group took their machinery and over two hundred head of stock, mostly horses, over a road which they cleared out along older hunting trails. Up Solomon Creek they went, up the Wildhay River, past Rock Lake and on over the pass to the Sulphur River. By descending that, they came to Grande Cache. Ever since, this way has been called the Moberly road.

The name Grande Cache goes far back into the days of the fur trade. In each of the years 1818 to 1821 Ignace Giasson, an employee of the Hudson's Bay Company stationed at St Mary's Fort near present-day Peace River town, travelled far up the Smoky River and on at least one of these trips crossed over the Rockies into British Columbia. On his return from the west side he brought back a large quantity of furs. Because of the deep snow, travelling down the Smoky was so difficult that he was forced to leave his furs in one large (Grande) cache. While we cannot prove that this was at modern Grande Cache, it is reasonably safe to presume that it was.

Around 1910, officials from Ottawa were frequent visitors to the Jasper mountains. In the spring D. R. Findlayson, assistant director of forestry, came out to set aside some of the lands adjoining Jasper Park, to create the Athabasca Forest Reserve. For some five years Alberta had been operating as a province, but all Crown lands were administered from Ottawa, and this reserve was a federal affair. Findlayson camped at Prairie Creek and talked his problem over with Shand, who showed him the eastern boundary of the park. The Athabasca Forest Reserve extended north some forty miles from Prairie Creek to the 15th Base Line and was bounded on the west by Jasper Park and the British Columbia border. Findlayson's visit boded no good for the natives of Grande Cache, but that came out later. In due course he completed his survey of this reserve and returned to Ottawa, and the forested hillsides resumed the even tenor of their ways.

In May 1910, when the new grass was two or three inches high and a fresh haze hung over the forests, when sticky leaves unfolded to fill the lazy air with their pungent spice, Shand and many of his foothills neighbours set out for Lac Ste Anne. Ostensibly they went to sell their furs and to buy supplies. In reality they yearned for the company of their "town friends" of Lac Ste Anne and for the sociability of meeting once more with other old friends who, along trails starting from many points in the Smoky River forest, all converged on the old village.

Shand's horses were not used to the heavy traffic now that the old trail had become such a busy road. They had been reared in the foothills and it took them some time to get used to the hustle and bustle. Of all the pack horses, Ewan Moberley had the best; he was very proud of his animals and every year or so brought fresh stock from the Kamloops area through the Yellow-head Pass. But the dislike of the mountain-bred pack horses for the strange sights of the tote road were as nothing to their surprise at their first sight of a mule.

Shand has a vivid recollection of his horses' awe at their first meeting with the long-eared, skinny mules working on the grade. He had the utmost trouble getting them to pass a fresno drawn by mules, and just then noon time struck. Now, mules are persistent and strong, and work wonders on construction. They are less friendly and docile than horses and have more clear-cut notions of their rights. At quitting time, either noon or evening, they seem to have built-in clocks, and when the proper minute arrives they stop and will pull no more. Shand's horses, cocking first one ear ahead and then the other as an indication of their distrust of this group of great-eared, cow-tailed beasts, carefully picked their way past. Suddenly, with one accord, the mules stopped, lifted their heads and brayed. The horses, as if the devil himself had come for them, flew for the bush, bursting tie ropes and banging packs against trees. Shand was two hours getting the mess cleared up, and ever after neither he nor his horses "hankered after" mules.

His native friends felt a similar astonishment when, in turning a bend in the pack trail west of Marlboro, they beheld their first locomotive and steam shovel, puffing, squealing and tooting as it cut into the cliff overhanging the McLeod River. Perhaps their surprise was caused as much by the fact that it should not have been there as by the actual sight of the mechanical monster. For it should not have been there.

The nearest rails were at Wolf Creek, over twenty-five miles away, and between these two points were two long unfinished bridges, the gap where the Big Eddy trestle was to go, and still another long trestle west of Bickerdike, which was likewise still a figment of someone's imagination. And yet, swinging and creaking in front of them, dipping and digging, were two steam shovels, a locomotive and a string of gravel cars. What the natives did not know was that by the remarkable determination of the contractors and the perseverance of hundreds of horses and mules, all this equipment had been carried over the icy roads in the heart of winter, so as to get on with the cutting of this difficult hillside as soon as spring came. The moment the steel reached Wolf Creek in February 1910, a work train of gravel cars and the two shovels pulled into the new town. A swarm of men descended on the locomotive, the shovels and the cars, dismantled them and loaded the pieces on a large fleet of specially built wide-bunked sleighs. Then, pulled by hundreds of horses and mules, the train of sleighs set off down the bank, across the ice of the McLeod, and up the other bank. Load followed load through the hoar-frosted pines, and wheels and rails, buckets and booms and a million other bits and pieces slid along the tote road. The boiler of the locomotive was blocked and nailed and cinched on to one huge sleigh, and its tender, shored up and tied down, followed on another. The whole train, pack, package and caboodle, disappeared into the bush. In a few days it emerged at the cut bank where ringing hammers and clanking spanners re-erected it into a work train and steam shovels. Before long, steam was raised, the shovels swung their jibs, and a long cut along the side of the cliff began to take shape.

Shand and his Smoky River Indian friends had indeed much to see and much to ponder. Down at the Big Eddy, where in the silent meadows generations of Indians had camped, where packers had turned their horses loose to roll and graze on the luxurious grass while they dangled a hook over the bank to tempt trout lurking in the shade, all was now uproar. Down one slope of the Sundance valley, across the old meadow and up the other bank for a distance of half a mile, vegetation had been uprooted and men were busy digging square holes, shovelling cement or pouring concrete to make footings for the new trestle. For the engineers had decreed that over this coulee was to be flung a huge curved wooden trestle, half a mile long, to carry rails, and ultimately trains, 125 feet above the creek – this creek twenty feet wide trickling quietly over its coloured gravel.

Men worked everywhere. Slowly but inevitably, a bent at a time, the trestle rose. Loggers with peaveys and canthooks swarmed over huge piles of logs recently pulled in from the forest. Horses treading slowly back and forth hauled a log at a time from pole pile to bent-builder. Carpenters worked at sawhorses, sawing and chiselling, cutting and shaping logs to be passed on to the fabricators. These fitted the logs into tiers twenty-five feet long, stretched out flat, ready to be hoisted into place. Far above, teetering on the rickety catwalk, projected out from the bank till it ended abruptly in the emptiness of mid-air, stood the donkey engine, belching sour, undigested coal smoke, waiting its turn to hoist. Suddenly, tooting to apprise its servants of its wishes, its drum began to turn, snatch blocks squealed and cables tightened as slowly, creaking and shuddering, one tier was hauled into place and set atop another. Soon in front of Shand's eyes one tier after another was yanked aloft to dangle and swing for a moment and then be secured until another bent of the trestle 125 feet high stood stark against the sky. In such fashion the trestle crept across the valley till finally its spider webs spanned the coulee where the shot-spattered logs of the Sinclair cabin had stood. The acrid smoke of progress replaced the serene softness of wood smoke rising from a trapper's cabin.

Rising above the hammering and sawing, the squealing and

the tooting, rang out the cook's gong. Tools were dropped, cables slackened and the bee-like busyness stopped, as men clambered from all over, out of holes or off platforms, to form ant-like lines straggling towards the cookhouse. The tooting and squealing stopped, the belching smoke ceased, and for a brief lull, as the sour blue smoke drifted off down river, the valley resumed its old serenity and silence.

Everywhere as Shand advanced towards Wolf Creek, he saw new evidence of the forward thrust of the railway. For the last few miles he rode along the completed grade. Everywhere, over bridge, culvert or corduroy, the grade snaked onward and onward. There was no problem, dense forest, deep coulee or bottomless muskeg, that the builders could not overcome. That they did not always succeed at the first try or even at the second, he was to see on the bank of the McLeod at Wolf Creek. But in the end, by their very persistence, they won. Shand clambered up the bank to join many other spectators who were looking at a cut that had slumped full again, and he realized some of the setbacks of railway construction. During the previous winter, three hundred men with picks and shovels and dynamite had toiled here for months. They left a cut some forty feet deep and many hundred feet long, with clearly defined sloping sides, awaiting the advent of the rails. Well over 100,000 yards of material had been wheeled out of the clay. Then, with the coming of spring, little trickles of water began to ooze out of the sides of the cut. The day before Shand's arrival, the massive bank had given way, and with a roar and a swoosh it slid in to fill the cut again. The sombre-faced engineer estimated that the quantity of material to be cleaned out now would be nearly equal to what they had taken out originally. Sometimes the terrain fought back.

The rails reached Wolf Creek in February and only then could work be started on the superstructure of the two bridges. The building of a false bridge caused a long delay and employed large gangs of men for a year. As a result, the temporary town of Wolf Creek came into being. Before the future divisional point of Edson boasted even one building, the town of Wolf Creek some six miles away fairly hummed. Five separate construction camps, each with two to three hundred working men, were set up in selected spots in the deep valleys, or stretched out for a mile along the grade. Scattered about with little semblance of regularity were places of business, conscientious or clandestine, including one bank, half a dozen stores and twice as many restaurants and stopping places. There were a few pool rooms, a drug store and barber and blacksmith shops. Even a real estate office had set up shop, for in the beginning speculators had hoped that Wolf Creek would become the divisional point. So busy were they in selling lands and booming Wolf Creek and cornering the land there that they forced the Grand Trunk to pass it by and to lay out its divisional point in the muskeg six miles west. Except for the speculators, what a city could have been built at the junction of Wolf Creek and the McLeod River – a city of hills and valleys and pleasant vistas.

Set somewhat apart were the offices and yards of Phelan and Shirley, the contractors on that portion of the line. To work for them and for Foley, Welsh and Stewart, who had a large contract west of Edson, came a constant stream of men who at Winnipeg or Edmonton had hired on and signed a "contract of work." Like cattle, these men were shipped to the end of steel. Seventy or eighty men were crowded into a battered old coach, having neither lights nor water, a coach without seats, standing room only. By turns men stretched out on the floor for an interval and then stood up to allow others to lie down, trying to take care that the jolting train did not make them step on the faces of the reclining men. Glad indeed were these labourers of all nationalities to reach the end of steel and set out on foot along the grades to the camps they were assigned to. The grade was a regular highway, with streams of men coming to work and quitting the job. As the contractors said, they always had three gangs of men, those coming, those working, and those on their way home. For often the working conditions were such that even the unorganized labourers of the day could not stand them and quit. Even when the conditions were satisfactory, some men were always on the move, tiring of work in one spot and off to seek some other camp which at the moment appealed to them. Almost any time a traveller along the grade would meet seventy or eighty men, each with his pack on his shoulders, marching two by two towards the front of the line or returning from it in disgust.

There was much to do and, from the contractors' standpoint, too few men to do it. The roundhouse at Edson was under construction; work had started on the grade going into the vast coal seams up the Coal Branch; and the Big Eddy trestle, half a mile long, made up of 170 bents and containing over two million board feet of timber, was under way.

Wolf Creek had one good hotel equipped with hot and cold water, as well as a regular bath. Stopping places of varying degrees of cleanliness down to mere flop houses filled the needs of the bulk of those who were willing to pay for accommodation. Set slightly apart from the main town were the two log buildings of the Royal North West Mounted Police. From these Inspector Tucker and three constables maintained order in the town and for miles along the grade. Considering their nature, Wolf Creek and the other construction towns as far west as the British Columbia border were remarkable for their quietness and their lack of lawlessness. The worst problem the Mounties had to combat was liquor and the bootleggers.

In Wolf Creek there was a host of decent labourers, contractors and conscientious businessmen. The shacks on the fringes of such a town, however, housed many a vulture. In spite of the counsels of the clerics and the vigilance of the police, many a man's stake fell to the cold callousness of a bootlegger, the cunning clutches of a gambler or was exchanged for the calculated caresses of a harpy.

Such then was Wolf Creek, a town of perhaps two thousand souls at the height of its short but active life.

Devoted preachers visited Wolf Creek and the camps, slanting their services in the direction of a breezy bit of a sermon and advising the men to keep away from the wickednesses of this world. They held services in bunkhouses, cook tents and pool rooms, sometimes with a quiet little poker game going on in an adjoining room, or even in sight, while as often as not a big grader stood just outside the meeting place drinking a bottle of rye and between gulps catching snatches of the sermon. Only courageous and dedicated men bearded the insults of a construction camp to preach under conditions often hostile and always discouraging.

As these ministers went to and fro along the grade, they often arrived in time to bury some of the scores of men who never returned to the bright lights to blow their roll or to their homesteads far back in the bush. The Reverend P. B. Bickersteth, in his book *The Land of Open Doors*, describes the death and burial of one such unfortunate. He went to visit him in one of the company hospitals. Next day he was dead.

The doctor had already ordered a rough wooden box from one of the men at the station, and, by the time he was washed and ready, they brought it over to the hospital. He was put into it, nailed down, and put outside; there was nowhere else to put him.

The doctor and I went back and got a wagon, on which we placed the coffin. I jumped up with the driver, who had much difficulty in restraining his language, because his team of grey mules was obstreperous; but the gravity of the situation made him do his level best, and it really was humorous to see a sudden outburst hastily smothered with a furtive look at me. Williams rode with us, and sat on the coffin, the only place there was. Our curious funeral procession went bumping along over a vile trail, and when at last we reached the place we found the grave ready and the men sitting round smoking.

After the service was over, they did not take long to shovel back the sandy soil. Another fellow and I cut down some small spruce trees, put posts and rails round the grave, and made a cross. We wrote the date on the cross, but not his name, as we did not know it for certain. So there we left him, and another is added to the number of those who never return. . . .

From Wolf Creek eastward Shand's horses followed the tote road beside the grade until they crossed the Pembina at Entwistle. Then, with relief, he and his horses turned from the right-of-way so disfigured with cuts, gouges, clearings and piles of tin cans, back into the old pack trail around Lake Isle. Even here, apparently, they could not escape all evidence of railways, for slashed through the bush was the newly blazed survey for the rival transcontinental, the Canadian Northern, which had awakened from its slumbers at Edmonton and was starting to advance west through Lac Ste Anne. When Shand explained to his Indians that yet another railway was to transverse this area and to run side by side with the Grand Trunk, they shook their heads in amazement at the ways of the white man.

Shand had expected that being bypassed by the Grand Trunk would kill Lac Ste Anne, but it was far from dormant. True, there had been some changes: Billy Connors had sold the hotel to Randal Chisholm, beer and whisky and other freight now came by train to Wabamun and was hauled twelve miles to the hamlet, and mail came three times a week by the same route. All the surrounding land was occupied by homesteaders, and roads and trails wandered from shack to shack. Some of the roads were quite passable for buggies and democrats, but the most startling change was the chug of Randal Chisholm's automobile which he had driven in along the old trail past Dan Noyes' place.

Perhaps of more moment to Lac Ste Anne than all these was the Canadian Northern survey that Shand had seen around Lake Isle. For there was no longer any doubt that the railway was going to pass through the hamlet. Shand and his team made several trips with his friend MacLaren, a Canadian Northern engineer. The Grand Trunk injunction which had kept the Canadian Northern Railway out of Stony Plain, however, did not deter the company for long and did not prevent waste on a far larger scale.

In September Shand bought a winter's grubstake and once more set off for Prairie Creek. While he had enjoyed a busy summer at Lac Ste Anne, he found on his way west that the Grand Trunk contractors had also been remarkably busy. During that interval of five months great changes had taken place in the line. In July 1910 the steel had reached Edson. As soon as it did so, Wolf Creek began to die. The process was very sudden at first, then it slowed up and it was nearly a year before the end came. In a short time Bickerdike, the new end of steel, enjoyed its brief reign of importance. But Edson did not languish when the steel passed on westward, for as the divisional point it was destined to have a future.

Passing west, Shand came to Bickerdike, or Mile 17 (that is, seventeen miles from Wolf Creek). In the fall of 1910 Bickerdike, as the end of steel, was far bigger than Edson, but its claim to fame hung by a thread and that would be severed whenever the rails reached Obed or Hinton farther west. Plans were afoot to start a branch line south into the Coal Branch, but so far this was a dream. While Edson had a future, Bickerdike's only future lay in the here and now. Its short reign was due to be briefer than that of Wolf Creek.

Nevertheless, it bore up well with its log shacks plastered with clay all in a row above the track, and behind them all the assorted buildings of the end of steel. Perhaps more pretentious than the buildings along this street were the rakish homemade signs indicating the business carried on inside: "Dad's Stopping House," "Short Order Resterant," "Poolroom," "The Old Man's Place." Signs or no signs, future or no future, Bickerdike was making the most of the present. Every other log shack or tent was a gambling joint, a pool room or a brothel.

Shand was glad to get away and ride over the divide to look once more at the clean, rugged mountains. That night as he spread his blankets beside his small fire, while his horses snuffed and grazed in a meadow, the slopes below him along the grade were alive with a host of twinkling fires. Far and near, freighters were stretching out, each beside his companionable fire, where joyfully for one night, one instant of eternity, his caravan had rested.

Prairie Creek had changed considerably during the few months Shand had been away. It was now rapidly being transformed into another construction town, because once more the railway was to be held up until a major bridge could be built over Prairie Creek. While normally the creek carries an insignificant flow of water, its canyon required a steel span 800 feet long.

The population before had consisted of a few people around Gregg's ranch and store a mile or so from the mouth of the creek. Now what the old-timers called "the new town" was springing up on the east bank of the creek immediately above where the contractors had started work on the bridge. Several log houses had been built, Fred Hood had put up a large store, Charlie Prine had run up a hotel and Sam Kushner was operating another store. Several large feed barns were in evidence and Fred Brewster operated his freight teams and packing business from his office and barn.

Down by the river the Grand Trunk contractors had built a long log hospital, divided into two wards each containing fifteen beds. Dr Shillabeer was in charge, and his hands were soon full, for typhoid fever was rampant. For a while the hospital overflow had to be housed in tents. In spite of a good physician and a hospital that for the time was very modern, the disease caused several deaths. During the worst of the epidemic he was assisted by Dr Richardson, whose normal duties consisted of patrolling the railroad grade on his horse and ministering to patients along it. Construction work continued farther west, and Dr Richardson had to care for the ill and injured in some fifty camps scattered for ninety miles from Wolf Creek to Jasper House.

Fortunately for Shand he was preceded at Prairie Creek by Inspector Tucker, Constable Nitchie Thorne and other police who had recently moved from Wolf Creek. Their arrival had a discouraging effect upon one gentleman who had built a comfortable little shack. Since his liquor business required the utmost privacy and since Inspector Tucker had located his detachment right across the street from him, he very quickly abandoned his shack and moved on. This was all to the good for Shand, who arranged to take over the new shack – the first one in Canada in which he had a proprietary interest. Previously he had spent the winter in a tent. His friend Thomas Monaghan had a shack nearby, and the winter of 1910–1911 was cheerful for both of them.

One day a string of pack horses drew in from the west, with some of Shand's old base line survey friends who had finished another season's work and were on their way to Edmonton. One of their horses, a good-looking mare, was thin and bedraggled, and her hoofs had been badly worn down by the summer's work on the mountain rocks. The surveyors decided that she could not complete the trip; since she bore a government brand and therefore could not be sold, they abandoned her in the hope that she would pick up on the neighbouring good pasture. Shand looked her over very carefully and decided that she was fundamentally a good horse, so he let her rest a couple of days and then took her over and turned her in with his other horses and with Jack Gregg's new stallion.

Next year she presented him with a colt which he went over to look at, promptly named Kate, and then as promptly forgot.

In this offhand manner Kate, who was to serve him till her death thirty-one years later, was added to his possessions.

Only one incident threatened to mar the winter's tranquillity. The shack's former owner asked Shand if he would have any occasion to store anything in the cellar. Shand replied that he had been in the habit of carrying all his worldly goods in the pack on his horse, and he had nothing to store.

"That's good. Got a few things stored down there. I'll come and get them later on," said the erstwhile bootlegger in one of those verbal exchanges where more is conveyed by what is left unsaid than what is spoken. "If you hear a noise some night, it'll be me."

Shand, never one to inquire into another's affairs or to run around telling all he knew, let it go at that.

Two or three weeks later, during a dark night when a lusty fall of snow shut out any possibility of moonlight, he awoke to hear a gentle scraping at the small rear cellar window. "Oh, oh," he thought, continuing to enjoy the warm comfort of his blankets. After a while the grunting and puffing below him ceased and he slept soundly till the morning. When the smoke rose from his stovepipe Inspector Tucker, very grave of mien, knocked at the door.

"What went on here last night?" he demanded.

"I don't know. What?" replied Shand.

"Who made the sleigh tracks behind your shack?"

"I haven't been out the door yet this morning, so I haven't seen any tracks."

"Well, didn't you hear any noise last night?"

"Not a thing – have a mug of tea."

The Mountie grinned. "Glad to," he said, and the matter was dropped.

Problems other than bootlegging occupied the attention of the Mounties that winter – problems which, by a long and honourable tradition extending back to 1874, they enjoyed solving. These involved dealing with the natives, who felt that of all white people the missionaries, the Hudson's Bay traders and the Mounties were the only ones who could always be trusted to deal fairly. Shortly after Shand returned to Prairie Creek he too became involved in helping the natives. By this time he had won their respect and open friendliness. A man's intolerance for other peoples and races – for "foreigners" – is usually inversely proportional to the breadth of his education. As a man's outlook broadens, he is not so positive that his religion or nationality is superior to all others, or that differing skin pigments denote degrees of worthiness. Shand felt no need to refer to his fellow men as damned Dagoes, bloody Bohunks, Chinks, Niggers or Nitchies.

At this time Vincent Wanyandi was camped some thirty miles north of Prairie Creek on the flats at the junction of Jarvis Creek and the Wildhay River. There, where they had ample pasture for their horses, he and a small group of neighbours and relatives tended their trap lines, which radiated out for miles north and west. Hay meadows and flats were favourite camping grounds all down the Wildhay, each succeeding one being on the opposite bank from the last. The Indians held a special place in their hearts for the Wildhay River, calling it manito-ca-pim-bi-it – the river which the Manito straddled as he strode along down it. The meadows, of course, occurred where each of his footsteps flattened out the earth, and there rich and succulent grasses sprang up – grasses that through the long winters nourished their pack ponies.

Vincent Wanyandi was by that time the only full-blooded Indian in the Smoky River country, and proud of this distinction. Though he could not speak English, he was the recognized leader of the natives in the area. There was some mild rivalry between him and Ewan Moberly for this claim to leadership, which was on a strictly informal basis, yet it was nevertheless clearly understood even by the Moberlys. All white men who were well acquainted with the natives recognized his leadership and dealt with Vincent on that footing. Shand developed a similar respect for the tall, open-countenanced, soft-spoken Indian and soon placed implicit trust in his integrity and absolute honesty.

Towards the end of March 1911, Vincent came into Prairie Creek to report the disappearance of his son Sam, who shortly before had gone out on one of his customary trips around his trap line and had not returned. Vincent asked Shand to go to the Mounted Police barracks to interpret for him. After the story was told, Constable Thorne, who later became well known in Alberta as Nitchie Thorne and who could talk and understand a little Cree, was detailed to return with Vincent to investigate. There was some reason to suspect that Sam had been the victim of foul play. His trap line extended north and east of Vincent's camp and at one point passed perilously close to the edge of the terrritory claimed by the Sturgeon Lake Crees – and there was no love lost between them and their neighbours to the south and west.

For days Nitchie and Vincent searched the area adjacent to the trap line but a fresh fall of snow blotted out much possibility of tracking. All they ever found was Sam's tea pail at one of his camps beyond the Berland River. Travelling was difficult as the snow was melting and the ice of the rivers had become unsafe. It appeared probable that Sam must have broken through the rotten ice on some river and been washed down under a log jam. In the spring when the rivers broke up, a further search was made for his body, but without result. His disappearance remained a mystery tinged with a suspicion of murder.

Gradually Shand became dissatisfied with his shack on the hillside above the railway bridge in the booming town of Prairie Creek. The bustle of a construction town at last became too much for him, so he moved over to the side hill above Jack Gregg's house and put up his tent. His landlord, rich from the money paid him for his coal interests, had just completed the big, white two-storied house which is still a landmark on the left side of the highway going west from Hinton. There with his wife Mary and her two daughters by a former marriage he lived in affluence and comfort. The two daughters, Lucy and Alice, were practically grown to women's estate, but they had never owned any store-bought clothes. Jack decided that the time had come to dress them up, and for days the big new house was filled with discussion of the clothes for which they planned to send to the T. Eaton Company. But, while it is one thing to study the illustrations in the catalogue, it is a far different matter to make head or tail of the text if no one in the house can read. Furthermore, the problem of filling in the correct descriptions on the order form, especially those involving various measurements, becomes complicated if one cannot write.

In the end Jack sent for Shand to measure the well-developed girls and to translate lengths and ample girths into figures filled in on the order form. The choice of styles was left to Mary and her girls, but Shand exerted his influence to toning down the more vivid colours into ones more acceptable to his taste. Finally, amid giggles and happy laughter, the measurements were taken and transferred to paper, and the long wait for delivery of the dresses began. After several weeks the parcel finally arrived from Eaton's at Winnipeg, and the happy girls decked themselves in their fine new clothes. Fortunately someone was on hand to take their picture, which is now one of Shand's dear possessions.

Civilization was reaching into the foothills, and the Gregg girls rode around by Shand's tent one day all agog over a new wonder that had worked West.

"It's a funny little thing," said Lucy. "The men have got it in the room where the man cuts hair."

"It's small – about the size of a mink only taller," said Alice.

"It's kinda' like a lynx, but it isn't one."

"And it holds its tail straight up and walks around rubbing against the men's legs."

"Nobody out here has ever caught one like it. What is it?"

"Oh," laughed Shand, "haven't you ever seen one before? It's a cat. People keep them like you do dogs, only they're no good for anything and never work."

"Then why do they keep them?" asked Lucy. "Do they eat them?"

"Heavens, no!" exclaimed Shand, and he was hard put to it to explain why white people do keep cats.

Pleasant as it may have been for Shand to live practically in the Gregg family circle, he was not long in setting out on another trip. In May he heard that there was a shortage of flour and other necessities at Tête Jaune Cache. A store was under construction there, but that did nothing to relieve the current shortage, so Shand and his friend Fred Kvass, a trapper from what today's maps call Kvass Flats on the upper Smoky River, decided to take in a load of supplies. They sent an order to Edmonton, and before long it arrived by train and freight wagon at Prairie Creek. Then, with two saddle horses and twelve loaded pack horses, the two men set out. Within minutes of their arrival at Tête Jaune Cache they sold every vestige of their supplies for double what they had cost laid down at Prairie Creek, and the purchasers were delighted to get them so cheap.

The trip west to Tête Jaune Cache and returning through the balmy air of May was delightful, even if uneventful. Furthermore, as Shand says, they returned with "the horses in good shape – no accidents." For it was always the horses that he thought about – the horses that at his bidding waded icy creeks, swam spring freshets, clambered over sliding scree or leapt logs in the windfalls, and trusted his leadership. A trip was successful if his horses returned in good shape.

"One night on our way out to Tête Jaune Cache," he reminisced, "we were camped by a little brook which was just beginning to trickle west, within yards of the summit of Yellowhead Pass. Fred, who was strolling about, called out to me.

" 'Come 'ere, Shand, and look at this tree.'

"I went over and saw that a good big fir tree had been blazed long ago – forty years before, in fact.

" 'It's sure a lot older than the trees the Grand Trunk surveyors blazed,' said Fred.

"It was still fairly easy to make out if you paid attention to it," said Shand. "It was right at the summit. Under a layer of gum I could make out the initials CPR and some figures reading 3700 or something like that. I don't remember exactly. Must have been blazed by one of Walter Moberly's party.

" 'It's a blaze left by the CPR, about 1872,' I explained.

" 'Guess I should've known that,' said Fred. But you know, Shand, I'll never take any prize for brains. I'll never be sure I have any till I see them.' "

"You know," said Shand, as he and Billy Magee and I sat talking, "Fred Kvass had plenty of brains. He was a smart trapper and a good woodsman, but I guess he couldn't have gone very far in school."

"Reminds me of the story old Bill Todd used to tell on himself," said Billy. "You remember him, Shand."

"Ummm," said Shand.

"He had never had much schoolin'," continued Billy. "He used to say that one evening the teacher came around and told his dad that he was promoting him to Grade Two. Next morning he got into trouble. 'You see,' he used to say, 'I was so damned excited I forgot to shave that morning.' "

Back at Gregg's ranch, surveyors, packers and freighters came and went. So did the natives from the Smoky River country coming in to get supplies. By this time Shand knew all the outstanding figures whose trap lines lay far back in the hinterland. One by one they came to know and to respect him. He was closest to Adam Joachim, the Iroquois whose education for the priesthood had been interrupted and who thereafter remained with his people far out on the remote river flats. Between these two a deep understanding developed.

The previous spring Adam Joachim had taken part in the great exodus led by Ewan Moberly when the natives moved from Jasper Park to the old Wanyandi lands in the vicinity of Grande Cache Lake on the upper Smoky. Now, a year later when he visited Prairie Creek, his house at Grande Cache was still not finished. So Shand saddled his horses again and set out with him to spend a few weeks completing the house. While snow still lay on the higher ridges, the trees shone in all the freshness of spring. Marsh marigolds glowed in the low places, and out of the water surrounding them a multitude of frogs greeted the new season with a wide range of bubbling, croaking, and occasional bell-like notes. In all the open glades green grass seemed to thrust itself up, even as one watched, while already the vetch family was represented by clumps of bean-like flowers, deep yellow, butter yellow and purple.

The long rolling ridges were mostly covered with a thick stand of pines, but at their top a few balsam displayed their spring array of frond-like needles. Lower down, forming a transition from the pines above to the black spruce and tamarack of the muskegs, grew white spruce, the largest trees of the Smoky River forest. A few of them, which appeared to have escaped the congested stands, stood as massive individuals in relative isolation bordering the clear-bottomed streams.

The flat lands showed evidence of repeated outbreaks of fire. Adam explained that these had been deliberately set by the natives to burn off the poplars and willows that threatened to encroach on their pasture areas. The river flats were lush in grass, but Adam assured Shand that if they did not kill the brush by periodic fires, the forest would quickly reclaim these meadows. For the richest soil was on these alluvial flats, and in ten years, if nature were left to take its course, this soil would support a rich growth of willows, and these, in fifty years, would be replaced by a stand of white spruce timber.

When they crossed the Berland, Adam told Shand tales of this area. He had been born on its banks, and a few miles upstream was the grave of his mother.

Travelling some fifteen miles a day through forests clad in the fresh raiment of spring, camping at night beside the murmur of busy brooks, the pair in a few days completed the trip of nearly one hundred miles to the verdant meadows of the Grande Cache. All along the way they camped in flats and in meadows, but while some of these were large and all were fair, the extent of rich soil in the valley of the Smoky at Grande Cache came as a surprise to Shand.

Of all his trips during the last five years, this excursion with an educated Indian companion of fine sensibility who, like his fathers before him, knew intimately every brook of his ancestral home and who seemed to anticipate his friend's unspoken request for more details of its story – to Shand this trip through the freshness of the foothills in spring was most memorable. Ostensibly he and Adam were going in to build a cabin. But even to Shand, who was accustomed to trips long and short, this was actually a holiday jaunt as the horses carried them towards each distant blue ridge, which when breasted revealed verdant valleys below and the blueness of more ridges beyond.

In due course the cabin was finished and Shand and his horses returned to Prairie Creek. For months at a time he had been used to living in a tent or camping in the open. Meanwhile he had been observing the Indians in their teepees and comparing these homes with the white man's tents. In those days all the Indians used teepees, and Shand soon came to recognize the superiority of the teepee over the tent for anyone leading a nomadic type of life. In the forest, teepee poles could be cut at a moment's notice, but this was not necessary if one frequented the main camping grounds. Nobody breaking camp ever took the poles along with him, so they were left standing and ready to be used by the next camper. Teepee poles, like so many other facets of life in the forest, were covered by an unwritten law – anyone could use them, but on no account must they be cut up for firewood.

The teepee was equal to the tent in the ease and speed with which it could be erected, but far surpassed it in the convenience of its heating arrangement. The teepee, unlike the tent, had its own built-in chimney. In fact it was all chimney : an open fire could be built at its centre and the smoke would rise and pass out of the opening at the top. Moreover, this opening was adjustable to suit the direction of the wind. With a tent, the fire had to be built outdoors, and in rainy weather or in the depth of winter this was of little use. If heat was needed in a tent, its owner had to carry a stove along, as well as several lengths of stovepipe. If heat was needed in a teepee, one merely lit a fire on the floor and sat around it to cook or relax.

Shand set about getting a teepee and learning to pitch it, and again he learned some more of the unwritten laws of the Indian world. He asked Dolphus Moberly, the superb native packer, to show him the tricks of erecting it. To his amazement, Dolphus merely looked at him and walked away. He followed Dolphus and asked him again, only to receive the scornful reply : "Ask a woman."

Not till then did he realize that he had insulted Dolphus by implying that he knew how to do a woman's work. Women were considered inferior beings, capable only of caring for men and cooking, of carrying loads and doing other menial work. The code of the Indians was very rigid. Women's status was clearly defined and their duties definitely delineated. They knew their place in the order of things and remained in their place. Doing that, they were loved and respected as mothers, wives and helpmates – perhaps cherished all the more for their careful compliance with custom. Cowards and weaklings might be punished by being banned from male society and thus from man's estate and set to do the work of a woman. But to suggest that a man do a woman's task was to offer him a grave offence. Accordingly Shand discussed the problem with some of the women.

"How much canvas will I need?" he had asked, and after a brief pause they announced that he should buy sixty yards of duck.

"The first chance I got, I went over and bought that much and handed it over. When you get sixty yards of white duck spread out, it seems to cover most of the hillside, but in no time at all half a dozen women went at it with scissors and needles. They enjoyed themselves, laughing and talking. Some of them held the canvas, others cut it up. They didn't use any patterns or anything – just started cutting here and curved around to there. Then they started sewing, and almost before I knew it there was my teepee."

Shand acquired the teepee because of its efficiency and simplicity. For a wandering packer and trapper this was a practical step to take. While he probably did not realize it at the time, it was a symbolic step – the step from a white man's dwelling to a teepee.

BY the spring of 1911 Shand looked upon himself as a seasoned packer and guide. During the last few years he had travelled the Edmonton–Tête Jaune Cache trail many times. His many side trips had taken him from the Brazeau River to the Smoky River and from the Swan Hills to Mount Robson, and to many localities within the far-flung boundaries embracing these points. His services had always been in demand, so that he was constantly on the move – constantly enjoying the anticipation he always felt each time he set out for another destination whether or not he had been there before. For in travelling he found some indefinable satisfaction. Every trail was enticing and every new one enchanting. The charm lay not alone in the witchery of the woods and the seductiveness of secluded valleys, but in the very action of travelling.

After spending a few weeks at Prairie Creek, it was only natural then that at the slightest excuse he set out once more for Lac Ste Anne on what was to prove his last trip there with horses. Supplies and merchandise were now being delivered by the railway to the new station of Hinton (Mile 65) three miles east of Prairie Creek. Since this was practically outside his door, taking a pack train to Lac Ste Anne was more sentimental than essential.

On his trip east he was amazed by the rapid progress in the infant communities springing into life along the new railway. Edson had changed the most. Even its name had changed, or rather was in the throes of changing.

"I thought the post office here was called Heatherwood," Shand said to one of the merchants.

"Well, it is and it isn't. I just got here two months ago, so it don't matter to me, but some of the real old-timers – homesteaders who came in here as much as a year ago – are pretty hot about it. They're sticking by Heatherwood.

"The railway says it's Edson – after Edson J. Chamberlain, one of their big nobs, and they've painted that name on the station. The station agent says he don't care a continental damn what name we put on our mail. To the Grand Trunk, he says, this is Edson. And if we want goods shipped here, they're to be billed to Edson. The Grand Trunk looks after its own mail and doesn't use the post office, so it's Edson to them but he don't care what we call the town."

"Well, there's a big argument goin' on," chipped in a bystander, "between the boys headin' up the post office department in Ottaway and the people here who want to call it Edson, so them boys call it Heatherwood. Seems they's already a post office in Alberta named Edison and Ottaway says the mail will get mixed up."

"That's odd," said Shand. "I homesteaded in Edison five years ago and *they* had quite a battle there too over naming the post office."

The name of the town might still be up in the air, but the town itself, although only six months old, showed every sign of having its feet solidly on the ground. The station and roundhouse had been built and many thousands of feet of siding tracks were balanced precariously on top of the muskeg, which had been shorn of trees for a large area. The main street running north up the hill from the station had been cleared out for two or three blocks, and already many pretentious stores opened on to the uneven wooden sidewalks. H. A. Switzer had opened a drug store, W. H. Jellis was in business as a hardware and lumber merchant, and Spanner Brothers' general store vied with that of M. Schwartz in attracting trade. There were stores specializing in men's wear, liquor, shoes and groceries, as well as the inevitable real estate offices. The population was about five hundred, and steps were under way to secure incorporation as a town. The Merchants' Bank was open, and plans were going ahead to build a two-room school.

Perhaps what interested Shand most was the new Grande Prairie trail. When the Grand Trunk reached Edson in 1910, it touched off a stampede of settlers who struck out for more than two hundred miles through the untrod wilderness towards Grande Prairie. The customary summer route, by way of Lesser Slave

Lake, was five hundred miles long, but in winter it could be reduced to four hundred by using the Sturgeon Lake cut-off. In a straight line the distance from Edson to the hamlet of Grande Prairie was only one hundred and ten miles.

Shand's old friend A. H. McQuarrie had spent the winter in charge of crews cutting a road through from Edson to Grande Prairie. Under his direction, ferries had been placed on the Athabasca, Little Smoky and across the Big Smoky at Bezanson, so that settlers bound for the Grande Prairie country could go in by this short-cut. This road started out at Edson and ran north and west till at Mile 53 it crossed the Athabasca River upstream from the mouth of the Berland River. In a few miles it crossed the Berland, then, after crossing the height of land, it kept in the vicinity of the Little Smoky River for many miles and finally emerged at Sturgeon Lake, where it intersected the winter trail from Lesser Slave Lake to Grande Prairie. This was the only road cut out through the Smoky River country that was passable for wheeled vehicles. Hundreds of settlers used this trail during the winter when all signs of muskeg and mud holes were buried under a foot of snow, and a great many hardy pioneers travelled it in summer as well.

After leaving Edson on his way to Lac Ste Anne, Shand and his horses took the tote road. Only a year before it had crawled with teams, but it was idle now and lonely in its idleness. All about was the evidence of the frantic activity of the year before. The remains of construction camps were shown by large clearings in the bush, dotted with abandoned shacks and barns, roofless now and with staring window and door openings, while all around lay piles of tin cans and other refuse. The depressing sight of Wolf Creek bore heavily on Shand. Here, for more than a mile along the track, were the deserted remnants of last year's boom town. Once the bridges had been completed and the steel moved westward, every living soul of the erstwhile town of two thousand people – except for three people – had moved on with it. Shand was glad to hurry along towards Lac Ste Anne, leaving the three residents of Wolf Creek to their gruesome enjoyment of the remnants of a town that might have been.

While at Lac Ste Anne, Shand undertook to act as guide for another mountaineering expedition. So in July he headed west once more. By this time the Canadian Northern surveyors were working west of Entwistle. Shand shook his head at the folly and the unbridled competition that resulted in building two transcontinental lines where there was not enough freight to make even one pay. For thirty miles west of the Magnolia trestle on the Grand Trunk, the surveys indicated that the two railway tracks would be right side by side, or at most a mere stone's throw apart. In the next forty miles they would never be more than six miles apart. And Shand could have guesssed that for the remaining 160 miles, till the two railways diverged after crossing the Yellowhead Pass, the two sets of tracks would be practically on top of each other. What useless folly, he thought, to permit the building of two rival lines side by side through difficult terrain in an area nearly worthless from an agricultural point of view, when the Peace River country was crying out for a railway.

Shand hastened on towards Swift's ranch to meet the party he was to guide to Mount Robson. It consisted of a mountain-climbing group headed by the Reverend G. B. Kinney, already famous for his previous climbs, with Conrad Kain, an Austrian mountain guide, as well as a party collecting mammal skins for the Smithsonian Institution, and headed by Captain O. A. Wheeler, Harry Blagdon and Charlie Walcott. Don "Curly" Phillips had outfitted the lot, while Byron Harmon, the famous Banff photographer, came along. Since Shand had been to Mount Robson two years earlier with the Amery-Mumm party, he was to guide this one in over the Moose River Trail, which left the railway grade near Moose Lake, some fifteen miles west of Yellowhead Pass.

Mount Robson was approached by going around its east side and crossing the Divide from Moose River to Calumet Creek, west of the uppermost tributaries of the Smoky. This approach, as Shand said, amounted to getting in behind it. The weather was good and the trip uneventful, except that one of his horses broke a leg amongst the rocks at the top of Moose Pass and had to be shot. "All the way along," says Shand, "the Smithsonian party exclaimed in glee as its members scurried about catching the various rodents that lived in the apparently inhospitable clefts in the rocks. What with picas, coneys and marmots, shrews, moles and voles, they fairly made my head swim trying to distinguish one from the other."

When they all returned to Swift's hospitality a few of them wished to see Maligne Lake, so Shand took them through Prairie de la Vache and over Shovel Pass. They were among the first intrepid white souls ever to see the lake. These early pioneers on Maligne Lake were a select few which included Mrs Mary Schäffer, who had seen it in 1908, and H. A. F. McLeod, who in the course of his duties as a CPR surveyor had visited it in 1875, when it was known to the natives as Sore Foot Lake – perhaps the first white man ever to do so.

On their return from Maligne Lake some of Shand's party went south to Banff, under the guidance of Curly Phillips, who took them along the route that we know today as the Jasper–Lake Louise highway. The rest of the party returned to Edmonton by work train, for by this time the Grand Trunk rails had swept on past Swift's place to the new town of Fitzhugh (Mile 111), which before long was renamed Jasper.

"You know," said Shand, "I always admired the Reverend Mr Kinney, and was sorry that he failed to reach the top of Mount Robson in 1909. It was such a narrow margin, and then he didn't have any elaborate party – came out all alone from Edmonton with five horses. Then met Curly Phillips and the two of them very nearly made it.

"By the way, he and Conrad Kain were the first to climb Pyramid Mountain in Jasper, while we were staying at Swift's in 1911."

"Wasn't it Kain," I asked, "who was with the party which did conquer Mount Robson in 1913?"

"That was McCarthy and Foster. Kain was an odd little cuss, but perhaps the greatest climbing guide and climber ever seen in Canada. I wasn't with that party, but they tell me Kain did a superb job going up, and finally the last stretch to the summit was a snow ridge. There Kain stood aside and said, 'Gentlemen, that's as far as I can take you.' And then he followed the other two the remaining few feet till all three of them stood on top – the first men to do so.

"He was just crazy about climbing mountains. One afternoon on that trip in 1911, when everyone else was resting, he set off alone and wasn't back by dark. We were all worried about him, but before breakfast he showed up and said that he had climbed Mount Whitehorn, which is five or six miles west of Mount Robson and something over eleven thousand feet high.

"Said he'd built a cairn on it and left a note in it. Now, everybody trusted him implicitly, but a story like that – going all alone and spending the night at some point on the way down – was hard to believe."

"Wasn't there some other party that climbed it a few years later?"

"Yes. Two years later, and they brought back Kain's tin can and his note.

"Kain," chuckled Shand, "may have known a lot about mountains but he sure got his eyes opened about construction camps. At Moose City, just this side of Moose Lake, he changed his clothes in the tent and slipped outside for a moment. When he came back the clothes he'd been wearing had been pinched."

"Conditions must have been pretty bad on the British Columbia side of the Yellowhead Pass," I suggested.

"They sure were. You see, the Mounted Police did not have jurisdiction there, and as soon as you crossed the line it seemed as if all hell had broken loose. The B.C. police were supposed to enforce the law, but they didn't show up."

"Before you go on, Shand, straighten me out about some of these camps and their mileages. I know Jasper was Mile 111. What were some of the others?"

"The summit was Mile 127, and at that point a new division started, so the numbering started from zero again. Mile 28 was the camp at the west end of Moose Lake, and Tête Jaune Cache was Mile 52.

"By the way," he continued, "Tête Jaune Pass is said to have been named after Jasper Hawse, who started Jasper House and was yellow-haired – tête jaune. I think if you check it up, you'll find that it was one of the Decoignes who was at Jasper House about 1820 who was yellow-headed. In any event, I believe the pass was named after him."

"By the way, did you know," I said, "that the Yellowhead Pass was also called the Leather Pass by the Hudson's Bay Company? Somewhat later they sent shipments of leather through it from

Fort Edmonton to the posts in the interior of British Columbia, where leather was scarce."

Shand went on to talk about conditions in the pass where, without police, the camps were wild. The only law was what each man took into his own hands. A bare hundred yards west of the summit – a hundred yards beyond the jurisdiction of the Mounted Police – a wide-open town had sprouted. There were the usual canvas-covered log shacks and general stores, and a Chinese restaurant. But, to Shand's surprise, in this little hamlet four saloons were operating without let or hindrance. There was more drunkenness in this one spot than he had seen in all the camps on the Alberta side put together. Sprawled around here and there were several drunks, sleeping it off.

No matter how bad or tough a town is, there is always some-one who, either because he can hold more liquor than the rest or because he drinks less, sets himself up as guardian of the drunks. At the summit was such a man who, joking all the time, laugh-ingly or cynically kept an eye on them. His job was to "roll them there corpses out of the trail so that the wagons kin pass," and he would intervene in the affairs of each new drunk and call on the bystanders to "lay him out there to one side so's he won't git stepped on." He did take the man's watch and any money he had and did not return them until the man came to.

The attribute of baldness seems to have been uncommonly high amongst bootleggers and other bad men in the camps. While stories get garbled with the passage of years, every Homeric incident involving these gentry is ascribed to a man named Baldy – Baldy Red, Baldy Robb, Baldy Yeoman or Baldy somebody else.

Shand recalls a Baldy Red whom he saw at Moose City. Baldy as usual was carrying a wad of money, and being well versed in the wickedness of camps, stepped into an establishment dis-pensing liquor and other pleasures. After a drink or two, he prudently gave his roll to the Madam for safe-keeping, while he went out to look over the camp to see what other delights or profits might come his way.

The town treated him royally, and it was late the next after-noon that he showed up at the Madam's requesting the return of his roll. She refused to give it up, claiming that he and some new-found friends had come in the evening before and drunk it up.

So Baldy set about demolishing her establishment. Sounds of battering, tearing and rending filled the air, interspersed with screams from the inmates and curses from the Madam. In the ensuing brawl she shot at Baldy. Her aim was poor and the shot winged an innocent man who ended up in the construction company's hospital.

Perhaps less drastic was Baldy's row with Dirty Mag. As Shand tells it:

"Baldy, I guess had been drinking and insisted that Dirty Mag set up a round of free drinks.

" 'Come on, Mag,' he said, 'for old times' sake.'

" 'Old times' sake don't pay no freight on booze,' replied Mag.

" 'Come on, Mag, you – –, set 'em up.'

"It grew to be quite an argument," says Shand, "and finally Mag chased him out – nearly threw him out. She was quite a woman.

" 'I'll show you,' said Baldy, 'I'll put you out of business.'

" 'You and how many more?' Mag flung over her shoulder as she went back into the tent.

"Baldy went away muttering to himself and headed for the barn. Presently he drove his team over and hitched them to the corner of Mag's place. Then, to show what the team could do, he eased them into their collars and gave the shack a preliminary jerk to show how nicely the whole caboodle could be pulled down. Then, as Baldy held the team but stood ready to urge them forward into a real lurch, Mag gave in to his repeated request."

Not all scrapes ended so easily. Not all shots ended merely in wounds. The camps in the pass had a dark reputation for every form of vice including murder by pistol shot or knife. Conditions were bad west of the summit, but bootlegging was not restricted to the British Columbia side. The police did not always catch all such Alberta gentry red-handed, but they did catch one at the bridge-building camp where the railway crossed the Athabasca within Jasper Park. Here one day the Mountie caught a French bootlegger. The Mountie and Maclaggan, the park superintendent, carried a load of bottles down on to the river, and smashed them one by one against the ice. That job completed, they strode up the bank and back to camp. But, while for a small space the whisky had spread over the ice, it eventually drained into a shallow depression. As the Mountie disappeared, Baldy Red, who had been an interested spectator, rushed down carrying a cup. Racing over to the little pool collected in the depression, he proceeded to dispense whisky to the small knot of bystanders at fifty cents a cupful.

After a few days at Swift's, Shand packed his horses and once more set out for Prairie Creek. Now that trains were running into Jasper Park, with tote roads all the way along and bridges over the streams, the trip was easy. It was no longer necessary to use the precarious old trail over Roche Miette, for now, where formerly the cliff had overhung the rushing torrent of the Athabasca, engineers with dynamite and steam shovels had scratched out a narrow toehold wide enough for two rails. Where not even a squirrel would have ventured to creep around the cliff, now trains and pack horses passed with ease.

This smooth way through and along the side of the sheer cliff had been won only at great expense and by great courage. For here engineers had to be let down from above with ropes fastened to a thick belt around their waists. While they worked, their fellows some eighty or a hundred feet above staunchly held the ropes. Here too men dangling from ropes had carried drills and dynamite so as to blast out a little notch above the swirling river torrent where other men could stand to tear out a wider gap.

This cut around the face of Roche Miette was only one of the difficult parts of the railway grade. An equally difficult though seemingly easy stretch of the line ran over the sand dunes on the east sides of Brulé and Jasper Lakes. The winds racing down the pass gain their full momentum as they sweep across the open expanse of these lakes, swirling a blast of sand before them, which day after day settles into sifting dunes on the east shores. Through these dunes the grade had to run, necessitating a cut of some 90,000 yards in one stretch and a fill of 120,000 yards a little farther along. But as fast as the cut was dug, the gales tried to fill it again. As fast as the fill was heaped up, the wind whipped it away. In the end, after much fruitless work, the contractor erected fences to break the force of the wind, and with brush and matting covered the exposed surfaces of the fill.

Bill Burns, an old-timer of the construction camps and of the north in general, often used to tell of his experiences here during the winter of 1910.

"For two days of each week terrible wind storms swept down the pass. The men working on this big sand cut could only average four days a week. Why, they couldn't see a rod ahead. Teams of horses freighting on the river would have to stop and take shelter in the woods. I remember when one man unhitched his team and the wind blew his sleighs and load four miles along the river ice.

"The first night that I landed at this camp about midnight one of those terrific storms blew up, and along about two o'clock in the morning I tried to turn over in bed. The wind had blown about three inches of snow and sand through the small cracks of the cabin logs, putting a heavy covering over the top of my bed. There were about a hundred men in the camp and we all had to sit up all night.

"The chore boy had not carried in enough wood for the whole night, so we set about cutting the bunks into firewood – it was so cold we couldn't keep warm at all. When morning finally came, not hearing the cook's breakfast horn at the usual time, and after waiting till about nine a.m., we all started for the cook camp. It was still dark, and we had to take hold of each other's hands in order to keep together and avoid losing any of our men in the darkness and storm. The benches at the table and the table itself with all its dishes were covered with about a foot of snow, and there was about three feet of snow and sand on the floor. The cook had mixed up a batch of bread dough and arranged it on boards over the cook stove. For protection from falling dirt from the sod roof, there was a thick layer of building paper nailed to the ceiling above the bread shelf. The snow had sifted in on this paper and the weight of it burst the paper through, covering the bread dough, bench and floor with a heavy covering of snow, sand and dirt. Those of us who could work at all set about with shovels. It took all of two hours, and in fact it was nearly noon before we got breakfast."

Shand, on his way home to Prairie Creek, was only a spectator at this struggle that had taken place with the shifting sands. When he reached there, he became a spectator at another struggle between man and the forces of nature. During the summer the parks department, to test the practicability of operating a small steamer on the upper Athabasca, had built a stern-wheeler at the mouth of Prairie Creek. She was ready for her trial run when Shand arrived. Jimmy Dunn, the park warden, was in charge of her and spent a busy hour or so while her fireman threw wood into her boiler. Clouds of black smoke belched in the air, and eventually the boiler began to hiss, and here and there spurts of steam escaped. All the residents of Prairie Creek lined the east shore of the stream to watch the experiment and to place bets upon her success or failure. Many prophesied that she could not stem the strong current of the Athabasca.

Finally, with a blast of her whistle, Jimmy ordered her moorings to be cast off, and the paddle wheel began to turn. Slowly she inched out into the little stream, churning the placid waters to foam, and Jimmy with a great display of confidence headed her for the stronger current of the Athabasca. She was making good headway as she thrust her snout into the rapid water, and her momentum carried her well out into the river. There, hollering for more steam, Jimmy turned her head towards the mountains. For a moment the issue was in doubt as she appeared to hesitate before the onslaught of the swirling waters. With Jimmy urging her and the fireman shoving in wood like mad, she began to crawl forward, but her boiler was too small and her engine too feeble. Her spirit was willing but her fireworks were weak. In the course of the afternoon she did make a mile or so up the river, but soon her fireman was exhausted and Jimmy had to swing her back downstream. The return trip to the mouth of Prairie Creek was a matter of minutes, and before Shand realized it she had sailed well by the little cove and was making record time heading downstream. She was beached near Hinton some miles below her launching site, and there she lay while volumes of correspondence passed between Jasper Park and Ottawa. In the end, she was taken down to Athabasca Landing and broken up. Only then did Ottawa begin to wonder why a steamer was necessary on the Athabasca when along this stretch of water for some fifty miles the Grand Trunk trains roared along one bank of the stream and the Canadian Northern surveyors were staking out a competing line on the other side.

The era of steamboats on the upper Athabasca lasted for one afternoon.

No sooner had Shand got over the excitement of the steamer than his knowledge of horses was put to work at another task. Over a hundred miles south and east of Prairie Creek the forestry branch of the Department of Interior was using a large batch of horses on the Clearwater Reserve. Fearing that they might not fare well on the forage there, the branch sent them up to the Athabasca River pastures for the winter. As Shand arrived at Prairie Creek from the west, these horses arrived from the south, and to him fell the task of taking them back into the pass to winter on the rich grasses at the mouth of Moosehorn Creek inside the outer range of the Rockies. There they wintered well, and the next spring found them all fat and frisky when Shand set out with them for the long trek back to Rocky Mountain House on the Saskatchewan River. Having delivered them, he returned to Hinton in style, for he caught a ride on a wagon from Rocky Mountain House to Bowden. There he caught the Canadian Pacific train to Edmonton, and thence sped along the old trails as a passenger on the Grand Trunk to Hinton.

The train trip and all it meant to the new country from Edmonton west gave him plenty to think about on his way home. As he says, the railway had replaced the pack pony. For five or six years now he and his horses had poked into many an unknown valley, had pressed across the summit of many a pass and at night had bedded along the banks of many a creek. Every trip had been taken with some definite purpose aimed at opening up the country. Each trip had been to study a coal seam, to look over a timber berth, to run a survey line, or to take scientists out to explore. Now that trains had penetrated the heart of the mountains and were already puffing their way towards the coal seams of the Coal Branch, there was less need for packers, and many of them were without work. Some, like Fred Brewster, were setting up organizations geared to taking tourists to see the beauty spots of the mountains, and a few of them would undoubtedly wax rich in this business. For Shand, however, the values he enjoyed had been taken out of the old way of life. Packing from here on would be at the whim of tourists, and he felt no desire to be at their beck and call.

His longing for the old trails and for the solitude of the trickling stream was as great as ever – perhaps even greater. He decided to find some other work so as to make his home in this area in the shadow of Roche Miette. Here where the chinook wind eased the winter snows, here where orange tiger lilies made the summers merry, here in the pine-scented solitudes he would stay.

Even though trains roared through Hinton, the beautiful Smoky River country seemed safe from harm. First of all, the Athabasca itself, a formidable barrier, prevented easy access. As Shand stood at Prairie Creek and looked north over the river, the forested hillside rising gradually from the valley to the long crest at the skyline seemed another protective buttress against the onslaught of the white man. Beyond that crest the land fell away to the broad valley of the Berland River. Beyond that it rolled away into other ridges and other rivers – the Muskeg, the Simonette, the Little Smoky and the Big Smoky. For the time being at least, this vast region seemed safe from civilization.

Moreover the federal government, which owned all the vacant land, had set up the Athabasca Forest Reserve and was starting to take active steps to save its timber from destruction. And it needed men to take over the duties of ranging the forest. The science of forestry was then in its infancy, but for a start the government needed men with a knowledge of the ways of the forest and a love of it for its own sake – for its beauty, its silences, its solitude, and for the infinite variety of growing plants that carpeted its lush meadows and its far blue hills. It needed self-reliant men who could take two or three pack horses and disappear into the wilderness in the spring, not to return perhaps till fall. It needed men who could live off the forest and who could gain the respect of the sparsely scattered natives, who for generations had made it their home.

A forest ranger's life suited Shand exactly. He had the necessary qualifications and could travel anywhere in the bush for any length of time. The period of employment was for the months of spring, summer and fall. During the winter he would be free to trap or to loaf, whichever suited his mood, and then, with the coming of spring, he could resume his ranger's work for another season. So in the spring of 1912 he was not long in accepting the offer to be the ranger in the Rock Lake–Grande Cache district, which embraced an area of some 4000 square miles.

The forest ranger was also expected to accept appointment as a game warden, but Shand refused to take on this office. He was well known to the natives and understood their way of life. They had to kill game out of season, it was part of their economy, and he refused to spy on them.

"I can't go amongst them and seek their help in protecting the country from forest fires and in showing me the various trails through all this area if they know I'm also a game guardian," he explained.

There were then no forestry cabins and no recognized forestry trails. Shand's job consisted of setting off with three or four of his ponies to familiarize himself with the country. In addition, he was to meet the natives and to explain to them the purposes of the new reserves – to preserve the forest from fire, which would be to the benefit of all men, white or red. The natives readily accepted the idea and cooperated. At the end of the summer's work Shand was expected to come in with notes and sketches showing the best pack routes in his wide wilderness. His notes showed not only the shortest trail but, perhaps more important, a trail such that at the end of each day's travel of five or six hours – every twelve or fifteen miles – pack horses could come to a good pasture for the night. From these notes the forestry department would compile maps which, as the years went by, would show a complete set of trails crisscrossing the area. During subsequent years these trails would be cut out to make them more useful for the rapid transport of supplies or of men who might be called upon to fight fires.

Shand spent a busy, happy summer, enjoying the thrill of exploring new valleys and being paid to do just what he wanted to do anyway. Amongst other duties, he had to post fire notices.

"They were signs about a foot high, printed on cloth," Shand explains. "I tacked these to the trees and they warned everyone of the dangers of being careless with fire. They also served as guide posts along the route of the pack trail. When I was told about putting them up, I suggested that since ninety-nine per cent of the people who would see them would speak Cree, the signs should give their message in that language. The authorities let me send to St Albert to get a hundred printed in Cree syllabics. The signs were colourful with large red and black letters – most attractive. When they came I tacked them to the trees.

"Next year when I went my rounds, every single sign was missing. Obviously someone had taken them down, but I couldn't see why – the people had been co-operative. I couldn't understand it till I met some natives and went to their shacks to eat. There in each cabin was one of my pretty red and black signs decorating the wall. I began to bawl them out for taking them down, and they listened with grave faces. Without any change in expression, except for a twinkle about their eyes, they explained why they had brought them home.

" 'Who lights the cooking fires and tends them?' they asked.

" 'The women,' I said.

" 'How many will see these signs nailed to trees? The women will never see them there. So we brought them home where they could see and read them.'

"Anyway," mused Shand, "even if their answers were more specious than sincere, the red and black signs did brighten the walls of the shacks. Next year I ordered another hundred just like them."

In the summer of 1912 Joe Errington and a small party, which included his wife, went out to stake claims on the north fork of the Wildhay. Errington already controlled the Blue Diamond Coal Company which was even then starting to open up its mine at Brulé. Tommy Groat, who a year or so before had married one of Ewan Moberly's daughters, was their guide. He too brought his wife and baby but took them over to live with the Moberlys at Grande Cache.

In the fall of 1912 John McVicar, a mining engineer, brought in several men to study the Hoppe Coal Claims on the Smoky. They worked away all winter. Donald Macdonald and the Round brothers took the contract for hauling supplies from Hinton to this party from time to time. Donald at that time cut out the first winter road from Prairie Creek to the claims.

When McVicar and his party were ready to go into the coal claims, Shand's summer's work was drawing to a close. The fall came on in its usual glow of golden magnificence, and all too soon snow fell on the summits of the trails. Shand turned his pack horses south again and headed for Prairie Creek.

A morning or two later, as he went down the trail to the Athabasca, the land was white. Everything, trees and trail, logs and bushes, was covered by fresh snow, and spruce branches sagged under their load. Then, of a sudden, the sun surmounted the bank of clouds to the east and flooded valley and foothills with a blaze of light. From every point of the compass, like so many diamonds, a million snow crystals shivered and scintillated. Far beyond Roche Miette the whole range of mighty peaks dazzled like a vast chain of jewels.

Shand, riding along, was reminded of the story of the prodigal son who, for several years, while his brothers had toiled at bench, counter and counting-house, had wandered off to the West. Returning east, broke, his father had pointed to the money his prudent brethren had saved, and said, "What profits have you to show for so many years of wandering?" And the wanderer had replied, summing up riches beyond the capacity of fat purses, "I have seen the Rocky Mountains."

That night Shand turned his horses out to graze on the Maskuta – Prairie Creek. Far to the west, silhouetted against the red sunset, stood Roche Miette.

CHAPTER
TWELVE

━━◆❋◆━━

SHAND spent a few fall days enjoying the hospitality of civilization. The old construction town of Prairie Creek had been completely abandoned and was a sorry-looking mess. Its place had been taken by the new railway town of Hinton three miles east which, because a coal mine was to be opened up there, was coming into some prominence. At the same time he prepared for the season's trapping. This year he planned to winter on the Smoky. Several of the old-time packers, all friends of his, were also going out to trap some part of the vast area well back from the Athabasca. Tom Monaghan and Fred Kvass were heading for favourite spots on the Smoky River. Montana Pete, who had filed on a homestead across the river from Prairie Creek, intended to trap many miles north and east.

Shand had done some trapping in previous years, but this was the first time he proposed to set out by himself for a whole winter. He took particular care in assembling his outfit and in selecting his supplies. It would be a very serious situation if he got settled down in his trapping cabin only to find that some important item had been forgotten So bright and early one morning he appeared at the store in Hinton with a carefully compiled list of his winter's requirements. The various articles of his grubstake, such as beans, tea and so on, he put into little canvas bags – the paper bags and other wrappings the storekeeper used would not last long on the journey back to the bush. The ponies, in threading their way along the pack trail, often bumped their packs against trees and stumps. In crossing a river the packs were frequently submerged and the canvas helped to keep the supplies dry. Moreover, if a number of paper bags burst, his groceries would end up as a hopeless mixture of salt and sugar, tea and tobacco.

Having bought his grubstake, he rounded up his ponies, put on their packs and cinched them up with the diamond hitch.

Then he rode over to the store, shook hands all around, and with a casual "So long" he set out. One of the features of these trips was the casualness of the departure. No one, least of all the trapper, gave more than a passing thought to the fact that he was leaving for six months or more and that during that time he might not see another soul. Then, as Shand says, "The following spring the trapper would arrive suddenly, all unannounced and unconcerned as if he had only left the previous week."

Shand and his horses set out down the hill to the ford across the Athabasca, and before long were climbing the long rise over the first ridge. All day long they had the trail to themselves, but there was no feeling of loneliness. While the leaves were off the trees and the glory of fall had passed, the woods were not lonesome. Here a squirrel challenged from a tree overhead. There a bush partridge clucked nervously, its feet pattering on the thick carpet of leaves until, becoming alarmed, it exploded into flight and went whirring off, skimming around the trees and finally disappearing from sight. Here and there a marmot sunned himself on an upturned root, or a weasel crossed the trail in a series of flashing, curving leaps, busy in his endless pursuit of food. Farther on, a hawk sat watching from a treetop or soared effortlessly overhead, now and then emitting its piercing scream. The forest was not lonely.

Shand, on this his first trip of the season, was also too busy to be lonesome. The ponies and their packs were not yet used to each other. Some of the saddles pinched. Some of the horses' backs were a little soft, and one or two of them tried to buck off their packs. All this caused minor delays, and neither he nor the horses were sorry when eight miles out they came to a camping spot. As always, this first day's trip was short. Trapper and horses were a team, and when the camp ground was reached some of the horses which had been over the trail before showed signs of recognizing it and would even walk over to the spot where earlier in the year they had been unpacked. There they waited patiently to have their packs and saddles taken off.

When the horses were rolling in the grass, Shand began to fix up his camp and get supper. At this point the inevitable pair of whisky-jacks arrived to keep him company and to see what tidbits they might pick up. Then, after a smoke and a rest, he piled up the saddles, checked them over for any damage that might need repairs, and finally covered them carefully with canvas pack covers to keep saddles and supplies dry during the night. Then he checked over the horses' backs, to be sure the loads were not hurting them and that no sores were starting. Each horse had its own saddle and blankets, and Shand was careful to look for loose nailheads in the saddletree or dirt or wrinkles in the sweat blanket that was next to the horse's back.

By this time the early dark was closing in. The whisky-jacks had deserted the camp fire. The red passion of the sunset had faded to the chilly blue of strips of evening clouds lying coldly serene in the western sky. At intervals the grazing horses snorted in satisfaction over the wealth of the ripened grass. The creek, a mere trickle this late in the fall, tinkled as it dropped over a waterfall six inches high. Shand poked up his camp fire, put on another tin to boil for tea, and leaned back against a tree in complete satisfaction with this serene world of himself, his horses, the creek and the cheery fire. After lingering over his tin of tea, he stretched out under a large spruce tree and was soon asleep.

After seven or eight days' travel, working his way over the great blue ridges, down slanting hillsides and along valley floors, Shand reached the Smoky River. Here he turned right to descend to Daniel's Flat and selected a congenial spot to pitch his teepee. The fur-bearing animals would not be prime for several weeks to come, but these weeks would be filled with many tasks so that when trapping time came Shand could bend all his efforts in that direction. Erecting his teepee took little time, and then high on a tree nearby he set about making a cache where his supplies would be secure from wandering wolverine, marauding bear or meandering mice. Isolated as he was in the bush, his life might very well depend upon the sanctity of this cache. To be on the safe side, he had taken along grub to last eight or nine months, including a margin to allow for visitors and to give away to anyone else who might run short during the winter.

"How much grub would you need for one winter, Shand?" I asked. "I'd like to put it on record."

"I thought about doing that once, but never got very far with it," said the old man, reaching over for a box. After a moment's search, he pulled out a roll of paper – a carefully written manuscript dealing with his life in the bush. Turning over a few pages he came to one on which he had listed the supplies he considered necessary for one winter.

"This," he said, "would do a man for a winter's trapping." And he handed me the list.

200 lbs Flour	10 lbs Raisins
8 lbs Baking Powder	30 lbs Dry Fruits
16 lbs Tea	30 lbs Cornmeal
80 lbs Sugar	20 lbs Graham Flour
25 lbs Salt Pork	1 bottle Mapleine
20 lbs Bacon	[Extract for Syrup]
40 lbs Rolled Oats	20 lbs Salt
25 lbs Rice	10 lbs Pearl Barley
40 lbs Beans	20 lbs Plug Tobacco
20 lbs Lard	100 Candles
20 lbs Butter	Matches (take plenty)
10 lbs Klim	Soap
[Powdered Dry Milk]	Ammunition (take plenty)

"These were the bare necessities of store-bought goods," he continued. "I expected to kill all the meat and fish I could eat. Of course, on a trap line a man eats much more meat than someone in civilization where farinaceous food fills a large place."

As well as groceries, Shand always made sure that he had an ample supply of medicines, of which he considered the following essential :

Carter's Little Liver Pills	Mustard
Gin Pills (Doan's)	Boracic Acid
Painkiller (Perry Davis's)	Iodine
Zambuk	Salts
Minard's Liniment	Hydrogen Peroxide
Permanganate of Potash	Plasters and Bandages

"As well as food and medicine, I always replenished my tool kit each fall. The following tools were indispensable" :

2 Axes (3½ lbs)	Hand Saw
1 Axe (1½ lbs)	Gimlet
Crosscut Saw	Chisel
Augers	Plane
Hammer	Wire Cutters
"Pocket case of Tools"	3 or 4 Files
Skinning Knives	Whetstones

Over and above these, in later years when Shand had built his own winter cabin, he had two or three items of what he called furnishings, which his horses packed in. The first of these was a "Teslin" folding cookstove, either in the two- or four-hole size. He preferred the latter: its firebox was longer and consequently he need not cut his wood so short, and the oven was large enough so that he could cook bread. Whenever possible he took in a galvanized washtub, lashing it carefully on the top of the pack on a gentle horse. When it was impractical to take in one of these, he could improvise by hollowing out a section of cottonwood log some three feet long and sometimes half as wide. He always insisted on the best quality blankets he could buy, and when these were spread over a good layer of fresh hay, he had an aromatic and very comfortable bed.

Having settled down in his winter home, Shand turned his attention to getting in a supply of meat. To be safe, he had to go out in the early fall and bring in enough meat so that even if he never shot anything during the winter, he would not starve. For over forty years Shand lived entirely on his own resources, far back in the bush, and generally far from help. If his food supply had failed or some accident had befallen him, he would have perished before anyone found him. I asked him if at times he had not worried about meeting with some misadventure.

"No, I never worried," he replied. "This was my life and I enjoyed it. Perhaps to some extent I enjoyed its challenge. An accident might happen to any man as it happened now and then to some of my Indian friends. Sometimes there are accidents over which one has no control. These are liable to befall any man who lives in the bush. When one does, the man does not show up the following spring, or ever – but that is a calculated risk. But most accidents are the result of carelessness or lack of sufficient preparation. Those of us who lived for years alone in the bush and survived were the careful ones – perhaps you might say the experienced ones.

"Oh, I nearly died one winter – I'll tell you about that later – but at the time I didn't know that I was so close. It never occurred to me that I might die until I had regained consciousness, and then, of course, I was better."

Once Shand got his camp established, he took a horse or two and headed south and west into the mountains. There, up in the high passes a day's travel from camp, he was in sheep and goat country. Here the mountain caribou ranged, and in any direction he was apt to run across a moose or a deer. It was bear country too – black and grizzly – but by that time in the fall most of them were hibernating. In a few days Shand had killed and brought in all the meat he needed. The weather was cold enough so that some of it would stay fresh, but much of it he dried over a slow fire and some of it he pounded and made into pemmican, to be carried along on his trap line. Another expedition later in the fall stocked his larder with moose meat, which could then be kept frozen.

One other source of meat was the beavers he trapped, and this, said Shand, was quite palatable. Porcupine meat, too, fitted nicely into a trapper's larder. "There's almost nothing in the meat line that a hungry man can't eat and get sustenance from."

"Even lynx?" I queried.

"Yes, even lynx. You think that's terrible, don't you – eating cat meat – and yet if you ask any trapper or woodsman he'll tell you that lynx meat is good. It's somewhat like chicken – much better than rabbit. Many a time when I've had plenty of moose and sheep, I've deliberately passed these up for a feed of lynx. It's not just a trapper's eccentricity.

"I'll admit," he said, "eating lynx is a sort of acquired taste – you remember how you spit out the first olive you ate. What about the green cheese you eat? I never get green cheese any more, but I like it. Once, years ago, I got some from Edmonton, but when I gave it to my half-breed friends they spit it out – thought I was trying to poison them. I doubt now if I'll ever eat any more lynx," he said wistfully.

Shand also had to prepare rawhide for straps and laces and for the fillings for snowshoes. "I bought all my moccasins from the native women. Indian women are hard workers and very skilled craftsmen. From moose and deer and caribou hides they make all the clothes for the family. Take moccasins alone – sometimes a pair will last only one day, sometimes you can wear them for a couple of weeks. Moccasins alone are enough to keep the women busy.

"And then there are all the fine points of making clothes and goods. Take snowshoes, for instance. To you they are merely pieces of rawhide fastened to a frame. But the Indian women know better. For the coarse webbing behind they use moose rawhide in half-inch strips. For the finer work in the front, only sheep rawhide is good enough.

"Day after day the Indian women work at making clothes, cleaning the skins, curing and smoking and scraping them. Here –" he said, reaching back to a shelf over his bed, "here is the scraper, *mich-ich-qun*, used by my old friend Anne Cardinal, a very old but a very skilful squaw. Many a time I've watched this old lady working away. This scraper probably doesn't mean much to you, yet it's made to very strict specifications. For best performance it must be made from a cow moose's foreleg – not caribou or elk, but moose – for some reason it lasts longer and does a better job. And not only moose, but cow moose. The grain in the bone is finer and tougher – at least that's what the Indian women say, and when dealing with things like this I believe there's just that difference in texture that makes all the difference between a mere tool and the tool used by a master craftsman."

When Shand felt that he had enough meat and rawhide for the winter, he spent a few days laying out his trap line. The weather was getting colder and a light cover of snow had fallen. Taking a couple of horses and provisions for a week or so, he set out, watching for signs of fur-bearing animals. He covered perhaps forty miles, swinging around in a long circle so that eventually he came back to his starting point. On this trip he put up a couple of lean-tos that would afford some comfort and protection from the weather later in the winter when he began trapping. He planned to work his traps in such a way that at the end of the first and second days he could sleep in these shelters, and on the third night he would be home. On his way around from one trap to another and from one cabin to another, he blazed trees – both sides of the tree, for he knew that some day he might wish to reverse his line of travel.

Some time later while the weather was still good Shand saddled up his horses and set out around his trap line, leaving a good cache of food at each of his shelters. The food he carried in this way, on horses now, would mean just that much less that he would have to take with him on foot when trapping began. Then, of course, he would be burdened with traps and, he hoped, with animals he had caught.

After he returned from this trip, he occupied himself for many days cutting and piling wood against the bitter days of winter. He cut enough to last till Christmas. After that the weather would probably turn very cold and trapping would slacken off. While he stayed home he could cut more wood, until the weather turned mild once more and the fur-bearing animals were on the move again. All these tasks kept him busy till trapping season started.

"Lonesome? Did I feel lonesome? No," said Shand. "I was busy every moment – busy and exercising. The days were almost too short for all I had to do. Then there were the horses. They would come around to visit and I would go to see how they were doing."

All of these preparations helped to ensure that no accident should befall him that care and forethought could prevent.

"You see, that's the difference between an experienced man and a greenhorn. When the steel of the Grand Trunk reached the Athabasca River a good many greenhorns went trapping during the winter. It looked to them an easier way to earn a living than working for wages in a railroad camp. And it was, if you knew how – but on that little word 'how' hung success or failure, perhaps life or death."

There was a young English college man and his wife who decided to put in the winter trapping, Shand began, thinking back, while I settled down to listen to another tale. The man had found railroad work hard and, having a little money, was able to outfit comfortably for the winter. Having no horses of his own, he hired a guide and a small pack train to take them out about thirty miles to a good locality for fur along the Wildhay River. After selecting a site for their cabin, the guide and outfit left them.

From laziness or inexperience, the shack they built was most uncomfortable, the roof so low that only in the centre of the floor could they stand upright without touching the joists. A small sheet-iron box stove without an oven was all they had for heating and cooking.

The weather up to New Year's was quite cold, although the snowfall was light. Fur was plentiful but the couple did not get nearly enough moose meat put by. Their first difficulty came when their moccasins began to wear out and they did not have any tanned moose hide to repair them. Neither did they have the necessary skill. Eventually the woman had to wrap her feet in gunny-sacking and canvas. Luckily about this time they fell in with a native family from whom they got new moccasins, but not before their feet had been slightly frostbitten.

The climax to their troubles came one day when they left their cabin to visit traps some miles away. They intended to camp out and to retrace their trail next day. Towards evening, however, the weather broke and snow began to fall. They decided to take a brief rest and then head home before the weather got worse, but within a short distance they found that their tracks had been covered by snow. In the growing darkness they missed their way. Instead of camping at once and waiting for daylight, they made the mistake common to most inexperienced persons in the bush. They pushed on, thinking they would soon strike some familiar spot. Before long they were lost. They had very little grub and very few matches, but they made a fire and sat by it during the long hours of that January night.

By daybreak there was more than a foot of fresh snow. They travelled all day and, as is usual in such cases, found themselves going in the wrong direction. Towards evening a native trapper crossed their trail. He recognized the snowshoes as white man's, and noticed that one pair was exceptionally small; his curiosity was aroused and he followed them. When he caught up with them they were in desperate straits, but he helped them to make a good camp and fed them from the food he was carrying. Next day he led them safely home, tired but very thankful for their narrow escape – and, except for sore feet, they were none the worse for their experience. They decided that they had had enough and set out for the railway again. Save for the timely arrival of this chance traveller, they would surely have remained lost and in a day or so would have perished.

Shand sat back and rolled a cigarette and then went over to put the kettle on the stove.

"Then," he said, "there was another time when two young fellows decided to locate a trapping country for themselves and brought out two or three pack ponies to carry their supplies. They followed the main trail for forty miles or so and then branched off it and built a small cabin on the Berland River. The weather was good, so they decided they'd push on twenty miles or so farther east to make a cache of grub. They planned to trap from both camps and to have supplies in each. This would allow them to cover a larger area.

"After making this second camp, they cut across and hit the main trail without any difficulty and returned to the railroad. They bought a further supply of provisions and went back to their first cabin. The weather was good, and they took their ponies some miles northwest to winter them on a good meadow. Fur signs were abundant near their first cabin, so they stayed there some weeks and thus made the fatal error of not carefully locat-ing the second cache and blazing a trail to it before the snow came.

"Early in the new year, when fur and grub was beginning to get scarce at their main cabin, they decided to move over and trap from their cache. They expected to reach it easily in less than two days, because travelling to it slowly with their horses in the early fall they had only camped out one night. Since they had plenty of food and ammunition at the cache, they carried very little grub and few cartridges.

"The snow in the bush was now several feet deep, and the look of the country had changed considerably. The partners felt sure, however, that they knew their way and camped when dark came on. That night it turned cold and snowed heavily. In the morning every tree and bush was laden with snow and many of the small spruces were bent double. They began to have misgiv-ings – which would be the better course, to push on or to return to the main cabin? They had not blazed their trail but generally had followed an old trap line where the trees had been blazed on one side only. To attempt now to follow their back trail would be difficult, as the blazes would be invisible on the far side of the trees and their own tracks had been wiped out by the fresh snow. They decided to push on and soon realized that they were completely lost. To make matters worse, one of them froze his feet badly.

"For a day or so these amateur trappers lived on what they found left by owls and coyotes in the shape of bits of rabbits, but they were rapidly getting weaker. Finally, the one with the frozen feet could go no farther and sat down. His partner built a good fire and pushed on, while his strength held out. After travelling seven or eight miles, he reached a bare ridge and a few miles beyond that saw smoke. He struggled on and at last came to some teepees.

"The natives spoke only Cree, but he managed to make them understand where he had left his partner. Immediately some of them started out to look for him. The next day the kind-hearted natives returned with the news that they had found the white man all right but had been too late. He had been in a crouching position over the ashes of his fire – frozen stiff. Furthermore, they explained, the fire had been built not more than a dozen yards from the main trail which the men had followed into that country in the fall.

"After resting a few days, the survivor was able to make his way out to the railway, where he spent some time in the construction hospital. The following spring, when he sent for his horses, they were all brought in in good shape. A year or so afterwards I saw the cache they had struggled so hard to reach, but by then, of course, the provisions had been destroyed by squirrels and other animals."

At this point Shand's neighbour, Billy Magee, dropped in. The kettle was singing on the little stove, so Shand made some tea, dug out a loaf of sliced store bread and unearthed a piece of boiled moose meat. After our lunch I returned to the subject of accidents, and he recalled one that befell his old friend Vincent Wanyandi, the full-blooded Iroquois.

It was about 1917, and Vincent was over sixty. Otherwise he might have come off without getting hurt. That fall he had shot a mountain sheep and brought the meat home. Then he found that he had left his hunting knife where he had skinned the sheep. Next day he rode back, found the knife and set off for home once again. The trail followed the bed of a small creek and was rough and slippery. About five miles from his teepee his horse slipped, falling on its side and breaking the old man's leg below the knee. The horse was unhurt and headed back to its companions near the teepee.

Toward dark Vincent's daughter saw the horse with the riding saddle still on feeding with the others. She immediately got help, followed the horse's tracks back up the creek and found her father by a small fire he had made. As they approached, they saw him sitting smoking, although he was quite unable to move and was in great pain from his badly swollen leg. It was too late to try to move him that evening, so some of the party returned to the teepee for blankets and grub. Meanwhile an old Stoney Indian, Washy Joe, did what he could to reduce the swelling, and then set the leg, putting on splints and bandaging it as well as possible with the material at hand. The operation was extremely painful. Next morning Vincent was moved on a sleigh to his home about forty miles north. Shortly after New Year's he could get about again with the aid of two sticks. No complications ever set in, and for years afterwards he was able to ride and move about as well as a man of his age could expect.

For a while Shand sat thinking and then he said, "You know who Conrad Kain was?"

"Yes," I said, "the famous Swiss guide."

"Well, he had a close call about the same time old Vincent did. Only it was a goat that nearly finished him off.

"In 1911, the winter after I had taken Kain and his party to Mount Robson, he decided to trap up on the headwaters of the Smoky behind Mount Robson. One day when he was up about the seven-thousand-foot level, he followed a billy goat who kept climbing a steep dangerous slope where at any moment he might start an avalanche. Conrad kept after him, and finally the goat disappeared around the corner of a peak. In a few minutes he showed himself again at the very top, peering over an overhanging snow cornice.

"Conrad, fully aware that he might start the snow sliding, kept on climbing, trying to get close enough for a shot. But he never did. All at once the avalanche started. For a few yards the snow carried him down with it quite slowly. Knowing what he was in for, Conrad sat down and placed his rifle across his legs. In a moment the avalanche was going full speed towards a precipice. Things happened too quickly to recall, but the next thing Kain knew he was feeling a pain in his legs and back and realizing that the sliding snow had stopped.

"It took him ten minutes to free himself from the snow, which was bloody from a wound in his back. Looking back he could see that he'd been carried over a twenty-foot precipice.

"Then, about ten feet to his right, he noticed a movement in the snow. He watched it for a moment, went closer and heard a faint groan. Then he realized that it came from the goat, whose horns and ears were sticking out of the snow. Conrad did not stop to think that he and the goat had been fellow survivors who had lived through a miracle together – he simply went over and cut its throat.

"Conrad knew what had happened to himself, but he could only guess how the goat had become involved. At the start of the chain of events, the billy must have been standing peering over the edge, fascinated by the sight of a man being carried down in an avalanche. Then the snow above the point where Conrad had set things moving must have started sliding too, because its supporting snow had been carried away. The first thing the goat knew this action had extended upwards to the cornice, which had cracked off, and the billy went head over heels in the wake of the man, to end up almost beside him when the slide stopped."

Shand's reminiscences next turned to moose.

"Most times," he said, "they'll keep out of a man's way, but in the rutting season a man wants to keep out of their way. Then they're more dangerous than a grizzly bear. Many a time in the fall I've heard an old bull moaning and roaring as he crashed through the bush. They go sort of crazy, and if they see or smell you they'll charge. I always gave them a wide berth. There were only two things in the bush that I was really scared of, a grizzly and a rampaging bull moose."

"What about wolves?" I asked. "Did you ever know of wolves attacking a man?"

"No. And neither have the natives. At times we've had several packs of wolves in the Smoky River country. In fact, that's Billy

Magee's job, to kill them off periodically." Turning to Billy, he said, "You've never heard of them attacking a man, have you?"

"No," said Billy, "but they'll follow you. You hardly ever see them, but they'll get on your trail and follow it – curiosity, I expect. I've gone back next day to where I've suspected that they were following me the night before, and there were their tracks, sometimes the tracks of six or eight of them. I sure wouldn't want them to take a notion in my direction. Three or four times I've heard them kill a moose perhaps half a mile away. Once I stood on a hillside and watched them.

"The moose was floundering around in the deep drifts, and seven or eight wolves were running on top of the snow and keeping up with it. One or two at a time, they'd dash in and nip at him, trying to cut his hamstring. When they missed, they'd swing away and come around at him again sort of from in front, and take another nip at his hind legs. Before long they brought him down and then, in spite of his kicks, and the sharp front feet and the flailing of his head, they ate him alive. Until they got him down they raised an awful ruckus, and what with their barking and howling it was awful. It's not so bad to see them do it, because then you can see what's going on, but its hair-raising to hear it happening somewhere near you in the bush and not see it. The snarling and bawling just scares the lights out of you.

"I went back the next day after they had killed the moose. D'ya know, there was just horns and hair left and dirty marks in the snow. No bones, no blood. They'd eaten every speck of him."

"But you never knew wolves to attack a man?" I asked.

"No," interjected Shand, "but you can't be sure they won't. One mistake on a man's part and he'd not be around any more to speculate on the question. It's like William Moberly. He was treed by them – perhaps they wouldn't have attacked him, but he's an expert woodsman and he felt that it was no time to take chances."

Then Shand told of Moberly's experience along the Wildhay late one winter afternoon. Travelling was hard, even on snowshoes, and he was making poor time. First he could sense that the wolves were following. Then from time to time he saw one, and then another, and at times two at once. Then as he crossed an open meadow ten of them followed him into the open space.

They weren't in any hurry and they made no noise. But there was a quality of relentlessness about them. They kept coming on, not racing, but gaining.

William had about three miles to go, but they were closing in on him and he felt he would never make that distance. It was no use to shoot one or two of them – the others would be upon him anyway. So he jumped for the lower branches of a dry pine and pulled himself up into it. The wolves stopped for a moment to take in this manoeuvre and then they jogged on and sat on their haunches at the foot of the tree. It was getting cold and Moberly didn't relish the prospect of sitting there all night.

Perhaps that is what put the idea into his head. He had plenty of matches and the tree provided plenty of kindling. He climbed about the tree, breaking off branches and twigs and dropping them very carefully so that as near as possible one fell on top of the other on the snow. At first he threw down three or four pieces, and one or two of the wolves got up and came over to smell them. Then, as more fell down, another wolf would come over to sniff at the twigs. Before long, Moberly had a fair pile of dry twigs. Then, carefully igniting one branch, he dropped it on the pile. It flared up and soon he had a small fire burning, which he was careful to feed by breaking off more branches. As the fire blazed up, the wolves became uneasy and in a short time they disappeared. After a proper interval, Moberly climbed down and hurried for camp. He didn't see any sign of the wolves, so presumably they had given up and had formed into a pack again, intent on chasing something else.

"But, while you still can't say that they attacked William, or would have," said Shand, "he always felt that he had had a narrow escape."

At Shand's teepee on the Smoky, the delightful fall finally gave way before the onset of winter, and he went out trapping. Up till about Christmas he made the rounds with some of his horses. In the meantime the snow was getting deeper. Then in January a cold snap set in and for a few days he stayed close to his teepee fire. After the cold snap Shand trapped for the rest of the winter, but the snow was too deep to use horses for transport, and he brought out his snowshoes.

"Why didn't you use dogs?" I asked.

"Well, dogs are all right in their place," he said, "on the prairies in the old days or up north even now, but they are not practical in the timber country – at least not as sleigh dogs. A dog can carry a pack weighing twenty or thirty pounds, but if the snow is soft or if much windfall has to be crossed, a dog is generally more bother than he is worth. Still, the Indians do use them to pack some of their stuff and make a pair of small pack bags joined together over the dog's back and secured by means of a wide, soft moose-hide strap passing around his chest. When you use dogs, it is usually necessary to go ahead and pack the snow down with your snowshoes. It's a curious sight to see a bunch of pack dogs on the trail, with perhaps five or six men on snowshoes going ahead and two or three others following the dogs. One has to be always on the lookout for moose or other game passing near, as the dogs are apt to make a bolt after them. This is especially so if the going is good, as on a river. If a dog gets away, he is almost certain to lose his pack and it might be very hard to find again."

"What about snow blindness in the spring?" I asked.

"Well, it's bad. If precautions are not taken to avoid it, it may easily prove fatal. It is especially dangerous when crossing a large lake, as you can easily walk into an air hole or get turned around and never reach the shore, or in the case of total blindness you could not find your way home, and the end would soon come. Blue-eyed people I have found more susceptible. It is very much easier to prevent than cure, and you should always take blue glasses or, failing them, blacken the face and nose. Charred stumps can always be found, and some of the black rubbed on the nose and face, especially under the eyes, is a very great help."

"Then you don't agree with your friend Jack Hornby that blue-eyed people are superior for the rigours of northern winters?"

"Poor Jackie – no, Jackie was a nice fellow in a lot of ways, but in others he was a little bit off. Perhaps I had better say eccentric. Nice chap, though, if he was in the right mood. His death and that of his two young companions was so needless – dying of starvation and scurvy."

"Did you ever have scurvy?"

"No, it is hardly known among the natives and old-timers who live principally on fresh meat, but it often causes considerable trouble to new-comers putting in their first winter or two trapping. If you should happen to be attacked, I was told many years ago by some Indians that boiling spruce shoots and drinking the liquid would cure it. I once had occasion to prescribe this, with perfect success, for a friend who had a bad attack, so I feel confident in recommending it to others."

"How many animals would you catch in a fair winter?"

"Well, I don't remember exactly, but each year I would probably end up with something like ten each of foxes and coyotes, perhaps twenty lynx, and maybe fifteen martens. Then I would have a few mink, some beaver and a sprinkling of the lesser animals like weasels."

"Didn't you come out during the winter?"

"No, I was quite contented there and usually pretty busy. And besides, it was a hundred-mile trip one way. The only way would have been to snowshoe out. It's funny how times change though. A few years later it became sort of fashionable for some of the natives to come out in midwinter, and now, of course, with the truck road open all year round, the old ways have all changed. Today, possibly once a month, several natives will chip in and hire a truck to bring them out to the bright lights at Hinton."

The winter of 1912–1913 was highly successful from Shand's standpoint. Several times he went over to visit John McVicar and the party which was drilling the Hoppe Coal claims. Once in a while he would snowshoe twenty miles or so to visit another trapper – Tom Managhan or Fred Kvass – or, in turn, he would have a visit from them. For a few hours or maybe lasting through two nights, the conversation would run on and on. Then the point would come where the two had talked each other out. For a while each would try to keep up the discussion, but inevitably one or both fell silent. Each had had enough of companionship and wanted to be alone, and the visitor would strap on his snowshoes and depart into the forest, not to be seen again perhaps till next year, when again he would be a welcome companion.

About the end of March, Shand packed up for good, and after a long day's trip on the ice of the Smoky, reached Kusta's Flat. Kusta was an Indian who had probably been christened Augustus, but on half-breed lips this became Kusta. In any event, he was away, but his small family and his wife, who had just had a baby, were in their teepee. In the only other teepee dwelt Swetyk, a very old woman, with her son and two daughters. The son, Margo, was seriously ill and Shand, when he went in to see him, decided that his end was near. All the men except Margo were out tramping their trap lines. Although there was plenty of food in the teepees, Shand was able to contribute a few of his delicacies, such as milk powder, in an effort to comfort Margo and to help Kusta's wife. Then he cut a good supply of wood and pulled out next morning to visit his old friend Fred Kvass.

A couple of days later he again visited Kusta's Flat and found that Margo had died. He set to work to dig a grave, and then along with Adam Joachim, who had shown up, he helped with the funeral.

"Old Swetyk," reminisced Shand, "was a very old woman. As near as I could ever make out, and I was quite curious about it, she would be about ninety. Rare as that age is, I believe old Swetyk was that old. I wish I had been more interested at that time and had known more about the early days out here, so that I could have questioned her about the Iroquois and their coming to this area. If she was ninety then, she would have been born about 1820, and I believe the original Iroquois came here about that time."

"Did she ever tell you any tales?"

"Only one that I really remember. She was very alert and had a good memory. When she told me this tale I was dubious, but the rest of the Indians believed it. Moreover, many years later I read about it in a book of the reminiscences of H. J. Moberly. Vincent Wanyandi believed it and so did Solomon Caraconté. So, coming from these different sources, I don't think there is any doubt about it."

Then Shand told me his version of the tale I too had heard before and believed.

When Colin Fraser was in charge of Jasper House about 1840, old Swetyk would be a buxom, black-eyed woman of perhaps twenty years. At that time a remnant of the Snake Indian tribe was camped near Jasper House on the point of land immediately upstream from the mouth of the Snake Indian River. Not far away was a larger camp of Stonies or Assiniboines, after whom, by the way, Fort Assiniboine was named. They laid claim to the territory between the fort and Jasper. At that time the Crees had not worked so far west as they did somewhat later, and the Smoky River country was the home of the Iroquois and, of course, old Swetyk.

Now the Assiniboines had long been enemies of the Snakes, and in many minor skirmishes had reduced them to this remnant that was camped near Jasper House. Perhaps the Snakes felt safe there, because the Hudson's Bay Company had a well earned reputation for treating the Indians well and for keeping peace between the various tribes. The Snakes' trustfulness, however, was their undoing.

One day the Assiniboines sent a messenger to the Snake camp, asking the men to come over to smoke and to arrange a permanent peace. It was foolish, said the messenger, to keep up this feud any longer. The Snakes, taken off their guard, went over – every able-bodied man of them, possibly ten or fifteen altogether.

No sooner were the Snakes seated along with a few of their hosts than the rest of the Assiniboines rushed up with their guns, and in a few moments all the Snakes were dead. The victors then rushed over and attacked the Snake camp, killing every remaining man, woman and child, except for three young women aged about seventeen. These they took captive and returned to their own camp.

But after the fleeting exhilaration of the killing, their consciences smote them. What they had done was not a crime in their eyes, even though it smacked of white man's duplicity, but they knew that the Hudson's Bay Company would be angry and maybe boycott them. They thought they had better move on, and so set out for Fort Assiniboine, some two hundred miles down the Athabasca. With them they carried the three girls.

When they camped near Fort Assiniboine they ran into a half-breed named Bellerose, who heard the story and learned that the three Snake girls were lying naked and bound in one of the teepees. Whatever may have been the Assiniboines' intentions, Bellerose thought that the three girls were to be killed next day – possibly tortured. It is doubtful if the Stonies would have gone that far, because it was Indian practice to adopt such captives and to treat them kindly once they gave up trying to escape. Eventually the girls would probably have been taken in marriage by some of the young men.

In any event Bellerose, being a brave man and obsessed with what he regarded as the girls' certain fate, sneaked into the teepee during the night, cut their bonds and turned them loose. All he could give them was his knife and his fire-bag containing a flint, a steel and some punk. The young women crept away into the September darkness and were soon in rapid flight up the Athabasca towards the mountains. Within a few days they reached the mouth of the Berland River, but there it seems they quarrelled, for they separated. Two of them made a raft and, taking the fire-bag with them, continued up the Athabasca. They were never heard of again – presumably they perished.

The third one travelled about thirty miles up the Berland. There she made preparations for winter. Berries were still to be had, and she managed to kill a few squirrels and with the sinews from their tails made snares for rabbits. Out of the rabbit skins she made herself a dress. She killed some porcupines and marmots too and dried their meat. She kindled a fire in the primitive way by revolving the point of one dry stick rapidly in a hole made in another. She gathered gum from poplars and collected a large pile of dry wood. By the time winter had set in she was ready for it, and lived at this spot till the following summer.

Then for several days she moved farther west. This would bring her into the vicinity of Berland Lake, some twenty-five miles east of where the forestry road from Entrance to Grande Prairie crosses the Berland, and into the country of the Iroquois. In the early fall, nearly a year after she had run away, an Iroquois from Grande Cache came upon her tracks. He couldn't figure them out. Since she had been unable to kill moose for moccasins, her footwear was poorly made, and he could not tell whether her tracks were animal or human. He concluded that they must have been made by a weetigo, that is, an Indian who had run amuck, eaten human flesh and been banished from the society of other Indians. When he told the other Iroquois about the tracks they came to the same conclusion, and for the time being the matter was dropped.

The next summer, after the girl had lived alone in the bush through two winters, a party of Iroquois were hunting in the valley of the Berland. The man who had seen the tracks the year before decided to go on to see if he could find the creature that made them. When he got back to the same area he saw snares set, trees barked and more of the strange tracks still fresh in the mud. This time he was sure it was a weetigo and decided to hunt and kill him. So, with his gun at full cock, creeping cautiously along so as not to be taken by surprise, he came to a high bank where the girl lived. A huge stack of wood was piled near the entrance of a small cave, and a little fire was burning nearby, but he could see no other sign of life. He hid himself close to the cave, and presently a wild creature in a short skirt of rabbit skins came up bearing a load of rabbits. Throwing these down, she bent over to stir up the fire, and the Iroquois realized that she was a woman, and knew at once that she must be one of the three women who two years before had escaped from the Assiniboines.

As soon as he moved she heard him, and with a wild cry started to run. In a few bounds he caught her, but she put up a frenzied battle and he had the greatest difficulty to get it through her head that he did not mean to harm her. Even then he had quite a struggle to take her into his camp. There, although she was more like a wild creature than a human being, the women were very kind to her. Finally, realizing that they meant to be friendly, she fell in with their ways and lived with them for two years. At the end of that time she went to Jasper House, where the factor employed her to help his wife. She lived there for two years and then married a Shuswap. None of her own tribe remained. She was the sole survivor.

"Old Swetyk died within the next year or so of telling me that tale," concluded Shand. "I've always been sorry that I didn't learn more from her, but I never saw her again after I left for Hinton that spring."

CHAPTER
THIRTEEN

———◦❊◦———

Aﬆer his winter's trapping, Shand went back
to work as a forest ranger. Crossing the Athabasca was easy now
because the Canadian Northern engineers had installed a ferry
above the mouth of Prairie Creek. Since the Grand Trunk had
built its line down the east side of Brulé Lake, the Canadian
Northern was forced to take to the west side and so had to cross
the Athabasca somewhere below the outlet of the lake. Accordingly, it surveyed its line so as to cross right opposite the Grand
Trunk station of Dyke. To permit work to go on along the north
side of the river and along Brulé Lake, the Canadian Northern
engineers had installed this ferry.

Shand was in his element carrying out the wishes of the
Department, and at the same time moving about from place to
place throughout the vast wilderness, rejoicing in its summer
beauty. One of his trips took him to the "Poison Lick," a place
where evil-smelling water emerged from the ground and several
horses had been found dead. Shand was asked to bring back a
sample of this water. When it was analysed, it confirmed the
suspicions he had formed when he drank some of it, that this was
a sulphur spring. The fact that the horses had died was a co-
incidence, because in the moist soil water parsnips grew pro-
fusely. In the spring, when grass was scarce, the horses had
probably eaten the parsnip and died.

"All over the country you'll find various Poison Creeks,"
declared Shand. "For instance, there's one that flows into Chip
Lake through Hattonford. Undoubtedly it got its name from the
wild parsnip."

"The names of creeks have always interested me," I said. "I'm
always wondering what story is behind each one. Take Carrot
Creek, which isn't far west of Chip Lake. Would you have any
idea how it got its name?"

"Oh, yes, it's because of the *oskatask* root, which is plentiful there. We would probably call it a carrot, only it's white really and long and thin, more like a parsnip. The Crees dig it up and make a spring tonic out of it – sort of bitters.

"Many of the creeks in the Smoky River Country," said Shand, "are named after various natives and early trappers who had cabins on them."

"I see there's a creek that flows into Teepee Creek, not far from the Muskeg, which is shown on the map as Shand Creek. That will be named after you?"

"I suppose so, but I don't really know why," said Shand modestly. "But a little farther south, where the 6th Meridian crossed one of the tributaries of Pinto Creek, there's a Polecat Creek."

"Yes, I've noticed that, but there aren't any true polecats here, are there?"

"Well, it's called that because of an incident that happened when Arthur St Cyr was running the 6th Meridian. One of his men, a green lad from Ontario – greenness is not confined to Englishmen! – saw a skunk there and disturbed it with disastrous results. He came running in to camp holding his nose and shouting about meeting a polecat.

"Speaking of the survey of the 6th Meridian," continued Shand, "perhaps the story of Pinto Creek is the most interesting. St Cyr, as you know, worked south along the 6th Meridian from the vicinity of Grande Prairie and arrived in this area late in the fall. He had arranged that during the summer a cache of supplies was to be brought in and left for him at Prairie Creek. Shortly after he crossed the Berland River his supplies began to get low, and he sent a couple of men with horses out to Prairie Creek. Somehow they went astray, and when they did not get back in time things began to look pretty hungry in St Cyr's camp. But he kept on and finally, where the line crossed what is now Pinto Creek, he had to kill a horse for food, and so he shot the pinto.

"That's only part of the story. Old Vassa Wanyandi was hunting nearby and he heard the shot."

"Now who is Vassa? – I thought I'd heard the names of all the Wanyandis, but I haven't heard of him before."

"Oh, Vassa was Vincent. The natives couldn't pronounce our

English names, and anyway he was undoubtedly christened Vincent by a French priest who pronounced the name differently to what we do. The Indians did the best they could to say it the way the priest did, and ended up by calling him Vassa.

"In any event," Shand continued, "Vassa heard the shot and came over to see what was going on. While they were cutting up the horse, he showed up. He couldn't speak either English or French, and none of the party could understand him. As he looked over their larder they showed him that they had very little food other than ten pounds of flour. St Cyr pulled out a ten-dollar bill and waving it towards Vassa said, 'Moose, moose, mooswa,' at the same time doing pantomime of a man aiming a gun. Vassa understood, but he pushed the ten-dollar bill away and in a pantomime of his own made them understand that he would get them a moose in return for half of the ten pounds of flour. As for the money, what use was it to him – but flour now, his family could eat that.

"Vassa was not long in carrying out the agreement. He had only been gone half an hour when the surveyors heard one rifle shot. 'Old beggar's had one of 'em tied up all the time,' said an axeman.

"In less than an hour Vassa appeared carrying some of the select parts of the moose. Then, taking his flour, he led a couple of men to where the rest of the moose lay."

In June, as Shand was working around Rock Lake, Vincent Wanyandi stopped there to camp. He was on his way to the Snake Indian River. Since Shand did not know all the trails crossing the various passes to the west, he went along with the Wanyandis over Eagle's Nest Pass. Gradually he was getting to know all the old trails and passes, and before that summer was over he knew the vast mountain hinterland as well as most people know the city where they live.

The route towards Eagle's Nest Pass lay up the Wildhay River past Rock Lake. Beyond the west end of the lake a low divide separates the headwaters of the Wildhay from those of the Snake Indian River. One night as Shand camped with the Wanyandis at the mouth of Mumm Creek, he commented on the number of meat-drying racks he had seen during the day. In many places along the trail stood these racks of various ages ranging from recent construction to decaying remnants built long ago.

Across the river from the mouth of Mumm Creek cliffs rose steeply for several hundred feet. While the rest of the valley and the table lands above them were clothed in a dense cover of pine trees, this precipice stood out stark and naked. Vincent was in a reminiscing mood and, pointing to the bare cliffs across the river, he spoke of his memories of long ago. Vincent had been born near Jasper House about 1850 when Henry John Moberly had held sway there. The old fort was then in its heyday as a post devoted to provisioning the many brigades that continually passed to and from the West Coast. The Hudson's Bay factor kept the Indians hunting and bought all the meat they could bring in. They hunted in all directions, but a favourite haunt of moose and buffalo was along the ridge separating the Wildhay River from the Snake Indian. The Indians killed big game here by driving them forward until with a final mad rush they could stampede them over a cliff. Such a buffalo jump was the cliff that Vincent pointed out.

"Long ago," he said, referring to the late 1860's, "when I was a boy big enough to start hunting with the men, we drove moose and buffalo over that cliff. The old men and the women and children would start out many days ahead of us and come here and camp. Then a day or so later some of the men would hurry over the ridge and take their places in two lines, two or three miles long, converging upon this precipice. Their job was to wait till we drove the animals forward and then to make sure that they did not break away to either side but that they were steadily headed towards their doom. Then, after waiting a few days to give them a good start, the rest of us would set out.

"We planned to scare the animals and to drive them ahead of us. Sometimes we shot a moose or two to eat, but we didn't want to kill more than that, so day by day, shooting off our guns now and then and barking like wolves, we drove the moose and buffalo forward till they met the lines of men sent out ahead. Then as we neared the jump, keeping in touch with each other by hooting like owls, barking like coyotes or howling like wolves, we kept closing in behind the buffalo and kept pressing them on. For days we had been disturbing the game, shooting and howling, and then during the last night when we had many between us and the cliff we kept up this noise, so that all through the night they were filled with fear. At daybreak, at a signal from our leader, we all yelled, shot off our guns and rushed forward through the bush, breaking branches and banging the trees with sticks. The moose and buffalo, nervous after many days' pursuit, would rush forward, only to be turned as they approached first one line of guards and then the other. And the faster they ran the nearer they came to these cliffs. Then suddenly it was too late. There was no place to go but forward over them. In a short time all of them would be driven over, and we would scramble down through the forests beside the cliffs. While we were doing that, the women and the old people would be busy slitting their throats and cutting them up.

"I can remember as a little boy camping here with my mother, and waiting for the fun to start. At night, far back up on the hill, we could hear the men calling and we knew that at daylight the buffalo would start tumbling down. First one or two moose would come and then a few buffalo, and then a whole lot of them crashing down onto the rocks over there. It was a time of great excitement as we all yelled and ran in amongst them – great happiness. In an hour or two it would all be over and we had meat piled everywhere. Some moose, some deer, but mainly buffalo.

"There were teepees here and there and all over, close together. The fires blazed while the women cooked moose nose and buffalo hump. Ribs roasted by the fire, marrow bones sizzled in the coals – great feasting, happiness and laughter."

"How many animals would you kill – how many moose and buffalo?" asked Shand.

"Oh, many, many. Sometimes just a few, but more often many, many. Sometimes the horses were heavily loaded when we went back.

"All day the women cut the meat into strips and hung it on the drying racks, while the little ones fed the fires which kept the flies away and dried the meat. At night we danced. All night the drums throbbed here at the mouth of Mumm Creek. For many days the women dried the meat and pounded some of it into pemmican. The saskatoons were ripe and the buffalo fat.

"Then after many days we packed the horses and set off along the north shore of Rock Lake and up Mowitch Creek, and then over the pass to Willow Creek and down the Snake Indian River to Jasper House where the meat bought many things – tea and tobacco, strouds and needles."

Shand decided that he would not trap the following winter, but would take it easy. So he bought a little shack in Hinton and for a few months enjoyed the social life of white people. Here he met Roy Woodley, who was working in Leslie Zorab's store, and the two took to each other at once. By then the Canadian Northern had built its grade to Hinton and had erected a station called Bliss a few hundred yards east of Hardisty Creek. The engineers were also at work on a bridge over the Athabasca, upstream from the mouth of Prairie Creek, and were laying out a townsite to be called Entrance, about a mile west of Dyke, on the north side of the river.

Roy Woodley planned to start a store on his own at Entrance, and that winter Shand helped him move across the river before the ice went out. Entrance was the last Canadian Northern station before the railway entered the National Park, and might be thought of as the jumping-off place or entrance to the park. It appeared to have a good future. The Canadian Northern bridge was expected to be finished in the spring of 1914, the headquarters of the Athabasca Forest Reserve was already being built at Entrance, and everything appeared propitious for the new town. Shand, too, decided to make his headquarters there, so he sold his shack in Hinton and moved over and camped on Orchard Creek, about half a mile west of the Entrance station. That was forty-six years ago, and today Shand, sitting on his front porch overlooking the Athabasca and the ghost town of Entrance, still regards old Entrance as the choice spot in all the foothill country.

Meanwhile the Canadian Northern construction crews were forging ahead with their railway. Since they could ship material over the Grand Trunk, they did not have to complete one portion of their line before they could move on to the next. Work on several sections of it went on at the same time. While the Grand Trunk engineers had chosen the east side of Brulé Lake, so as to avoid cutting a tunnel through the shoulder of the Bedson Ridge, the Canadian Northern had no option but to blast it out. This work required several months, and at times Shand and some of the natives rode along the west shore of the lake to watch them work at it.

The trip around the lake was extremely pleasant, particularly through the open valley of Solomon Creek, which came in from the north and emptied into the extreme lower end of the lake. Three or four miles back up the creek Montana Pete had built a cabin, and for years this valley was the home of Solomon Caraconté, the old Iroquois. How far back this particular little band of Iroquois had lived here, Shand did not know for certain, but their fathers had probably chosen this spot before 1829 when the first Jasper House had been moved from the mouth of Solomon Creek to its later location at the lower end of Jasper Lake. White men had named the creek after Solomon, but in Shand's time the natives referred to it as Old House Creek.

"Did you ever know the exact location of the old Jasper House? Did you ever see it?" I asked.

"Oh, yes, when they found that I was interested, the natives took me over to see it. It was on that little point of land that sort of sticks out into the lake, where Solomon Creek comes in. Actually it was perhaps a hundred yards back from the lake and maybe two hundred yards west of the mouth of the creek. Often when I was hunting I would wander over the ruins – a pile of stones where the chimney had been, and a depression which was once a cellar."

"I'd like to see it some time."

"Well, it's all gone now. The last time I saw it the stakes for the centre line of the railway were stuck in the chimney mound. Then, when construction started, all traces of it disappeared in the grade. It was a charming spot, though, with the beautiful expanse of the lake in front and the blue mountains sweeping up from the green water."

"Yes," I said, "it impressed all travellers in the same way. Some day I'll bring up Sir George Simpson's diary of his trip through here in 1824 and let you see what he thought."

George Simpson was a Scot who was much more concerned with the bawbees of business than the beauties of his bailiwick. But on October 11 even he had written "the situation of Jaspers House is beautifully Wild and romantic, on the borders of the

Athabasca River which here spreads itself out into a small Lake surrounded by Lofty Mountains. . . . The country seems rich in large and small Animals, as we saw numerous tracks Daily, the banks finely Wooded and as we approach the Mountain high and prominent and the face in many places exhibiting strata of Iron & Coal."

This is among the first references to the high quality coal which was later mined at Brulé. Sir George's diary for that day contains another entry which is of particular interest.

". . . This is merely a temporary Summer post for the convenience of the Columbians in crossing; the Winter Establishment was last Year on the borders of the Smoky River about 80 to 100 Miles to the Northward, but it was this Season determined that it should be removed to Moose or Cranberry Lake situated more in the heart of the Mountain near the height of Land and where we suppose Frazers River takes its source; the object of this change is to draw the Freemen further into the Mountain than they have been in the habit of going, where they are expected to make good Hunts as it has been rarely Wrought and thereby the lower parts of Smoky River and the Country they used to occupy towards Lesser Slave Lake will be allowed to recruit . . ."

Simpson's reference to the establishment in 1823 of a wintering post "about 80 to 100 Miles" north is interesting. I asked Shand if he had ever heard of it.

"No, I've never heard the natives talk of it. Undoubtedly it would be on the upper Smoky in the vicinity of Grande Cache, and it was probably at the same place where Ignace Giassson made his Grande Cache about the year 1819."

After a pause I said, "And so, Shand, eventually the coal Sir George Simpson mentioned when he wrote up his diary by the light of the fire at Jasper House was hauled out on railway tracks passing right over the old fireplace."

"Yes," he mused. "Everything changes – everything but the river and the mountains. And yet every July the tiger lilies burst into spurts of orange flame and cover the hillsides overlooking Brulé Lake or old Jasper House, and the purple columbine and the bluebells still flourish where the old post stood. I was down there the other day, just standing and looking out over the lake, and there at my feet a beaver swam slowly past. Sir George's old post is gone – diesel trains roar over it – and yet the beaver that brought the post into being still survives, and in the evening flips his tail as he crawls up the bank to cut a new generation of poplar trees growing where the old palisades stood.

"Yes, everything changes. The Canadian Northern engineers were in a tizzy to get their railroad built. From its old divisional point at Tollerton, just south of Edson, it swept on through the tunnel at Brulé Lake and then past Jasper to establish another divisional point at Lucerne on the west end of Yellowhead Lake. Then it went on to Tête Jaune Cache and turned south towards Kamloops and Vancouver. And, just when they got it finished, during the First War, it went broke, and so did its rival, the Grand Trunk. The Dominion government had to step in and made the Canadian National Railways out of the two older ones. Right away, parts of each newly built line were abandoned. A few months later, steel that had been laid a year or so earlier was taken up and shipped east and to Europe for wartime railways. Parts of each railway from Hinton back for a hundred and fifty miles to Lac Ste Anne were forsaken. From Hinton west the Grand Trunk ran on its original track through to Jasper. For many years trains kept running on the Canadian Northern track from Hinton through Entrance as far as the Brulé mines. Then in 1926 the railway decided to abandon this piece of line through Entrance. At the same time they were anxious to get away from the sand dunes on the east side of the lakes. So they built a new piece of line from the old Grand Trunk station of Dyke and a new bridge across the Athabasca. In this way old Entrance was by-passed, but the new route of the line saved the railway a lot of headaches and at the same time served the Brulé mines. The old Pocahontas mine on the Grand Trunk had been shut down years before. Then, because Entrance had acquired considerable fame as a jumping-off place for hunting parties, the railway decided to rescue its name from oblivion, so they changed the name of the former station of Dyke to Entrance. As a result, Entrance is now across the river from where it was, and the old Canadian Northern bridge, together with its old grade, have become part of the highway going through here to Brulé. Here at the gateway to the mountains we have seen many changes."

"Well, the Smoky River country hasn't changed much."

"Maybe not in any essential quality, but it, too, has seen some changes since I first started working for the Forestry Department about fifty years ago."

During the summer of 1914 Shand went back into the hills again as a ranger in the Rock Lake district. He cut out more trails and posted more fire notices. In general, while he kept busy all summer, his work was merely a repetition of previous summers – practically unrestricted freedom to roam the valleys and passes, with a pay cheque waiting for him at the end of the season.

Next spring Shand was back as a ranger, and with him he took his young mare Kate – the one foaled on Jack Gregg's ranch by the mare that the surveyors had abandoned. This was the beginning of a long association of horse and man that was to last twenty-seven more years, till Kate's death in 1942.

Fire prevention and fire fighting were in their infancy – the Forestry Department had not reached the stage of lookout towers in the Athabasca Forest Reserve – but Shand and his colleagues were expected to do what they could to put out any fires that got started. The rangers, by this time, lived in forestry cabins scattered here and there and connected by telephone. To assist them a pack train of fifteen or twenty horses was kept ready at Entrance during the months when fire risk was high, to take extra men and fire-fighting tools out to the scene of any outbreak. Many a hot day Shand put in "turning a fire." One phenomenon of the woods that helped to sustain the flames and which was itself the result of forest fires was windfalls, the bane of all men who travelled in the bush. A fire passing through a forest of spruce and pine in the foothills was usually accompanied by a great wind, and had a tendency to travel in the tops of the trees and to run slowly down the trunks, charring them but not injuring the heart wood. After being fire killed, the Banksian or Lodgepole pines, having very deep tap roots, often stood for years and remained perfectly sound. Eventually, however, the tap roots rotted and a windstorm blew the trees over. Lying crisscross on top of each other for miles and miles, such forests of dead trees formed a serious obstacle to travel and caused endless work in keeping trails open.

After the hazard of fires was over for another year, after the forest had flamed out into its golden flush of fall, and after this too had died out, Shand set out for his trap lines once more. This time he planned to spend the winter of 1914–1915 by himself in the cabin he had built on the Smoky. So, after making the rounds of his friends at Entrance and saying goodbye to Roy Woodley, he turned Kate and his other horses up the hill and rode on over the ridge alone. Ten days later he turned his horses loose on the banks of the Smoky. As he entered his cabin, he had his first real experience with pack rats. The pack rat, a greyish-white little animal with a bushy tail and a most unpleasant smell, is adept at taking over an empty cabin. He gathers up all the shiny objects he can find, such as spoons, cartridges and tins, and packs them into a corner where in their midst he makes a warm snug nest, composed of moss, feathers and any hair or wool available. As a rule, not more than four rats occupy a small cabin at one time. Shand says that when he pushed his cabin door open the place stank to high heaven. For two nights after he had killed the rats he camped outside while he cleaned and aired the cabin.

Shand could not stand vermin of any sort. The natives and most of his fellow trappers were apt to look askance at his yen for cleanliness. He always advised greenhorns to be particularly careful to keep clean. Not only did he feel that doing so was much more healthful, and certainly more comfortable, but keeping his person and his cabin clean Shand believed to be one of the best antidotes against "going to pieces" in the solitude of the forest and against becoming what newspapers are fond of depicting as a "wild man of the woods."

He felt very strongly on the question of lice. When he went in to the Smoky River country most natives, and in fact most of the very few white men, were lousy. He always kept a canvas handy to draw over his bed if there was any prospect of native visitors. When he became acquainted with his neighbours, these visits were frequent. At first he did not want to take a chance of offending them by mentioning the matter, but after he came to know them well he broached the subject. They laughed. "Why, we're lousy, everybody's lousy and always has been and always will be – might as well try to stop the leaves from falling or the fuzz from blowing off the cottonwoods," they said, "as to try to get rid of lice."

"I know," Shand said, while they sat around reaching into their shirts to scratch, "but don't they nearly drive you crazy? They bite and tickle, and keep you awake – I don't have lice."

"Well, you don't seem to scratch," they agreed grudgingly.

"Look at my blankets – there's no lice in them," he continued, pulling the cover off.

They examined these with interest, and then, seeing that the blankets were old and patched like their own, shook their heads.

"How?"

"I wash and scrub – I scrub me – I scrub my blankets and hang them up to air. If you do that, you can get rid of lice. And what's more, from here on I'll give you all the soap you need, or at least I will next time I come back from Entrance." And he handed around two or three cakes of soap. The battle against lice was a strenuous one, but soap eventually won the day.

"From then on," said Shand, "they've kept themselves free from lice. The soap I brought out from the stores was infinitely better than what they used to make from moose fat and ashes. What they made was soap of a kind, but strong-smelling stuff and not very good."

Shand says that except for tuberculosis the half-breeds of the Smoky River country were on the whole fairly healthy. They were also cleaner than might have been expected. So long as they kept to themselves and remained fairly isolated in the bush, they stayed that way. When any of them became hangers-on around the white man's settlements they deteriorated rapidly, and as Shand said, then they equalled the low whites in dirtiness.

Shand explained that the game laws worked a severe hardship on the natives. All the people of the Smoky River country, the Wanyandis, Caracontés, Joachims, and so on, are technically white men. Some, like Vincent Wanyandi, were full-blooded but never took treaty. Because they all lived together he too was considered as legally white and therefore, unlike treaty Indians, was subject to the game laws. In theory the natives are no longer allowed to kill big game except during the open season. Much of their food, which consisted principally of meat, was made up of beavers, rats and lynx.

"Pretty good eating, too, mind you," said Shand, "and, of course, they ate rabbits. They tried to conform with the law, but if they came across a moose with a broken leg or a deer that was lost, well, they couldn't turn their backs on good meat, could they? Sometimes, too, during the closed season, a ram or a mountain goat slipped off a crag when no ranger happened to see it.

"One sore spot with them was and is that both the Stoney Indians and the Chippewas, who only recently took treaty down near Rocky Mountain House, together with members of these tribes who still reserve the right to do so when it suits them, invaded the Smoky River country. Of course they are legally entitled to kill game all the year round. It's pretty hard on my friends back on the Muskeg to see these invaders killing their game when they can't. There's no love lost between the two peoples."

He went on to explain that trapping was almost the only way that the natives could get ready money to buy the few things they needed from the stores. Their livelihood was threatened by the possibility of white men exterminating the fur-bearing animals. The greatest danger came from white men who went in with large outfits of grub and traps, with the sole object of making a "stake" and getting out again after two or three years. These men built several cabins along their lines and carried on their operations in a thoroughly business-like way, with the result that they cleaned out a district in a very short time. Now the natives and old-timers, of course, trapped to make money, but without the intention of finally going to live in civilization. Therefore, it was in their own interests to see that the stock of game was not reduced to the vanishing point, as they had made permanent homes in their trapping districts.

"The natives were always very friendly with old-timers like Montana Pete, Tom Monaghan and myself. We all trapped over the same area and here and there our lines crossed, so that we met now and then and knew what everyone else was doing. Many a white man would steal your fur if he came across something caught in a trap, but all of us helped each other. If a native found one of my traps with a mink in it, for instance, he would hang the trap up with the animal still in it, so that any passing animals could not damage it. Everyone who did that was always careful to leave the mink or whatever it was in the trap. You see, if it had been taken out, one could suspect that a less valuable skin might have been substituted."

"What about the depression of the Thirties? Was that felt up here in the bush too?"

"At the beginning of the depression the game wardens were pretty strict, but in a year or so when it was obvious that these people had to kill to eat, they were left alone. To make matters worse, the depression drove many white men to trapping and there was an invasion of white strangers who planned to trap till times got better."

"Didn't the natives resent the intrusion of these white trappers?"

"Oh, yes, but what could they do? Besides, they are fundamentally law-abiding."

"What was the story behind the killing at Obed Lake in the early Thirties?"

"Oh," replied Shand, "the natives were not involved in that. That was a white man's squabble." And then he went on to tell me his version of this tale.

For years a white trapper by the name of Andy, who long ago has gone to his reward, tended his lines in the Marlboro–Obed country. He was a solitary individual and maybe a bit queer, but he was well liked by everyone in the area and by the two or three merchants with whom he dealt. For some years he had lived in a cabin on Obed Lake and trapped out from there. Now the muskrats liked Obed Lake, and its marshy shores were dotted with their houses. Since by right of having trapped it for years this lake was Andy's exclusive domain, he felt free to practise his theories of conservation on it.

For a couple of years the price of rats had been low, but Andy knew that possibly the next year the price would be up again. So during the years of low prices he did not trap the lake, and the rats had multiplied about as much as the food supply or natural diseases would let them. In any event, in the year of the trouble, whenever Andy walked around the lake it seemed filled with muskrats swimming about or hunched up eating lily roots. As summer advanced into fall, it became clear that the price of muskrat skins was going to be up. Andy's practice of conservation was going to pay off. The lake teemed with rats and the price was up. Just to be sure that he would reap his bonanza, he warned all the natives in the area that no one was to trespass on his lake. They understood and stayed away. They knew that at times old Andy could be most cantankerous.

Just when the ice was forming at the edge of the lake and when Andy was busy checking and repairing his traps and whittling an extra supply of wooden stretchers for rat skins, a construction train parked beside the railroad track a mile from the lake. The train remained there for some weeks as various repairs were made to the track. Now the cookee in his spare time was accustomed to stretching his legs by taking his ·22 and wandering through the forest picking off bush partridges. As was to be expected, his nomadic feet took him to the lake, and as he studied the marshy shore with its countless muskrat houses his eyes fairly popped. He hastened back to the cook-car, confided in a companion, and the two of them sent to Edmonton for a supply of traps.

The hogger on the locomotive saw the traps when they arrived. He was an Edson man and for years had heard of Andy and his temper, so he made a point of warning the cookee.

"Better watch yourself, son, if you're aimin' to trap Obed Lake – that's Andy's preserve and he's a cantankerous old cuss. If you bother his rats there'll be trouble and we'll have to get a new bull cook. Stay away from Andy's rats – and I'm not foolin'."

Meanwhile as Andy patrolled his preserve he noticed the bull cook's tracks where for some hundreds of yards he had wandered along the shore. These were made by a white man's boots and not by a native's moccasins.

"The breeds know better than to come sneaking round here," he muttered, and resolved to keep watch.

One evening a day or so later the cookee and his friend set out for the lake with a score of traps dangling from their shoulders. Next morning the head cook in the caboose on the railway was in a vile mood as he banged about in his kitchen preparing breakfast for the gang and cursing because his helper was not there. The hogger, when he came in to eat and discovered that the bull cook and his companion were missing, was the only man really alarmed. Putting two and two together, he would not allow anyone to go to search the shores of the lake. "Too damned dangerous," he said. "Send a wire to the Mountie at Edson. He knows old Andy and he's the man to investigate."

When the Mountie came he cautioned the rest of the gang to let him go alone to visit Andy. At the shore of the lake, where a small open point projected out from the spruce trees, he found the bodies of the cookee and his companion, and hurried over to the trapper's shack. He found Andy busily whittling stretchers and charged him with the crime, taking extra precautions to warn him that anything he might say would be used against him. But Andy needed no warning. "Don't know anything about it," he said. And even when lodged in jail at Fort Saskatchewan he protested his innocence.

Meanwhile the Mountie sent the construction crew to bring in the bodies, pointing out a bizarre feature of the case. The bull cook had been shot through the head. His companion bore no marks of any wound. Evidently only one shot had been fired. That shot was the last sound the companion had heard, as from sheer terror his heart had failed before he pitched over to lie beside the bull cook's body.

News of the murder spread over the area, and no one doubted that Andy was guilty, yet everyone hoped that the crime could not be laid at his door. More than one friend offered to put up the money to see that he got a good lawyer. Others were ready to testify as to his good behaviour and the respect in which he was held. When he came up for trial the following spring, his lawyer used all the tricks of his long experience. When Andy faced a jury of his peers he was found not guilty.

"I didn't know Andy," said Shand, musing over the story, "but I often speculated about his guilt with a friend of mine, an ex-Mountie. As we talked he would say, 'You wait, some time I'll get a drink into old Andy and I'll find out.' A year or so later he had his chance, and as he told me the story it went something like this:

" 'Old Andy came to Edson one night,' said the Mountie, 'and two or three or us invited him over for a drink. After a while I got him talking and asked him what he thought of all this business of lawyers and juries and judges.'

" ' "Lotta damned fools," said Andy. "Even my lawyer – mind, he was sure good to me and I like him, but all of 'em's a pack of fools. You know what he said at the trial? I was sitting there and all the people were around and he got up and spoke for a long while and at the end of his speech he pointed to me and he said 'Look at my client. He's an old man, grey and stooped, and failing rapidly, poor old man. And the prosecutor says that in the evening, as it was getting dark, at two hundreds yards across the bay of the lake my client shot the victim between the eyes. Why, at that distance, in the half light, he wouldn't have been able to hit a man, let alone drill him between the eyes.'

" ' "Then," Andy continued, "the jury voted to let me off. Why," he said, "the big fools. I'd like to show 'em how to shoot. Why, at two hundred yards I could hit a silver dollar every time." ' "

"So Andy went back to trap?" I inquired by way of rounding off the story.

"Well, yes, he did," said Shand. "But not to his muskrats. You see, since he was in jail all winter there was no sense letting a lake full of rats perish from starvation or a hard winter, so the Marlboro natives moved in and made a killing. Andy came back to an empty lake."

"Those rats must have been a godsend to the natives during the depression."

"They were."

For the next several years after 1915, Shand was busy as a ranger in summer and a trapper in winter. Little of moment occurred, although he did have an encounter with grizzly bears one day after he and his horses had crossed Rocky Pass and had started down the Muskeg River. As he rode along he spotted two cubs playing on the river bank immediately below the trail. Now, grizzly cubs are always a danger signal, and so as not to blunder into trouble he stopped. If the mother bear should turn out to be right with them he could ride away, and the bears, his horses and himself would all be relieved. He expected to see the mother on the gravel bar below the cubs, but while he sat his horse, searching for her with his eyes, his ears were assailed by a woof and a grunt from the hillside above him. In spite of his care, he had got into the most dangerous situation the woods held – he had come between a mother grizzly and her cubs.

"She was sure gallopin' down the hillside," he said, "straight for the horses and me. I just had time to get my 38·55 Winchester off my saddle and let her have it. Luckily I hit her in the throat and she rolled down almost to where the horses and I had been – I say had been, because we sure didn't wait for her.

"I was sorry to have to kill her and was worried about the cubs, but since it was in September they were a fair size and I hoped that they could fend for themselves. The next fall I saw a young grizzly near the same spot. It could well have been one of those cubs. This time, of course, we had no trouble and I was able to go on without molesting him. I've shot lots of black bears, either for food or because they were hanging around my shack and were bothering me, but I have only shot three or four grizzlies, and that was when we have had arguments along the pack trails."

In the spring of 1916 after Shand's ranger duties started, a Mounted Policeman stopped at his Muskeg River cabin. He wanted Shand to go with him to act as interpreter while he visited the various natives who were living in the Athabasca Forest Reserve. He was accompanied by Supervisor Charlie MacFadyen of the Forestry Department.

"What's the matter now?" asked Shand, putting on the kettle.

"Well," said the policeman, "I have orders to evict all half-breeds who live on the reserve. They're trespassers and will have to get off."

"You've taken on a man-sized job," said Shand. "You'll have your hands full for a while."

"I know," replied the Mountie, "but first I have to warn them all."

"But," said Shand, "they don't have to move. I was at the meeting at Jack Gregg's when they were told that, if they gave up their lands within the park, they could move on to Crown land anywhere else, and I distinctly remember the word 'anywhere.'"

"Well, you come along with me and interpret."

When Shand became proficient in the Cree language, he often acted as official interpreter. All government men dealing with the Indians preferred to have a white man act in this capacity, because they felt that his rendering of both sides of the discussion was apt to be more correct and to the point. They were suspicious, and usually with some justification, that a native interpreter might soften the impact of what they had to say and, especially in criminal cases, might shade his translation of a fellow native's testimony in his favour.

"Sure, I'll be glad to come," assented Shand, "but as soon as I tell them what you want, they'll ask me what I think about it."

"I suppose they will."

"And then I'll tell them that in my opinion they don't have to move."

"Well, that's up to you. Under the circumstances, I would do the same thing. As a matter of fact, I think you're right, but my job at the moment is to give them official notice to move. And I want you as interpreter, because you'll do it correctly and not soft-pedal what I have to say to them, but tell them exactly what I say."

So they set off to see Ewan Moberly. As usual amongst the sociable natives, several others were gathered at Ewan's, so other families got the news at the same time.

"Ewan," said Shand, "the Mountie is here because orders have come out from Ottawa that everyone has to move off the forestry reserve."

Then he explained very carefully the reason for the move. Ewan looked at him for a moment and then said, "But we've built houses here, we've cultivated some crops. Besides, we like it here and we obey all the laws and also help with fighting fires. It's only a few years since we moved from Jasper Park and now they want to make us go somewhere else."

There was a pause while Shand interpreted and the Mountie made notes.

Then Ewan said, "Shand, what do you think – do we have to move?"

"No, I don't think so."

"What's he say?" asked the Mountie.

"He asked me if they really had to move, and I told him that I didn't think so."

There was much more discussion. Then they went in to Ewan's shack, had tea and a bite to eat and went on to break the news to the other natives. It took several days to go around to all of them, and as soon as the job was over Shand went back to Entrance.

He didn't forget the problem facing his friends in their threat of eviction. Neither did he let anyone else forget, for he rounded up all the men who were still in the country and who in 1910 had been at either of the meetings when the exodus from Jasper Park was first discussed. From these men he obtained statements of their understanding of what the half-breeds had been told. According to the Ottawa version of the meeting, they had been told that they could move on to any *vacant surveyed* Crown land. While Shand hesitates to suggest that this exception was added as an afterthought, he is firm in his belief that at the meeting the exception was not pointed out. In the end, after long and voluminous correspondence with Ottawa, the matter was dropped. Some years later Malcolm Norris, the President of the Alberta Métis Association, wrote asking him for a sworn statement of his version of the original verbal agreement, because there was some fear even then that action still might be taken against the natives.

CHAPTER
FOURTEEN

—◦{✳}◦—

Iₙ the fall of 1918 Shand built a new cabin on the Muskeg River about sixty miles north of Entrance. Ever since his championship of the cause of the natives, he had been held in the highest esteem, and more than ever he was a welcome visitor in shack or teepee. In the Smoky River country the natives were well off, and all owned bunches of horses and some cattle. They had comfortable log houses in which they lived in winter, with cookstoves, furniture and many modern accessories, such as gramophones and sewing machines. They also had many necessary farm implements to cultivate the land where suitable. Nevertheless they preferred to live by the chase instead of by agriculture, especially since the climate was rather too severe for extensive cultivation. In summer they lived in their teepees, moving about as their fancy dictated, always camping where there was good feed and water for their considerable herds of horses. Theirs was a happy, carefree life.

All summer long the men brought in meat, and all summer the squaws dried it or made pemmican. The hunters might be lucky enough to get lots of fresh meat during the winter, or they might not, but the squaws usually had a good supply put by. Wood could be cut any hour of the day or night; the horses that lived had colts the next spring, and that would take care of that; but food had to be conserved. At times they went hungry, but rarely.

And of course no one went hungry so long as any neighbours had food. As well as being kindly and hospitable, the natives were generous. In conformity to custom ages old, food was common property, freely taken, gladly given, and prestige sat at the hearth of the skilful hunter.

"The only real case of selfishness I can remember," said Shand, "ended in the death of Kusta Wanyandi. Several of the natives, on their way out to Entrance in the spring of 1921, had stopped near Cabin Creek one noon to light a fire and to boil a kettle of tea. In one of the sudden changes in weather it had turned quite cold and a light snow was falling. When all the other men had eaten and were ready to go on, Kusta complained of the cold and said he would sit by the fire for a few moments longer and then would soon catch up to them. As they left, the men commented on his strange action, but soon forgot about it. At dark when they camped for the night, Kusta had not come up with them. For a while they speculated about what had become of him, but since at times in the past he had been unsocial and secretive, they went to sleep, expecting to find him in camp in the morning.

"Next morning he was still missing, so they started back to see if any misfortune had befallen him, but could not find any trace of him till they got back to their previous campfire. There he was, sitting with his back to a tree and his legs spread out with the fire between them just as they had left him, except that the fire was out and he was frozen stiff. By the look of the tracks, they decided that after they had left him he had never moved from his sitting position. In a matter of seconds they found out why. Between his legs was a bottle of moonshine with perhaps an ounce of the liquor still in it. Inclined to be somewhat unsociable, he had obtained this liquor some time in the past and carried it with him. To his companions around the fire the previous noontime a drink would have been most acceptable, and divided between the five or six men, its effect would have been cheering without doing the least harm. But Kusta was selfish, preferring to keep it to himself, so he had made up a pretext to stay by the fire.

"Liquor is the curse of the natives," concluded Shand.

The friendliness and sociability of the natives were unfailing. Throughout all the decades Shand lived amongst them, the genuineness of their welcome to each other and to him contrasted strangely with the bickering and enmity in white communities. Simple people they might be, leading a simple life in a severe environment, yet their sincerity far outweighed their lack of material culture.

In spite of distance, they visited back and forth. Twenty miles was no barrier to a social visit. Gladly they went that distance to exchange news, to see or to help those who from sickness or bad luck were in need. These visits were always enjoyed and caused no trouble or extra work to the host. The visitors became one of the family, helped with the work or went out to hunt partridges or fish, or whatever else was needed in the larder. People travelling in the bush nearly always carried their own blankets. A teepee never appeared to be quite full and there was always room for just one more; or if the visitors were really too numerous then a lean-to would be erected outside close at hand for sleeping quarters while the meals were taken in the teepee. A visitor's moccasins were always mended, or a new pair given him before he set out again on his way. The conventional short visit of civilization was usually prolonged into two or three days when one had come a long distance, and the time passed all too quickly in conversation or in poker. This could be called the national game of the fur country. Everyone, white man, Indian or half-breed, knew and enjoyed it, and as the games were always played for trifling stakes, they never became dull. Indians who could not speak a word of ordinary English could understand and speak "poker English."

The acme of sociability, however, was reached in the "tea" and "give-away" dances. For all peoples, dancing is a fundamental emotional outlet. What the Red River jig was to the Prairies, or the square dance to the west, or the more sophisticated dances to the early settlers, the tea and give-away dances were to the natives. The tea dance centred around a copious and ever replenished supply of tea, strong and black as sin. Of all the gifts of the white man to his red brother, some of them of dubious value, none was more welcome or more pleasurable than tea. Tea may be the national drink of Englishmen, but in the vast muskegs, the endless forests or the unending barren lands, tea is the universal drink.

For a tea dance the floor of teepee or shack was cleared and an incredible number crowded into the confined space and, to the beating of drums, danced around the fire in an endless shuffle. These instruments were homemade by forming a wide flat loop of willow or spruce and covering it with a sheepskin dressed in the same way as parchment, and they were beaten with a short round stick. When two or three players performed at once, the effect was lively and gay. The women and girls joined in at certain times with a wordless melody, while the dancers stepped slowly around the fire. With rests or intervals, the dance might go on all afternoon or even through the night.

The give-away dance was more lively. In it, men and women asked each other to dance, but before doing so had to give the partner a nominal present. These presents or tokens of them were held by each throughout the dance. The excitement was great, and young people often gave practically all they possessed – silk handkerchiefs, blankets, rifles and horses. Tea and refreshments were always at hand, and sometimes when lots of people were gathered together, as in summer at a trading post, one of these dances might last for two or three days and nights. At times, in place of actual gifts exchanging hands, tokens were substituted and were later redeemed. A long stick, for instance, might represent a horse, and a short one a dog. Shand had an interesting experience along these lines. At a give-away dance a young woman, on asking him to be her partner, gave him a short stick for which he exchanged some trifle. Next day she redeemed her pledge by taking him over and giving him a vicious husky dog which was tied nearby. He had to be kept tied up because he hated everyone except his mistress. No one else could touch him. Yet there was no guile in the girl's gift. She valued this dog and had given Shand what was perhaps her dearest possession.

Shand, too, was leery about the dog, but he could not refuse the spirit of the gift, and he resolved to make friends with the beast. He had never owned a husky, but conceivably he could put this one to some use, and secretly he was grateful for the girl's obvious kindness and felt that he could not let her down. So he decided to make the men who had laughed do so on the other side of their faces. He knew better than to try to lay his hand on the brute. Instead, he left him tied up for two or three days, but every now and then went over and gave him pieces of meat. At the end of that time, while he knew that the dog would still resent any attempt to handle him, he fed him once more and untied him.

"Come along," he said. The beast, hitherto accustomed to curses and blows and the usual starvation of Indian dogs, followed Shand, the only man who had treated him kindly. In the course of a week or two the dog responded to kindness so much that he became his inseparable companion – a wise guardian and an unquestioning servant.

"New Year's," continued Shand, thinking back to many a celebration, "what we Scots know as Hogmanay, has far greater meaning to the natives than Christmas. Since in general their white ancestry is Scottish or French, and since both these races set great store by New Year's, the natives do likewise. Moreover, they are mainly of the Catholic faith and devoted French priests minister to them.

"In the Smoky River country their spiritual headquarters is Lac Ste Anne, and every year that they can do so, they make the pilgrimage there in July. For years Father Beaudry travelled amongst these people – a fine gentleman and well educated as are all priests. Perhaps he was close to them because his mother had been a half-breed from the Winnipeg area and was one of the Grants so famous in Red River history. Amongst Indians and half-breeds everywhere the Roman Catholic Church has established many missions where children are educated free and taught various trades if desired, and their efforts to help the people is beyond all praise. The priests are untiring in their ministration to the sick and dying, and in summer or winter undertake long trips by horse, canoe or dog train wherever their presence is desired. They live humble, frugal lives and are one of the chief factors in the wonderful peace and lawfulness of the back area.

"A squaw's life is hard, but it has its rewards in the respect in which she is held. Of course squaws are like white women. Some are fine, patient old souls, some are embittered and scold. When this scolding becomes too much for the men, they talk back and shut the old lady up by calling her an *Iosegun* – a sour berry – a bitter one. The word means gooseberry, and not far from the highway about halfway between Whitecourt and Valleyview lies Iosegun Lake.

"But sour or not, all of the elder women are experts at making clothes out of hides. They make the most beautiful moccasins, gloves and shirts out of tanned moose and caribou skins. They are good housekeepers too – clean and tidy. Of course you'd expect tidiness from a nomadic people. One thing that always interested me was the amount of sphagnum moss they used.

Along the trails there were many muskegs, and here and there in some of them grew this particular long-fibred moss. During the summer the women used to pull great quantities of it, and the willows nearby would be bent over where they had hung it to dry. Then, some other time, they would gather it and store it away. Cloth was scarce and was too precious to use for wiping rags and scrubbing. So for scouring and cleaning the women used sphagnum moss. A wad of it always lined the papoose's backboard, both because it was soft and comfortable and because the mother could change it as a white woman changes her baby's diapers. The women used this too for sanitary purposes.

"The squaws have a rare sense of humour too. It is restricted, of course, to the purview of their environment, but they laugh and joke and have a merry old time."

The winter of 1918–1919 stands out in Shand's memory. That fall when he left Entrance for his winter's trapping, great things were happening in the vast world of civilization. For one thing, the end of the war was in sight. But war or no war, only the slightest echoes of the turmoils in the civilized world ever penetrated the Smoky River country. Once he rode over the hill above the Athabasca, then for another six months civilization was shut out. Shand looked forward to another pleasant winter in his cabin on the Muskeg River.

Even the horses seemed glad when they reached home once more, and Kate crowded up close to the cabin door waiting her turn to be unsaddled. Shand went about his customary preparations for the winter. While he was waiting for the colder weather when the furs would become prime, he rode over to visit his friends at Grande Cache and spent a few days with them. They too were settling down into the winter, were well and happy and optimistic about the trapping prospects.

Although the weather was relatively mild when Shand returned to his cabin, he felt chilly and hastened to light the fire. He prepared his usual supper, but strangely enough had no appetite for it, although for a long time he sat by the fire sipping cup after cup of tea. "Must have a cold coming on," he thought as he sought the warm comfort of his blankets. He had a fitful sleep, but dozed off for a few hours before morning. When he woke up he felt as if his head was on fire, and his lungs and throat were choked with phlegm. A great lassitude had come over him.

"I've really got a cold this time," he thought, and putting more wood on the fire, he took out a bottle of pain killer and drank some. It burned his throat, but cheered him up a little and made his breathing easier. Before he knew it, he had swallowed a whole bottle – an incredible dose.

The next time he woke up the fire was out, and even in his warm blankets he was cold, but his breathing was much easier. It was late in the afternoon, so he believes that he had been asleep or unconscious for nearly twenty-four hours. In any event, he felt better and soon started the fire and made more tea. It was two or three days, however, before he had strength enough to do more than keep the fire going.

Then, about the time he was able to get up, Adam Joachim came over to seek his help, for in time of sickness Shand's common sense and his medicines were often called upon. "And," said Adam, "this is a time of great sickness. Half the people of Grande Cache are sick, and already five are dead." Could Shand come over and help?

When Shand described his own experience, Adam nodded his head. "That's it," he said. "Today a headache – great weakness. Tomorrow, dead." Some great evil was abroad in the land.

So he gave Adam several bottles of pain killer and what other medicines he could supply, and promised to come over as soon as he felt strong enough to catch and ride a horse.

Two or three days later, he arrived at Grande Cache. Dismay and fear filled every face, and in a corner of every cabin lay someone gasping for the air that could not enter the lungs. Already ten had died.

The survivors spoke gently to each other, wondering what the morrow would bring. Death had never been a stranger in teepee or cabin, but it had none of the dread mystery of this savage scourge which struck so swiftly. Some it spared. Some it smote lightly, and they lived. Others – mainly the young adults, the vigorous hunter and the buxom squaw – it cut off. The crones and the callow were left to mourn. One cabin, where three of a family of four had died, lay empty.

Shand and some of his friends who had recovered or had been

spared did what they could, bringing in meat or wood, spooning out pain killer, and laying out the dead in the empty cabin. In the Grande Cache settlement one person died in every five. In every family, the Caracontés and the Wanyandis, the Moberlys and Macdonalds, the Joachims and the de Lormes, some gap was left. At the end of three weeks, twenty bodies, frozen stiff, lay piled on the floor of the abandoned cabin.

Then as silently as it had fallen, the scourge lifted. On a gravelly knoll above the stream Shand and the other men scratched graves out of the frozen gravel. With bowed heads the men listened as, amidst the anguished wail of Indian women, Adam Joachim consigned the victims to their eternal rest. As the gravel was heaped up, the pine trees sighed and swayed before the wintry wind – the clean wind that had swept away the scourge. In a few days Shand and the men had fashioned the little roofs that mark the graves of natives – the roofs that symbolize loving kindness and protection from the evils that beset man here and hereafter – the roofs that ward off the digging claws of wandering wolves.

The Spanish flu of 1918 had passed on.

The summer after the flu was dry. Scorched leaves and dry pine needles baked in the sun. Shand and the other rangers dreaded the forest fire that would surely come. When it did come, they fought it manfully with horses and hand shovels, with buckets and trenches. Eventually, after terrible damage to miles of forest, it too became history.

That summer on the Prairies, unknown to the people of the Smoky River country, the drouth seared crops and even wild hay was sparse and scraggly. In the fall of 1919 many small farmers sold all their cattle, for they had little feed. The larger ranchers shipped cattle to farms in the bush lands where hay was plentiful. Some of them sought large wild meadows and marshes secreted in the unknown forest, to which they might drive their cattle for a winter's feed.

That fall Shand, loafing at Entrance for a few days, sat on the porch of Roy Woodley's store while the train slowed to a stop. As he watched, two men, dressed in the neat, practical clothes of cow men, got off and piled their luggage on the platform. When they brought out two well-kept saddles and other riding gear, Shand pricked up his ears. They disappeared into the station for a moment, and then the agent came out and waved.

"Shand," he said, "here are two men who are looking for a man like you." And he introduced a man by the name of Dillon and his companion.

It turned out that they wanted someone to take them out on a trip, and they waved their arms in the general direction of north.

"How far back do you know this country?"

"I've been pretty well all over it back to the Smoky a hundred miles north and then many miles beyond that downstream."

"That's good, you're the man we want."

"Where do you want to go?" asked Shand.

"At the moment that's a secret. We'll tell you after we get out a way. You'd better take along grub for at least twenty days. Can you leave in the morning? You buy the grub, and we'll help you pack it."

"Well," thought Shand, "that's odd, but they look like decent fellows, and they act as if they had some money."

As soon as they started to help him pack he realized that these two knew horses and packing. Next day as they stopped on the trail for a bite of lunch, he again asked where they wanted to go.

"Keep on along this trail towards the Smoky, and tomorrow night we'll tell you. I'm sorry to be so secretive, but we don't want any news leaking back."

"It's funny," Shand thought, "they're not the kind to be running away from anything. They know pack horses and must have had a lot of experience. Surely they're not looking for gold – not in this country. Maybe it's coal."

At the first night's camp they helped with the supper and were easy to get along with and easy to talk to, but their secret gnawed away at Shand. After supper they went for a walk and seemed to be talking over their plans. It was not until twenty-four hours later, when they were camped on Moberly Creek eating supper, that they told him what was on their minds.

"It's been a dry year out on the Prairies," they explained. "We both have pretty big cattle spreads near Calgary, and this winter we're going to be short of feed. We've heard about tremendous hay meadows up here on the Big Smoky. We want to find some of these where we can come in and get hay and either haul it out or send some cattle in here for the winter."

They produced a map of the area and held it out. "Where are the meadows?"

"Why didn't you tell me before?" said Shand. Then he indicated on the map the large area he had travelled over during the last few years.

"You certainly are the man we want," said Dillon. "Now where are the meadows?"

"There just aren't any," Shand replied regretfully, shaking his head. "Oh, there are little meadows and pastures that will carry a few head of horses, but big meadows, no. There are none anywhere that I've been, and from what the natives tell me, there are none farther down the Big or the Little Smoky, or the Simonette. The only meadows that I've heard of that might measure up to your requirements are those on the west end of Lesser Slave Lake, although I've never seen them."

Their disappointment was evident in their tones and their faces. The meadows had meant so much to them.

"Next morning," relates Shand, "we set out once more for Entrance. I heard a year or so afterwards that they had gone back to Edmonton and taken the train for Lesser Slave Lake and were successful in their search.

"After a man has lived in an area for many years, all sorts of people come to him looking for information," Shand reflected. "I guess I'm a sort of 'old man of the mountains'!"

Shand's visitors also include surveyors, scientists and geologists – men for whom he once packed – or else men seeking out his advice on some new problem. Some visitors come because word has gone abroad of the very modest man whose long life in the forest makes him worth visiting.

"But not all my visitors come looking for undiscovered riches in the hills. Some have personal problems. One day some years ago, a woman drove up to my shack alone in an expensive car," Shand reminisced. "She was well dressed and well spoken, and yet she reminded me of someone I knew, but I couldn't place her. Like all city women, she had lipstick and powder and lacquered nails, but because of her black hair and something indefinable in her features, I knew that somewhere in her ancestry lay Indian blood.

"She introduced herself by her married name. Then she said, 'Of course, Mr Harvey, that won't mean anything to you. I used to be Gladys——.'

" 'Oh,' I said, 'are you Gladys?' And I was very glad to see her.

"Then she explained that she worked for one of the large retail stores in Edmonton and was doing so well that she was being sent to the United States on a buying trip. That was why she had come to see me. In order to enter the States she had to have a birth certificate or some proof of age.

" 'I think I was born in this country about the beginning of the First War. Could you tell me what year, or give me any information? You see,' she went on, 'I was undoubtedly baptized by the priest, but when the old church at Lac Ste Anne burned down many years ago, all the records were lost.'

"I looked at her for a minute and said, 'Yes, you were born around the end of October 1912. By and by I'll look up the exact date in my diary. I remember it well. Your dad was packing and guiding for Joe Errington's party when he was looking for coal on the north fork of the Wildhay. He had brought your older sister and your mother to live with her folks, the Moberlys. I was camped within a few miles, and on the day you were born Philip de Lorme came over and asked me if I would find your father and tell him that everything was all right. I remember you as a little girl, until you were perhaps six or seven years old.'

" 'Could you give me some sort of written document stating that?' she asked.

" 'Certainly,' I said. 'I'll write it out and we'll get a Justice of the Peace to witness it. Let me see now, Gladys, wasn't it?'

" 'Yes, Gladys Margaret.'

"So we sat and talked for a long time, and I told her many tales of her childhood. After we had sort of talked each other out and she was ready to go, I sat back and looked at this fine woman who was doing so well in Edmonton. 'Well, well,' I said. 'To think that you are little Gwennin.'

" 'Gwennin,' she said, 'who's Gwennin?'

" 'You were, of course. Your mother could not pronounce Gladys very well and called you Gwennin.'

" 'Oh, am I Gwennin? Well,' she said. 'I've always wondered who Gwennin was. You see, I have a snapshot at home showing Mother with two girls and a baby, and the names are written on the back of the picture. I've never been able to figure out who Gwennin was. I thought that she must have died and that I must have been the baby in the picture so wouldn't remember her.' "

As Shand told the story, he added, "She was quite surprised to find that she was Gwennin. Once in a while she still comes out to see me, and every year she sends me a Christmas card."

During the fall of 1919, after Shand had returned from his trip with the two ranchers who were in search of hay, he spent a few more days at Entrance. Then, about the middle of September, he set out once more for his cabin on the Muskeg. There was nothing to indicate that the West was entering the hardest winter of a generation. The weather was glorious. The muskegs were red and russet, for the shrubbery had ripened, and bearberry leaves clothed the ground in a red carpet. The blueberry bushes with their pinker red glowed in the sunshine. And to the north and east as Shand neared the Muskeg River, the great Simonette ridge was a mass of gold as the aspens ripened in the haze. A magnificent hill it was, this height of land, the father of four streams. Off it to the west started the Simonette, while farther round towards the east the Little Smoky gathered up many tributaries for its two-hundred-mile voyage through the autumn woods towards the Peace River. Farther around, dropping off its southeast corner, ran streams plunging down to the Berland, which was on its way to the Athabasca. Off it, too, came Lone Teepee Creek, rushing on to join the Muskeg a mile or so north of Shand's cabin. The Simonette ridge was a prominent landmark.

But for all its mildness and for all its beauty, September could be deceptive too. Shand, ever one to be cautious, kept an eye on the weather. Glorious golden days lasted till near the end of the month, and then one afternoon a haze spread over the west. Within a couple of hours a blizzard as vicious as he ever remembered lashed out over the valley of the Muskeg. It meant little to Shand working around his cosy cabin, but he was to remember that day long after others were forgotten.

For that day Sam Mahon froze to death. He and his brother-in-law, John McVicar, had been studying the coal deposits in the area, and that day their whole party was pulling out for the season and was well started on its way to Entrance. They had crossed the Muskeg and come to the unnamed creek that ever afterwards was to be known as Mahon Creek. It was a lovely day, and all were travelling in their shirt sleeves. There was some possibility that coal might outcrop on this creek, and for a final fling Sam and his companion Tom decided to walk down it for a mile or so to prospect. Then they planned to cut across the second leg of the triangle and thus intercept the pack trail. After that, by hurrying, they proposed to catch up with the rest of the party before they made camp for the night.

As the pack train swung along an hour or so after they left, the storm struck. Its sudden onslaught sent them all scurrying to untie their coats from the pack saddles. In a few minutes the aisles of the forest were hidden in the blast of the blizzard. Within an hour the deep carpet of leaves was buried under two or three inches of snow. The pack train kept on its way, but McVicar was worried about Sam and Tom who were afoot and coatless. Both were well versed in the ways of the bush, but even then he knew that they would have a miserable trip till they caught up. Soon camp was made, and while the kettle boiled everyone kept an eye on the backward trail.

When the early dusk was falling and the men had not come in, McVicar and one or two others set out along the trail, carrying the men's coats. But after dusk they came back alone. Beside a blazing fire they kept a sleepless vigil, firing two shots from time to time to apprise the wanderers of the location of the camp. At daylight all set out to look for the lost ones. Even the packer, who knew the country, had trouble following the trail now that it was buried in this faceless snow.

After going back four or five miles, the guide yelled. As the others came up he pointed to the fresh tracks of a man who evidently had stumbled along in the snow and crossed the trail without recognizing it. Two men hastened along the tracks, while the others followed back along the way he had come, looking for his partner. In a few minutes both parties were back, the first helping in an exhausted man, and the second coming in to report that Sam Mahon had died of exposure within two hundred yards of the trail.

The story, briefly told, was that the previous evening the two men had set out for the trail about the time they had planned. While on their way back the storm had struck, and they could not make out the pack trail. Soon, shivering with cold, they knew they were lost. They had no matches, which they had left in their coats. With matches they could have started a fire with some birchbark, without them they were helpless. There was no use in wandering further, and so as to keep moving without going astray, Tom selected one tree and tramped round and round it all night. After daylight he set out again to find the pack trail and it was his track that McVicar's packer found.

Sam Mahon, in his weariness, sat down with his back to a tree. There in the morning his friends found him dead from exposure.

This September storm was winter's opening gun, and never once during the next six months did it relax its grip. Snow fell frequently, and soon it filled the valleys to a depth of three or four feet. By January the last of the natives' cattle, unable to paw through the snow, had died. By the end of February most of their horses had starved, and March saw the death of all but a dozen of them. Once in a while a feeble chinook blew, but it only made matters worse by putting a crust on the snow. Shand's favourite mare Kate, now a pitiful wreck, hung around his cabin, the spaces between her ribs resembling a stretched accordion, while behind them her flanks fell away, contracting against her empty stomach. But Shand did not lose her or her companions either. Each day when the pawing horses could barely reach the grass, he went out with his shovel and laboriously cleared away snow till they could get food for another day. Within the area he had shovelled they were yarded by the depth of the surrounding snow. By his efforts alone his horses survived.

Men hungered too. Daily they strapped on snowshoes and hunted the silent forests. They came back with stories of moose yarded up in the alder thickets, dying, when the snow was too crusted and deep for them to break out to new browse. Wolves in packs pulled down many an antlered monarch or killed with abandon in the moose yards. Shand went abroad hunting. One day across a little opening he saw a moose, his splendid antlered head and his withers and the dark line of his back showing above the snow. Shand slipped off his mitt, brought his gun up and then hesitated. The moose did not move. He shouted, but it paid no attention. Then Shand snowshoed over the icy crust and approached the beast with his knife at hand and his gun ready. But these precautions were not necessary. The moose had been dead for days and was frozen stiff. It had plunged forward through the snow till exhaustion had stopped its struggles, and there it remained to freeze slowly. It was so thin that Shand left it where it was.

The natives too grew thin on their slender diet, but were never near starvation. As the winter hung on, with some settling of the snow and some thawing in April, although very little, everyone was anxious to get out to Entrance for more flour and supplies. But it was the first week in June before they could do so.

"But," says Shand, "I got all my horses back to Entrance without losing any." So ended the severe winter of 1919–1920, with snow falling till June.

CHAPTER FIFTEEN

S HAND is an old man now. Some days he walks with a cane – not a polished malacca or black briar but a spruce stick. Most of his old friends are dead: Adam Joachim, Vincent Wanyandi, Ernie Harrison and Montana Pete. Roy Woodley is gone too. So, for that matter, is his store, and indeed the village of old Entrance which held it. Even the railway steel which years ago curved around the hill near the water's edge is gone. Long ago it was taken up, and now the grade serves as the highway going west to Solomon Creek and Brulé. But amongst spreading spruce trees overlooking the roaring river and a few hundred feet back from the old track and far above it, Shand's shack remains.

This snug cabin which he built on Roy Woodley's land in 1921 amongst tiger lilies and purple loment has been his headquarters ever since. For many years, while he roamed the forests trapping, it served as his home during the short intervals when he returned to the society of Entrance. Then in 1946, when he sold his Moberly Creek cabin and gave up trapping as a full-time vocation, it became his permanent home.

What remains of old Entrance is kept alive because the forestry headquarters stayed there. Today from these buildings a gravelled highway leads up the hill to the right on its way to the Muskeg River, the Big Smoky and even to Grande Prairie. Another follows the old railway grade west for a few miles to Brulé Lake and then strikes out twenty-five miles to Rock Lake – another of Shand's old stamping grounds.

Shand's friend Billy Magee, a forestry employee charged with predator control, owns the old Woodley land. Billy, a much younger man, is not only an ideal landlord, but is Shand's most frequent visitor. Billy, too, knows every creek and meadow of the Smoky River country, and many an hour these two spend together. And then, across the old railway track and looking right down on the river, live Bill and Jackie Hanington. Bill also earns his living out of the vast wilderness, for he is a technical forester who moved out from Montreal when the new paper mill opened up at Hinton. He is a nephew, two or three times removed, of the Hanington who, with Jarvis in 1875, explored the passes north of Entrance, trying to find a route for the CPR. Bill thus travels over much of the area trod by this predecessor.

Among Shand's many visitors are the natives from Grande Cache and Muskeg River. In days gone by they came out to the store at Entrance, turned their horses out to graze with his and set up their teepees nearby. Now, with a gravelled road running far back into the Smoky River country, they hire somebody with a truck to bring them out over the road in two hours – a distance that used to take eight days by packhorses. In any event, they still come out, and when they do they go up to visit Shand and keep him posted on the happenings in the area he knows so well.

"But," says the old ranger, "each year fewer of them come. Each year someone of the generation I knew comes no longer. In most cases their sons and daughters visit me, and now and then, but rarely, their grandchildren. I can't keep the grandchildren straight – whose sons or daughters they may be. Anyway, things are changing with the natives too, and the young people are seeing too much of civilization before they are morally prepared for it. They are not the honest, sturdy people their grandparents were."

Shand continued to trap from his shack on the Muskeg River until 1923. Then he set out for Scotland for a rather extensive trip. Finally after many months he rejoiced as his homeward-bound locomotive puffed out of Hinton. There, once more, Roche Miette, the old guardian of the pass, stood out bold and blue against the evening sky. In a moment, with a roar, the train swept along high above Prairie Creek and plunged into the dark seclusion of the forested river bank. Shand reached up for his bag, and in a few moments the weariness of the long train trip was all over, and he was heading for the warm welcome of Roy Woodley's store. Once more he was home.

As in every other little town, the people of Entrance assembled to watch the arrival of every train that stopped at the little station. About the time of Shand's return, however, there was one train which they awaited with particular interest. Shand does not remember how the word reached Entrance or who received it, but about 1925 a message came saying that one of the area's earliest white residents – a man out of the legendary past – was on his way to the Coast and would pass through Entrance on a certain train. Everyone had presumed that long ago he must have passed to his eternal reward. The old natives shook their heads in wonder and, reckoning far back into the dim years, stated that the old man must now be over ninety. Nevertheless, they all turned out to watch for the train. Most in evidence was the whole Moberly clan, three generations of them, for word had come that the passenger was to be the patriarch who seventy years ago had ruled Jasper House, Henry John Moberly.

No, the long passenger trains did not stop in Entrance, but it was expected that the old man would be standing on the back vestibule and would wave as the train flashed by. Then all would see the man whom no one, not even his sons, could remember, but who indeed had fathered this tribe of resolute mountaineers. Eventually, up Hinton way, they heard the train whistling for the crossing and then roaring as it flashed over the Prairie Creek bridge. Finally boring into the darkness came the great headlight. With one accord the crowd swayed closer to the rails as with its usual roar the train clattered by. But, alas, Henry John Moberly, the patriarch, was apparently fast asleep in some berth.

After his return to Entrance in 1924, Shand went back to his trap lines and now and then varied this with a spell as a forest ranger. Back and forth he travelled, on one venture or another, traversing every foot of his beloved foothills country.

In the fall of 1960, when the old domain in which Shand had spent over fifty years was accessible by car, Frances and I were anxious to see it. One day Shand undertook to show us some of the old trails and his old cabins and camping spots. On a morning in August, the three of us and Billy Magee drove some eighty miles along the forestry road north of Entrance to the site of Shand's cabin on the Muskeg. The round trip, which used to take him two weeks, was done by car in about five hours, with many a stop to look at scenery and points of interest.

From Old Entrance we headed the car up the hill and in fifteen minutes were at Jarvis Lake.

"We've covered this distance in a quarter of an hour," said Shand, looking at his watch. "We usually made this lake at the end of the first day's trip from Entrance."

At Jarvis Lake we were over the first ridge, the height of land between the Athabasca and waters flowing via Jarvis Creek into the Wildhay River. The series of lakes on our right, which Shand called the Chain of Lakes, include Cache, Graveyard and Gregg Lakes, and he told us what he knew about the derivation of the names.

"Cache Lake gets its name because Hawkins, the DLS who ran the 15th and 16th Base Lines, had a supply of iron pins and grub packed into a cache there. In the timber on the east side of Graveyard Lake lies an old Indian burying ground, and Gregg Lake, of course, is named after Jack Gregg."

As we continued down the hill, we came to Twelve-Mile Creek, which by the old pack trail was that far from Entrance. As we continued the descent to within a mile of Moberly Creek, Shand asked us to slow up because we would soon be intersecting the 14th Base Line which fifty-three years previously he had helped to establish. On a side hill a painted sign proclaimed that it was on the base line, but without it we would never have known. The slash eight feet wide cut through the forests of 1907 had long since grown up.

A little farther on we crossed Moberly Creek where about forty years ago Shand had built a cabin. By walking a couple of hundred yards from the road, we came to it. The sod roof was falling in, and in general it was in a sad state of repair. Shand was most critical of the man to whom he had sold it for neglecting it so and for the general untidiness of the place.

Another seven or eight miles brought us to Pinto Creek. After driving about the same distance beyond that, we stopped to have lunch at the government picnic shelter on the bank of the Berland River. Three of four cars were parked there while their owners were out fishing. After a picnic lunch we set out again and soon were ascending the slope rising from Cabin Creek, and here Shand indicated another point of interest.

"Do you remember me mentioning the native who drank moonshine till he died? Well, the old trail was about a hundred yards off to our left, higher up the ridge. By the big tree there, Kusta Wanyandi froze to death in 1921. At that time I was living at my shack at Entrance, and the natives came in and told me about it."

Before long we reached the Muskeg River, a charming clear stream perhaps twenty feet wide. Here for a mile or so stretched meadows lush with grass. Here, too, was a neat Catholic church with its cemetery hard by. Trails branched off in all directions to perhaps a dozen neat log shacks back in various clumps of trees. For this is the present-day native settlement on the Muskeg River.

"Well," said Shand, "I knew about the church, but I didn't expect to find so many people living here. Joe Macdonald, my old trapping partner, lives here and so does Louis de Lorme. I wonder which is Joe's shack?"

As we drove along we came to a space cleared out of the spruce trees and bulldozed flat by the road crews.

"This was a road construction camp," said Billy Magee.

"Yes," said Shand. "I heard that they had chosen the same spot I picked out in 1917 when I built my shack here. It stood right here," he continued, locating himself by the trees behind and by the elbow of the stream that had been in front of his cabin.

Then, noticing a tent in the trees close to the road, Billy Magee and I walked over to greet this native family, while Shand and Frances came along more slowly. We were met by a woman whose iron-grey hair and forthright look stamped her with an air of authority. It turned out that her maiden name had been Caraconté and that now she was a widow with some children. The patience of her steady gaze and the wrinkles deeply incised in her face made her look old, although in reality she was about fifty. One of her daughters, a demure, neatly dressed girl of perhaps fourteen, showed little trace of Indian blood. The other one, perhaps two or three years older, was unmistakably Indian, and clad as she was in jeans and a red blanket coat she had the fresh sultry look of an Indian maiden ripe and confident. "If youth but knew what age can tell," I thought, looking from daughter to mother, from vernal voluptuousness to wrinkled visage.

As soon as Shand came up, the widow's wrinkles softened into a smile, and for a long while, oblivious of the rest of us, these two talked in the quiet musical cadence of Cree. Nearby, on the bank of the clear stream, the tent was pitched, and from it to a point high up in a nearby spruce ran a long yellow aerial wire. Blankets hung over branches to air, and on the ground, at the foot of another spruce, a bed had been made. Pack horses grazed along the stream. Wooden pack saddles hung in the crotches of two or three trees. A minimum of furniture was revealed by the wide open flaps of the tent, but from somewhere well back inside came the loud, continuous yowl of some radio singer endlessly reiterating his determination to end it all if he could not have "You, You, You."

But through it the soft flow of Cree continued as Shand asked for news of his old friends of the woods. Finally I heard the name "Dan'l" as he asked, "Where is Dan'l?" It turned out that Dan'l lived in a house nearby. The widow called a boy and sent over to get him.

Now Dan'l, I knew, would be Daniel Wanyandi, and in a moment he emerged from the bush, rolling a cigarette, and beaming at Shand. Daniel was a fine-looking man of medium height, with a friendly open face. While he smiled and shook hands, he professed not to speak English. For a long time Shand and his old crony chatted away, while Billy and Frances and I struck up a broken conversation with the Caraconté widow, who seeing that we were friends of Shand's, developed a command of English previously concealed.

Eventually we parted with smiles all around and set out to look around the small settlement, taking in the church and the cemetery, with its little roofs over the graves. Finally, after a call on one of Shand's early trapping partners, a swarthy Indian named Joe Macdonald, we set out for Entrance.

As we neared Entrance, Shand brightened up, and insisted that we have supper with him. While the kettle was boiling, he brought out a bottle of whisky and four glasses.

"Bottled on the Tay," he said, "and Tay water always did make the best whisky. That's the only luxury I allow myself now. It's the only luxury I need. When friends come, we can talk better over a drink or two.

"This is a special occasion," he continued. "It just struck me a moment ago. Fifty-five years ago today I reached Edmonton, so there's a special reason for a wee drop. You'll have to have a cold supper. For dessert there's some cakes from the store over at the railway, and I've got a nice piece of moose cooked up."

Some weeks later, about the middle of September, we paid Shand another visit. We planned to enjoy a day or so in Jasper, and during that time to check the manuscript with him to clear up some minor points and to correct others. This was to be our last visit to Shand for the purpose of getting his story, and was to be a sentimental journey, to follow the trails that Shand had trodden long ago and to follow in the steps of the railroad builders. From Lac Ste Anne we drove along the long-abandoned Canadian Northern grade, past Lake Isle, until we came out where the modern Jasper highway passes under the present Canadian National Railway at the Magnolia trestle. Then we swept on over the magnificent highway, which for most of the distance from Evansburg to Obed was laid on top of one or the other of the old grades, stopping now and then at some of the old railway construction camps. We paused at Evansburg to look at the footings of the long-abandoned high level bridge. A few miles farther on we were back on the old grade. Here, along this grade, heaped up fifty years ago with shovel and wheelbarrow, thousands of men had moiled, hundreds of men had died, and in the trees hard by lay the unrecognizable graves of the men who did not make it through to see the coming of the steel.

Our next stop was old Wolf Creek town. To reach it we left the highway, drove around by the modern hamlet and then walked along the track to the high banks, where the two bridges had been flung across the canyons. Little remained of the old town. The log and frame buildings were gone. The canvas-covered barns, bunkhouses and warehouses had left no trace to show where they had been. The tent-roofed gambling shacks and brothels had vanished as completely as the payrolls of their transient clientele or the girls who here had plied their trade.

We hastened back to the highway, through the thriving town of Edson, and some six miles west turned into the Coal Branch road. We followed that for a mile south, and turning off it for a few hundred yards came face to face with the Big Eddy trestle. It, too, was losing the fight for survival. In front of it, modern multi-yard scrapers had thrown a tremendous curving fill across the valley of the Sundance. Beyond it the famous old trestle was being dismantled. Here on the high bank we stood looking out at the Big Eddy from about the site of Ben Berthoux's store. At this spot at the north end of the old trestle, the Canadian Northern tracks had once had a stern struggle to cross those of its rival. But the struggle had long since ceased, and now some old concrete abutments bore mute testimony to the rivalry of the two roads.

Then after a peek at Bickerdike and the old Marlboro Cement Plant, we continued our trip. Soon, far to the west, Roche Miette stood sentinel over the gateway to the pass.

Spending the night in the luxurious comfort of the Athabasca Valley Hotel at Hinton was a far cry from the nights the packers had spent on the banks of Hardisty Creek a few hundred feet away. Next morning we continued our sentimental journey. Three miles west of Hinton we walked in along the high banks of Prairie Creek to the end of the railway bridge where fifty years before Shand had lived in the bootlegger's shack. Holes in the ground marked the remains of small cellars of the once booming end-of-steel town. Here many men had died of typhoid, and their graves must be somewhere about. Here, too, we thought, the Gregg girls had seen their first cat.

Returning to the car, we soon sped past the farms of some of the Moberly clan, and a short distance farther on Jack Gregg's old white frame house appeared to have weathered the years remarkably well. From Hinton to Fiddle Creek the modern highway has forsaken the old grade. Beyond the creek, however, we picked it up as we approached the remains of the mining town of Pocahontas. Five minutes later our car whisked us around the spur of Roche Miette – old Disaster Point. No longer do horses struggle up and down over the mountain ridge. No longer do Grand Trunk trains creep round the projecting rock. For dynamite and diesel-driven shovels have carved a way for a broad pavement to bend leisurely around the old dangerous point. No longer indeed do horses or even steam locomotives travel this way, for in the modern world of fish-tailed cars and diesel trains, horses and steam, like the disused pack trail or the deserted grade, are mere memories.

For a few days we lived in the comfort of Gordon Bried's

Palisades Motel. Here, amidst hot and cold water, an electric refrigerator and propane heat, we sat looking out the window at the site of Swift's ranch. For the motel is built on the only freehold land in the Park – the land on which Lewis Swift settled sixty-seven years ago. While Swift's buildings are long since gone and the Palisades Lodge occupies the bench on which they stood, the clear mountain brook still flows as of yore. On it, still in its old location, Swift's handmade waterwheel occupies a place of honour, for Gordon and Gwen Bried treasure all the relics of the days that are past. Close by is the old farm cart with its wheels cut from Douglas fir logs. So is the anvil Swift resurrected from Walter Moberly's Athabasca Depot, together with many another memento of the old Jasper Trail.

For a few days, under the clear blue skies of mid-September, we tarried. When we continued our tour we drove up the Miette River on the gravelled road which is not yet too proud to reveal the fact that it is the old Canadian Northern grade. Before long on the shore of beautiful Yellowhead Lake we passed the extensive ruins of a town that might have been – a town situated in one of the beauty spots of the mountains – Lucerne, the old Canadian Northern divisional point.

Here at the summit, visions of the men of years ago – Sandford Fleming, Reverend George Grant, Walter Moberly, the old railroad builders – crowded in upon us. Here, somewhere buried in the old Canadian Northern grade beneath us, lay the roots of the tree Moberly had blazed in 1872 and about which Shand had told us.

Through this pass from time immemorial had come a procession of Indians – Shuswaps, Snakes, Stonies and Crees, moving back and forth. Through this pass a hundred years ago had tramped the fur trade brigades, carrying buffalo leather from Edmonton to supply the posts in the northern interior of British Columbia and calling this the Leather Pass. Fifty years ago here at the summit had stood one of the hell-hole towns of unregulated construction. Here, for a few bustling years, surveyors and packers had been busy with their tasks: Oscar Englund, and Featherstonhaugh, James Shand-Harvey and Fred Kvass, Dolphus Moberly and Rod McCrimmon. Here, too, Baldy Red and Dirty Mag had acted out their little drama.

These mountains all around, so solemn and silent now, had once reverberated with dynamite blasts and echoed to the rending and clanking of steam shovels. Here mules had lifted up their voices to announce lunch time. Here too rose the steady thud of station men's picks, as foot by foot they built up the grade, or the clink of their shovels as, with bared heads, their fellows stood by while they filled in the grave of someone who had worked on the grade – someone whose name even they might not have known.

Finally, clanking and groaning, a rail at a time, the track-layer had edged forward, leaving the mountains ringing as brawny men pounded spikes with their swinging hammers. But then it turned out that it was not final after all. For, within a year or so, other men came to take up the rails, and for decades the grade lay abandoned – a pathway for wandering cougars.

Finally we descended the Fraser, and suddenly the splendour of Mount Robson's sheer face burst upon us. We continued to the old Tête Jaune Cache. On this flat the remains of once sturdy log buildings jut out from the trees. In many cases the roofs have fallen in and big poplars now grow within the rotting walls, but the old buildings are still there. As we moved from one to the other, we wondered what part each had played in the march of progress known as the railway. This building with the pipe-jack still in the high gable end – was this Baldy Red's destination with the seven dressed hogs which, when the police stopped him, turned out to have three bottles of whisky artfully sewn into each of their belly cavities? Or was it from this old ruin that Rod McCrimmon used to start his father's six-hundred-dollar team of great grey mules on their way, laden with freight for farther down the Fraser? Perhaps it was to this building that Fred Kvass and Shand had brought supplies after urging their pack saddles to Tête Jaune Cache.

At Tête Jaune Cache we had come to the end of the duplication of the railway grades. From here back to Edmonton, 280 miles away, two grades had run side by side. From here back to Edmonton one set of rails had been taken up within a handful of years after it had been laid, and for nearly fifty years its empty grade had been left to stare at an empty sky.

In spite of the appalling waste, however, some good resulted.

Much of the money poured out to build these two grades found its way into the pockets of the homesteaders. For working on these two lines west of Edmonton provided them with a grub stake when they needed it most – a fortuitous subsidy to the settlement of the West.

And the rivalry of the two grades thrusting west to Tête Jaune Cache has provided us with a fascinating chapter in the story of the opening up of the West. It is said, probably with little exaggeration, that for every mile of grade some man lost his life by accident, pneumonia or typhoid. In resting places unmarked these fifty years alongside the grade, or actually within it, lie many forgotten men who toiled to build the West.

Next morning we set out once more for Shand's cabin and for home. Once more we left the pavement at Prairie Creek and soon were crossing the Athabasca on the old Canadian Northern bridge, and moments later drew up before Shand's door.

For an hour or two we discussed various sections of the manuscript and settled many points where it had been unclear. The September sun streamed through the open door, while squirrels, gathering their winter's food supply, scurried about in the branches overhanging the cabin and rained spruce cones on its roof. As we sat sipping a drink bottled on the River Tay, the golden valley below exuded a sense of peace and well-being. Then from far away came the faint thunder of an approaching train. Minutes later the rumble had swelled to a roar, as along the far bank of the river diesel engines, pulling a hundred cars, flashed by. As we watched, four or five pack horses grazing on the hillside wandered past the shack.

"See the bay there with the blaze on her face?" said Shand. "She's old Kate's granddaughter. I don't own any horses now, but at times as these pass I give them some salt or sugar. Reminds me of the days when old Kate and I used to pack in to the Muskeg together."

As we left, Shand insisted that we take a bouquet of sweetpeas with us. "They'll only freeze in a day or so," he said quietly. So he and Frances wandered about in his little garden, gathering the flowers. Then he helped her into the car, closed the door, and handed her the bouquet. For a couple of hundred yards we let the car coast down the hill, and then before turning on to the highway, stopped to wave.

Below us flowed the river. Behind us was the russet hillside smelling of ripening herbs and rising to meet the great blue mountains. A short way up Shand stood before his cabin. As we stopped, he waved. Then putting the car in gear we drove on to the abandoned railway grade.

"A rare individual," I commented.

"Yes," said Frances, "and infinitely content."

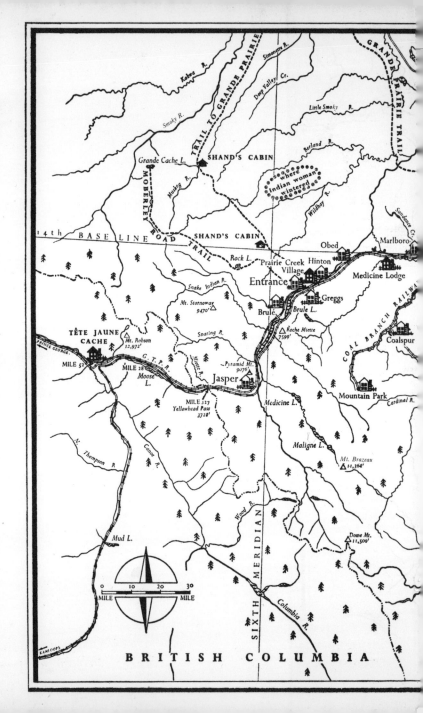